T0327350

RESEARCH IN MARITIME HISTORY
NO. 15

MERCHANT ORGANIZATION AND MARITIME TRADE IN THE NORTH ATLANTIC, 1660-1815

Edited By
Olaf Uwe Janzen

International Maritime Economic History Association

St. John's, Newfoundland
1998

ISSN -1188-3928
ISBN -0-9681288-5-8

Research in Maritime History is available free of charge to members of the International Maritime Economic History Association. The price to others is US$15 per copy.

Back issues of *Research in Maritime History* are available:

Research in Maritime History would like to thank Memorial University of Newfoundland for its generous financial assistance in support of this volume.

CONTENTS

CONTRIBUTIONS

CONTRIBUTORS

ANNA AGNARSDÓTTIR is Associate Professor and Head of the Department of History at the University of Iceland. She has published extensively in historical journals and books both in Iceland and abroad, as well as editing several books. Dr. Agnarsdóttir is currently working on a book on the Iceland trade during the period 1800-1820 and is editing *The Iceland Correspondence of Sir Joseph Banks 1772-1820*, one of the volumes of the Banks Archive Project, a joint project of the Royal Society and Natural History Museum, London.

JOHN F. BOSHER is Professor Emeritus at York University, Toronto and the author of six books, including *Business and Religion in the Age of New France: Twenty two Studies* (Toronto, 1994), *Men and Ships in the Canada Trade 1660-1760: A Biographical Dictionary* (Ottawa, 1992); and *The Canada Merchants 1713-1763* (Oxford, 1987).

OLAF U. JANZEN is Associate Professor of History at the Sir Wilfred Grenfell College campus of Memorial University of Newfoundland. He is the author of "Newfoundland and the International Fishery," in M. Brook Taylor (ed.), *Canadian History: A Reader's Guide. Vol. I: Beginnings to Confederation* (Toronto, 1994) and he is the co-editor of *The Northern Mariner/Le Marin du nord*, the journal of the Canadian Nautical Research Society.

SILVIA MARZAGALLI is maître de conférences at the University of Bordeaux, France, where she teaches modern history. Her PhD thesis dealt with the responses of the merchants of Bordeaux, Hamburg and Livorno to Napoleon's continental blockade. She has published several essays on eighteenth and early nineteenth-century European maritime and merchant history. She is presently working on the Franco-American trade network from 1783 to 1815.

R.C. NASH has been Lecturer in Economic and Social History, University of Manchester since 1975. His general research interest rests in the economic and social history of Britain 1500-1800 and of the American colonial empires, 1450-1850. He has published a number of articles in his specialist research areas, which is the development of the Atlantic economy, particularly trans-Atlantic trade and shipping, the economic and social development of South Carolina and Huguenots in the Atlantic world.

JOHANNES POSTMA is Professor of History at Mankato State University since 1969. Born in the Netherlands, Postma came to the United States as a student in 1958. His major publication is *The Dutch in the Atlantic Slave Trade, 1600-1815* (Cambridge, 1990).

DANIEL A. RABUZZI is Assistant Professor of European history at Luther College in Decorah, Iowa. He specializes in the economic and gender history of early modern Germany and Scandinavia, with a particular interest in maritime and merchant milieus. His articles have appeared in *Central European History* and *Eighteenth-Century Studies*

HENRY ROSEVEARE is Professor of History at King's College, University of London and editor of *Markets and Merchants of the Late Seventeenth Century: The Marescoe-David Letters 1668-1680* (Records of Social and Economic History, New Series XII, 1987). He is currently working on the history of the Port of London between 1660 and 1800.

IAN K. STEELE is Professor of History at the University of Western Ontario. His specialty is the British Atlantic Empire in the century after 1660. His books include *Warpaths: Invasions of North America* (Oxford, 1994); *Betrayals: Fort William Henry and the "Massacre"* (Oxford, 1990); *The English Atlantic, 1675-1740: An Exploration of Communication and Community* (Oxford, 1986): *Atlantic Merchant-Apothecary: The Letters of Joseph Cruttenden* (Toronto, 1977); and *Politics of Colonial Policy: The Board of Trade in Colonial Administration, 1696-1720* (Oxford, 1968).

AINGERU ZABALA URIARTE teaches in the Department of Modern History at the University of Deust. (Bilbao). He has researched the mercantile and maritime history of the *Ancien Régime* extensively, with particular emphasis on the eighteenth century. His most important works to date are *Comercio y tráfico marítimo del Norte de España en el siglo XVIII* (2 vols., Zarauz, 1983) and *Mundo irbano y actividad mercantil Bilbao 1700-1800* (Bilbao, 1993). Professor Zabala is currently extending his field of research to take in the seventeenth century.

NUALA ZAHEDIEH is Lecturer in Economic and Social History at the University of Edinburgh. She is author of various articles on the Caribbean and Atlantic trade, and of a forthcoming book, *The Capital and Commerce: London and Colonial Trade in the Late Seventeenth Century.*

Preface

This volume of *Research in Maritime History* comprises of papers written for presentation at Session C.10 of the Twelfth Congress of the International Economic History Association, which was to have been held in Seville, Spain in August 1998. That session, built around the theme "Merchant Organization and Maritime Trade in the North Atlantic, 1660-1815," had its origins in my research into an attempt by Scottish merchants early in the eighteenth century to break into the Newfoundland fish trade. I was particularly interested in the social and economic context of this venture, but soon found myself exploring larger questions about the way in which credit and marketing networks were developed in the eighteenth century; how trade was organized; and, in general, about the means and circumstances which caused merchants to invest in trades that were already well-established but which were new to them.

Recognizing that these were questions which had long engaged maritime economic historians, I concluded that they could serve as the focus of a session at the IEHA Congress. I therefore approached a number of specialists in maritime commerce, inviting them to participate in the proposed session by preparing papers with an emphasis on the logic and strategies employed by merchants in coping with the many challenges of trading within the North Atlantic region during the period 1660 to 1815. I was much encouraged by the positive response to that invitation, and I wish to say here how much easier my task of organizing this session has been, thanks to the contribution of scholars who have complied so generously and so willingly to my every request. Naturally, with nearly a dozen papers analysing maritime commerce from Iceland to the West Indies and both sides of the Atlantic, the risk was great that the very diversity of the North Atlantic mercantile experience would overwhelm the underlying unity provided by the session theme. Special thanks are therefore owing to Professors Ian K. Steele and Henry Roseveare, who accepted the unenviable task of preparing the introductory and concluding essays for this volume which reaffirm that unity.

From the beginning I decided to publish the papers in advance of the Congress largely to make them as accessible as possible. This decision became serendipitous when the Seville Congress was unexpectedly cancelled for reasons which, at the time of this writing, remain as unclear as the cancellation itself is controversial. It now appears that the Congress will proceed in Madrid. That all this will have a damaging effect on attendance is undeniable — several B Sessions and some C Sessions have already been cancelled. All the more reason, then, to thank the participants in Session C.10 for their perseverance: the success of this session within the context of a severely disrupted conference is entirely to their credit and their unflagging cooperation in bringing this volume together. I cannot conclude, however, without also expressing my deepest gratitude to Margaret M. Gulliver, the Managing Editor of Maritime History Publications, in making this volume ready for publication, and the invaluable assistance and advice provided in its preparation by Prof. Lewis R. Fischer, the Editor-in-Chief of *Research in Maritime History*. Without their help and encouragement, *Merchant Organization and Maritime Trade in the North Atlantic, 1660-1815* would never have been produced.

Olaf Uwe Janzen

Introduction

Ian K. Steele

Although these essays concentrate on merchant initiatives, they are themselves innovative perspectives on early modern economic life and previews of substantial scholarly work in progress. Most new European trading ventures of the early modern period were not spectacular initiatives to exotic peoples and places. These nine essays amply document how challenging things could be for those entering a trade within the relatively familiar bounds of the North Atlantic world. Free of the "North Atlantic triumphalism" that can affect the study of early modern world trade, these studies emphasize the opportunities, aspirations and methods of the mercantile intruder into established trades, and of the innovator attempting their reorganization.[1]

What did merchants need to know in entering an unfamiliar trade? How much "mystery" was there to specific trades? Fur, fish, rice, molasses, and wine were each complex staples, capable of dictatorial economic power over the rhythms of life in their producing areas and, as we have been learning more recently, ultimately dependent upon consumers whose tastes varied and changed over time. As scholars learn more of the totality of these trades, it becomes even easier to presume that merchants needed to know a great deal. The American exporters to Northern Europe, discussed in Professor Daniel Rabuzzi's paper, were very anxious to contact knowledgeable and trustworthy merchants there. Professor Olaf Janzen recounts the misadventures of young Edward Burd Jr., sent as supercargo to buy fish at Newfoundland and paying the obvious price of ignorance compounded by bad luck.

Merchant adventurers were primarily wholesalers, or *négociants*, those "gains-from-trade" dealers engaged in a seemingly eclectic exchange of goods bought where they were thought to be cheap and sold where they were expected to be expensive, with the proceeds reinvested to repeat that

---

[1]Sanjay Subrahmanyam, "Introduction," *Merchant Networks in the Early Modern World* (Aldershot, Hamps., 1996), xxii, regarding the theories of Max Weber, R.R. Rostow, and Immanuel Wallerstein.

1

profitable process.[2] Armed with some understanding of calculation and languages, and one of the many printed merchant advisors of the period, bolder traders attempted to apply some general knowledge of commodities, shipping, customs brokering, marketing, and debt collecting to whatever opportunities presented themselves. The Gaigneurs of La Rochelle, discussed by Professor John Bosher, seem to have entered the fur trade in complete ignorance, and remained wholesalers who neither bought furs directly from Amerindians nor sold hats in retail shops. What they needed to learn about trade with Canada could come from experienced partners, investors, suppliers, shippers, and workers. Professor R.C. Nash studies the Huguenot merchants of Charleston, South Carolina, who needed to learn about quality in buying rice and naval stores but, like the London merchants in the West Indies trade, they sought trustworthy suppliers who would trade honestly in order to gain long-term business advantages. Were the risks of innovation always high? Do these essays suggest that merchants were pushed by business necessity as much as they were lured by profits?

The gathering of capital was a crucial, if almost invisible, aspect of new trading ventures. A posture of trustworthiness, as explained by Dr. Nuala Zahedieh, was a general prerequisite. Families were a major source of investment, bound together as they were by mutual regard, or at least by an informal tontine that promised inheritances to survivors. Arranged marriages in early modern merchant families, like other business partnerships, said much about their economic condition and aspirations. Exogamus marriages, whether to gentry or craftsmen's families, represented real or anticipated social mobility and social adventuring. Intermarriage of merchant families reinforced the trust required to be in business, strengthened the social confidence of a caste or even an oligarchy, and celebrated continuing commitment to the mercantile way of life. Migration and subsequent marriage into an alien society by a family member were life events of special business significance. The apparent difficulties of cross-cultural migrations and marriages, compared to those within the more familiar bounds of an empire's culture and legal system, seems obvious but noteworthy.

---

[2]Jacob M. Price, "What Did Merchants Do? Reflections on British Overseas Trade, 1660-1790," *Journal of Economic History* XLIX (1989), 267-284; Charles P. Kindleberger, "Commercial Expansion and the Industrial Revolution," *Journal of European Economic History* IV (1975), 613-654.

Religious fellowship has long been regarded as a central source of credit and trust among post-Reformation merchants, and religious persecutions of Jews, Huguenots, and Quakers forced migrations that created international networks of credit, trust, and investment. The essays of Bosher and Nash invite us to test such propositions concerning the Huguenots of La Rochelle and of Charleston. When a religious community was strong, and most marriages occurred within it, the power of religious fellowship and the power of family combined and became indistinguishable.

Were connections of trust, credit, and investment increasingly built through commercial experiences of mutual advantage? Merchant letterbooks of this era invariably contain more complaints than gratitude, more dunning than thanking, but trust could be built if honesty combined with good fortune. When venturing into new trades, even more than when continuing and expanding existing businesses, a referral from a satisfied business associate was a precious thing. Consuls, those merchant representatives who came to bear a crest of trustworthiness from their governments by the end of the eighteenth century, were well placed to conduct business themselves in the regions to which they were posted, and to introduce their countrymen. When merchants sent out circular letters inviting investors, one suspects that the early modern was blending into the modern.

The gathering of capital and credit for North Atlantic maritime ventures was, largely but not exclusively, a European activity in this period. Perhaps the more limited colonial capital resources could often be more profitably employed locally, at less risk. When looking at the new trades between the United States and Europe in the wake of the American and French Revolutions, it becomes instructive to learn whose capital was employed in the trade, as distinct from the shipping. Was the initiative necessarily with the capital in the restructuring of these trades?

One striking feature of these essays is the extent to which government initiatives, legal, diplomatic, and military, created mercantile opportunities. Government regulation was commonplace in the "age of mercantilism," and it usually involved the harnessing of privately launched enterprises that had proven successful enough to be subjected to the purported needs of the state. None the less, Professor Aingeru Zabala Uriarte's study of Bilbao demonstrates the creative uses of regulation to seize control of a trade from foreign merchants and to concentrate economic power in a growing port. Bosher's essay documents how a

French government religious offensive against Huguenots made a gift of the Canadian fur trade management to favoured Catholic merchants. More of the opportunities described below derive from formal "deregulation" or politically inspired changes that removed existing controls. Surinam was allowed to trade legally with English North American colonies after 1704. By the terms of the Act of Union of 1707, Scots traders were allowed into the English Atlantic empire, including the Newfoundland fishery. The American Revolution and the French Revolutionary wars entirely remade American seaborne commerce with France and northern Europe, as the essays of Rabuzzi and Dr. Silvia Marzagalli demonstrate. The Anglo-Danish war of 1807-1814 gave British merchants a government-encouraged opportunity to invade the trade of Iceland and, in this instance, both consuls and gunboats forcefully demonstrated the power they represented. However, trades that were encouraged by wartime foreign and economic policy were best pursued with some caution, for those trades could easily die with peace and a change in policy.

This bouquet of scholarly papers could be arranged by country, by trade, or by type of trade. Bosher, Zahedieh, Nash, and Janzen study new initiatives within trading empires, and Dr. Johannes Postma examines the growth of a trade between empires. The essays of Professor Zabala Uriarte, and Drs. Rabuzzi, Marzagalli and Anna Agnarsdóttir all concern changes in international trade. Agnarsdóttir's concluding essay fittingly concerns a new trade that was both between European countries and between the Danish and British empires. While there are several suggestive ways to pattern this gathering of new scholarship, the historical context and trajectory is best seen by reading the papers in approximate chronological order.

The most direct example of government intervention creating an opportunity for particular traders occurred with the French government's siege of La Rochelle in 1627-1628. Bosher demonstrates how this brutal religious consolidation included a transformation of the Canada trade into a *négoce dévot* under the Company of One Hundred Associates. The Gaigneur family were prominent in what became a Catholic Reformation crusade, to be paid for through a monopoly of the Canadian fur trade. The Gaigneurs entered this trade without any evident experience or substantial financial resources. This initiative was linked to their mushrooming family network of influence in the reorganized governance of La Rochelle itself.

The family moved "upstream" in the fur trade by sending agents to Canada. Was this to capture a profitable part of the fur business that could be managed without expertise, or to contribute to the Catholic reconquest of New France, or both? The family certainly did not insist upon doing business only with Catholics, as the study of charter parties, loans, and partnerships indicates. Were the Gaigneurs a front through which the Huguenots still operated, or just a safe place for those forced out of the trade to invest their money? Why were Catholics and Huguenots investing together in the shipping to New France under this new regime? Did the marketing of fur in Europe require money and expertise that could not readily be gathered by these new French Catholic investors? If the government of France intended to put the fur trade into Catholic hands all the way from the Huron hunters to the retailers of France and Germany, its success was limited. The story of the Gaigneur clan reminds us of the continuing place of family networks of trust and profit, and the strengths and limits of government policy before the age of "mercantilism." The government could violently disrupt trade in the name of religion, and both make and break the fortunes of a family, but could not control international investment, shipping, and marketing even when these were a target of national and religious exclusion.

Whether the sober subject of a Dutch painter, or the foil of a Restoration playwright, the early modern European merchant epitomized prudence, sobriety and, where the culture allowed, respectability. For Max Weber and R.H. Tawney and their many admirers, this profitable sobriety has been rather tortuously connected to the ethical demands of Calvinism. Zahedieh reminds us that commerce made its own demand of respectability upon all merchants, who needed a reputation for honesty and prudence, as well as financial substance. Focussing on London merchants exporting consumer goods to agents in the British West Indies in the 1670s and 1680s, Zahedieh analyses the great need for trust, and the preferred techniques for displaying one's own trustworthiness and for determining it in others. Quaker and Jewish communities provided additional social controls that reassured creditors, and Quaker avoidance of courts prompted them to be particularly prudent, since Quaker creditors lost the legal threat frequently used in other mercantile correspondence. The reputation for success that the Quaker merchant community maintained had another source; any unsuccessful Quaker merchant had difficulty marrying within his community, and would be disowned if he married an outsider.[3] Zahedieh emphasizes the internal discipline within these groups, rather than the better-known "advantage" of persecutions that scattered a ready-made network of these, Huguenot, and Jewish mercantile refugees.

Risks of misplaced trust remained very high, but mechanisms were developing to spread risk. The Royal African Company eventually collapsed because of difficulties with their plantation debtors, very unlike the only other American monopoly that held regular London auctions of its imports, the Hudson's Bay Company. It should be remembered that credit for colonial purchases of slaves or consumer goods were usually riskier than loans for more durable capital investments, such as land and major sugar works. These capital loans were more likely to come from family, could be better secured by mortgage, and were increasingly recoverable through the courts. Another important risk-shifting development for metropolitan sugar or tobacco merchants of this period was the "commission system." Substantial planters bypassed the merchants or agents in their colonies and shipped produce directly to England on their own account, paid the freight, and took all risks until the goods arrived in Britain. The metropolitan merchant charged a commission of about three percent to market the produce and to purchase returns for the planter.[4] Within the next generation, trade and shipping risks were also reduced by the development of colonial vice-admiralty courts and by much more reliable marine insurance. Perceived trustworthiness, the precursor of a statistical "credit rating," remained essential to mercantile success.

Nash offers a convincing study of the Huguenot merchants of colonial Charleston, and uses his results to refine and synthesize recent scholarly argument about that community. As was true for pioneering investors in most other colonies, Huguenots who arrived at or near Charleston's founding (1680) could not immediately become Atlantic traders of some staple export that was still to be discovered. By the time the Carolina staple trades in rice and naval stores were developed, these

---

[3]Barry Levy, *Quakers and the American Family: British Settlement in the Delaware Valley* (New York, 1988).

[4]K.G. Davies, "The Origins of the Commission System in the West India Trade," *Transactions of the Royal Historical Society*, 5th ser., LII (1952), 89-107; Jacob M. Price, *Perry of London: A Family and a Firm on the Seaborne Frontier 1615-1753* (Cambridge, MA, 1992), 49-50.

Huguenot pioneers had already invested in agriculture and their mercantile connections with merchants in London had become rather dated. Those Huguenot merchants who arrived around 1700 brought fresh creditworthiness, backed by their metropolitan families and co-religionists. They applied these resources effectively in the burgeoning new trades, and participated in a flourishing Huguenot religious community marked by an active church, endogamous marriages, and business partnerships. While those of Huguenot heritage remained a significant minority in the Charleston business community beyond 1720, they did not display cohesive ethnic behaviour, and were integrated into the English community even faster than rural Huguenots. Could there be a clearer example of Philip Curtin's observation that such networks, created by the scattering of trading communities, had an inherent tendency to work themselves out of existence?[5]

Trade between European empires in America is known to have been of increasing importance in the eighteenth century, but much remains to be learned about it.[6] Postma provides a very suggestive interim report on his promising research concerning trade between Surinam and British colonial America. Trade laws guarded the Dutch monopoly over this plantation colony, but practical necessity led to a little "deregulation" (1704) that formally permitted British North American vessels to import needed food and horses. Despite the resentment of British West Indian planters and imperial administrative zealots, such trade was perfectly legal for British colonials in peacetime.[7] The merchant network for this very unbalanced trade, in which New England returns were largely in Dutch bills of exchange, deserves attention; it would have been even more complicated if the entire trade had been illegal.

Postma's pioneering work on the horse trade between New England and Surinam is particularly intriguing. Those who presumed a

---

[5]Philip Curtin, *Cross-cultural Trade in World History* (Cambridge, 1984), 1-14.

[6]Richard R. Johnson, *John Nelson, Merchant Adventurer: A Life Between Empires* (New York, 1991); David Hancock, "The Invention of Madeira Wine, 1703-1808," *Journal of Interdisciplinary History*, forthcoming.

[7]The legal issues, as confronted by the Board of Trade, are sketched in I.K. Steele, *Politics of Colonial Policy* (Oxford, 1968), xv-xvi, 88-89, 157-158. The Molasses Act, by imposing a differential duty on imports of molasses and sugar from the foreign West Indies, only confirmed the legality of the trade.

Dutch affinity for windmills might notice that Barbados had many and
Surinam had very few, if any; seven degrees of latitude was the difference
between reliable trade winds and prevailing calms created by rising
equatorial air. Governor Robert Lowther of Barbados complained in 1715
about the New England horse trade to the foreign West Indies as allowing
the latter to compete with the English, "as We grind the Sugar-Canes with
Wind-Mills, ... [while] they are necessitated to do it by an Engine that's
drawn by Horses and Cattle."[8] Horses were nearly impossible to breed in
the tropics, but were important both for the mills and for the proper
conveyance of the European master class. Barbados reportedly had 2471
horses on its 1309 plantations in 1710-1712, though these animals were
seldom used in sugar mills.[9] The entire West Indian market for horses
would have been quite large, and could be supplied only by a maritime
trade over long sea routes. As countless European military venturers
discovered, horses did not fare well at sea, often injuring themselves
during loading or in transit, and they were difficult to supply with
adequate fresh water and food while aboard. Nearly 35,000 horses were
imported into Surinam alone between 1683 and 1794, suggesting a
significant trade that, until now, has been without an historian.

Although the Newfoundland fishery had been active for nearly a
quarter of a millenium by 1726, it could still be brutal in initiating new
players. For prominent Edinburgh merchants with some experience
exporting Scottish fish to pay for the Iberian wines they imported, the
addition of a fish-buying "sack ship" voyage to Newfoundland would seem
a perfectly natural and profitable extension of their trade.[10] Janzen
analyses the troublesome voyage of the seventy-ton Christian through the
self-justifying journal of her inexperienced supercargo, Edward Burd, Jr.
The Edinburgh merchants seem to have spread their personal risks
adequately and were well advised on various aspects of the venture.
However, they did not have the information to be able to help their novice

---

[8]London, Public Record Office, Colonial Office 28/15, fol. 101, quoted in Frank
Wesley Pitman, *The Development of the British West Indies, 1700-1763* (New Haven,
1917), 202.

[9]*Ibid.*, 372.

[10]Peter Pope, "Adventures in the Sack Trade: London Merchants in the Canada
and Newfoundland Trades, 1627-1648," *The Northern Mariner/Le Marin du nord* VI, no.
1 (January 1996), 1-19.

supercargo with the marketing of their fish or with the assembling of a return cargo; some London merchants of the same time period expected to learn enough by regular Spanish packet boats to be able to leave their "sack ship" masters additional letters of instruction at Iberian ports.[11] Burd's ignorance as a fish buyer was particularly expensive, but Janzen is right to notice the two other factors that were bound to be emphasized by the disappointed Burd: the slow and leaky ship, and the repeated bad luck. It is refreshing to see luck included prominently in the explanation of commercial failure; too many historians insist on the rational controllability of events, and are therefore unwilling to allow chance to have a significant place in any explanations.

Business initiative could also be achieved through institutional change, as evident in Zabala Uriarte's careful study of the Consulado of Bilbao in the last half of the seventeenth century. Serving as a guild and a mercantile court, the Consulado of Bilbao had been authorized in 1511. The consulado had given this growing port, famous for the export of high quality wool and iron, some independence from its powerful hinterland rival, Burgos. A century and a half later, Bilbao merchants used the opportunities provided by an export boom (1655-1670) to strengthen their control of trading in the city. Foreign merchants were defeated in their attempts to have consuls appointed to arbitrate their trade disputes, and the consulado strengthened its reputation and commercial expertise, regulated and resolved disputes concerning bills of exchange and promissory notes, supervised changes in the flow of money, and attacked counterfeiting. Finally exploiting their port's natural advantages fully, the merchant elite of Bilbao used their noteworthy institutional change to assist in wresting control of the wool trade from Burgos, and particularly from those foreign merchants who had come to dominate investment in the wool industry. Behind the well-recorded institutional initiatives, one suspects a network of individual mercantile ambitions; but that would be another, and longer, story.

The half-century before the "age of revolutions" within the North Atlantic community is represented here solely by Postma's study of Surinam's trade with British North America. Dutch trading primacy faded in this period, with the British and French gaining dominance. Within the

---

[11]I.K. Steele, "Instructing the Master of a Newfoundland Sack Ship, 1715" *Mariner's Mirror* LXIII, no. 2 (May 1977), 191-193.

British empire, Liverpool emerged as the port for new midland industrial centres and the accelerating slave trade, the Scots captured the tobacco trade at both ends, and the North American colonies developed new European trades in grain, iron, and flax seed. French colonial sugar production expanded rapidly, coming to dominate the re-export trade to much of western Europe. Tropical consumables, predominantly addictive and heavily taxed, became prominent in the transformation of the spending and eating habits of western Europeans. This was also a time without major "trade diasporas," indeed a time when they were apparently becoming obsolete.[12]

The revolution in commercial relations that attended the American, French, and Haitian revolutions brought new opportunities as well as commercial disasters. Rabuzzi draws mainly on the tobacco traders of Baltimore in exploring some pioneering American ventures in the northern European markets. These new opportunities could have been exploited by European merchants establishing agencies in the United States, or by American merchants establishing agencies in Europe, but neither method was significant. Rabuzzi documents the preference for the less structured, and more tentative, ventures by American shipcaptain-supercargos into northern Europe. If this type of wandering merchant had been largely superceded in the "ecumenical" North Atlantic trades, it was a trading method that was being revived.[13] Recent dramatic changes in circumstance may have prompted caution and flexibility. In any case, the Baltimore merchants had a "surplus" of tobacco for under-supplied European markets, though alternative suppliers emerged quickly. The Baltimore traders also had access to underemployed American shipping, and eventually they had the major advantage of neutral status in a wartime European shipping world. While a few American traders were seeking European capital, the trade described here was predominantly employing American capital. Seen as a potential contest between northern European and American merchant venturers for mastery of a new trade, the Americans had initial advantages.

The need for knowledge and trust are very evident here, as in some other new trades. Rabuzzi explores the limited American knowledge of northern Europe, mentions American monolingualism, and the paucity

---

[12]Curtin, *Cross-cultural Trade*, 230-234.

[13]*Ibid.*, 88-89, 111-115, 127-135, 245.

of Americans who migrated to Europe, married there, and became permanent agents. This may have been cultural, but one wonders whether, in different economic conditions, American merchants could have found German-speaking immigrants (or even ex-prisoners of war) happy to use family connections or to become agents in Northern Europe themselves. The networks of established mercantile acquaintance through the British, and through the Dutch colonial trade that Postma explores, proved central. The American consulates and political acquaintances helped. One suspects that the "cold call" circulars were less effective, and might have been entirely useless if circumstances had not forced uncommon risks upon northern European importers caught within Napoleon's continental system.

Comparisons with the Franco-American trade in this era are particularly helpful. The great eighteenth-century French tobacco "farm" had built a large French market for Chesapeake tobacco, then the supply network collapsed with the American Revolution. French trade with her West Indian sugar colonies was disrupted by both the Haitian Revolution of 1791 and the war with Britain from 1793; the French needed American neutral carriers bringing tropical produce, especially from the expanding economy of Spanish Cuba. Diplomatic and military links between France and the United States were close, and the language barrier was not severe for Yankee traders whose community had long fought or traded with Acadia, Canada, and the French West Indies. Marzagalli's preliminary study emphasizes American consular records, which are made to reveal the general levels and patterns of trade and ship ownership. Marzagalli rightly seeks to determine who initiated this flourishing new trade, which seems to have developed much more easily than the US trade to northern Europe. Ownership of goods in transit is harder to discern than ship ownership or trading routes, but the evidence examined indicates more French than American capital was engaged in this trade. French and French West Indian merchant migrants to the United States, and to Cuba, provided more of those essential links of trust than did American migrants to France's fastest growing port in the eighteenth century, Bordeaux. Why did those new colonial American wheat and rice trades to southern Europe, developing rapidly after the mid-eighteenth century, apparently provide no personal bridges to the French trade of this period, at least not at Bordeaux?[14]

A clear demonstration of new methods of commercial intrusion, and of the opportunities that war might bring in trading with a rival's colony, is provided by the British trade with Danish Iceland between 1807 and 1817. The British government was unwilling to annex Iceland, even when nudged by Sir Joseph Banks, but was happy to encourage trade, provide some naval support, and send a consul. Agnarsdóttir's thorough exploration of this modest trade, totalling thirty-seven ships over eleven years, details the serendipitous establishment of contacts between a prisoner of war and a merchant needing tallow, the British use of forced trade, and the limits of a trade that was ultimately not well suited to either partner. Did Napoleon's "continental system" deprive British fish merchants of European markets that would have made a small triangular trade with Iceland possible, on the Newfoundland "sack ship" model?

Do these papers, quite coincidentally and unintentionally, exaggerate an evolution from imperial to international trade within this integrating North Atlantic world?[15] Was trade within empires easier than international trade, whether one considers migration of merchants within a culture, capital offered within a familiar legal system, postal communications, shipping routes, or government interests and assistance? Imperial trade grew in both absolute and relative volume and value throughout early modern time, without ever matching the international trade within Europe. Without considering mercantile initiatives central to the frequent migration of Europe's dominant trade entrepôt, from Venice to Antwerp to Genoa to Cadiz to Amsterdam and then to London, it is easy to underestimate major inter-imperial and international trading opportunities that were created throughout this period.

Were there significant changes in the nature of merchant networks between the 1620s and the 1810s? The scattering of family and co-religionists, to live, trade, and marry in alien lands, became less crucial.

---

[14]Paul Butel, "Traditions and Changes in French Atlantic Trade between 1780 and 1830," *Renaissance and Modern Studies*, XXX (1986), 124-145; Kindleberger, "Commercial Expansion."

[15]Compare the Atlantic world described in Ralph Davis, *The Rise of the Atlantic Economies* (Ithaca, NY, 1973) and K.G. Davies, *The North Atlantic World in the Seventeenth Century* (London, 1974).

Were worlds of imperial legislation and international commercial diplomacy evolving together to provide growing confidence for alien and remote investors? Did the growth of trade through agents, and protection through consuls, reflect a set of new conditions, assumptions, and conventions that were increasingly shared by the North Atlantic trading world? Or did an early-modern Atlantic world end abruptly?[16] Were the British consuls and gunboats at Iceland a hint of a developing informal empire of unequal commercial and industrial advantage that would provoke new restrictions within Europe, and new empires beyond?

---

[16]John R. McNeill, "The End of the Old Atlantic World: America, Africa, Europe, 1770-1888," in Alan R. Karras and J.R. McNeill (eds.), *Atlantic American Societies: From Columbus through Abolition, 1492-1888* (London, 1992), 245-268; Peggy K. Liss, *Atlantic Empires: The Network of Trade and Revolution, 1713-1826* (Baltimore, 1983), 222-241.

The Gaigneur Clan in
the Seventeenth-Century Canada Trade

J.F. Bosher

There are two good reasons for singling out the Gaigneur family. The first is that they and their many relatives sent more ships, more goods, and more people out to Canada than any other trading firm in their time, which stretched from 1628 almost to the end of the century. This reason will be universally understood, but the second reason may puzzle the business historian who has not studied the reign of Louis XIII: the Gaigneur family and their relatives were all Roman Catholics established at or near La Rochelle, where so much business was still in the hands of Huguenot families. This is an anomaly that invites us to set aside the normal assumption on which trade is studied without reference to the religion of the traders. Close study of the Gaigneur clan shows that their trans-Atlantic trade can best be explained with reference to the religious and political events of their time. Those events count for a great deal because the Gaigneur clan's motives and purposes can only be inferred from what they did: they left no explicit statements, no letters or memoranda, that might tell us what they thought they were doing. The same may be said of most merchants engaged in shipping or trading with New France during the seventeenth century. Few indeed left any reflections on their lives; we can only try to deduce why the merchants in the Gaigneur clan traded with Canada and Acadia.

The year 1628 was a strange time to begin sending ships over to those colonies. The armies of Louis XIII and Cardinal Richelieu had been besieging La Rochelle, a Calvinist stronghold, since the spring of 1627; it surrendered on 28 October 1628; soldiers, royal officials and Roman Catholic missionaries immediately invaded and began to catholicize the town. The public in France and throughout Europe followed these events with passionate interest. Only people unfamiliar with French history in those times could imagine that shipping to Canada was driven entirely by business motives and that religious purposes were secondary in it. This being so, the problem for the historian is evidently to determine, or to disentangle, the parts played by business and religion in the Canada trade.

Because merchants's thinking must be deduced from their actions and their circumstances, the problem is difficult and its solution debatable. This debate requires a measure of scientific detachment from religious or other ideological commitments.

The Gaigneurs' Entry into the Canada Trade

Pierre Gaigneur (c. 1624-1692) was the central figure in the story of his clan's trading, but he was not the founder of it. He inherited an interest in trading to New France from his father, Louis Gaigneur, who in turn was brought into this trade by his relatives in the Tuffet family. Studied for its trans-Atlantic trade, then, the Gaigneur clan first attracts attention in the activities of Jean Tuffet who fitted out at least six ships for Acadia between 1628 and 1632.[1] There is no trace of any earlier trading across the Atlantic by relatives of the Gaigneurs; indeed, trans-Atlantic business before the siege of La Rochelle (1627-1628) was almost entirely in the hands of Huguenot merchants. At first Jean Tuffet worked out of Bordeaux, where he had taken refuge during the siege. This was because he was already an active *dévot,* or Catholic zealot: during the campaign Louis XIII waged in 1622 against the Huguenot towns in the southwest, Tuffet served as a *munitionnaire*, managing supplies and large sums of money for the Catholic army in Aunis commanded by the Comte de Soissons.[2] Neither Tuffet nor anyone else left a written statement explaining why he began fitting out ships for the trans-Atlantic colonial trade during the siege of 1627-1628, then engaged a nephew, Louis Gaigneur, Catholic like himself, to act as an agent or partner at La Rochelle, and went on trading out of La Rochelle where he moved a few years later. But close study of his circumstances leads to the conclusion that he was moved by religious and political events.

---

[1]Claude Massé, "Jean Tuffet et ses activités en faveur de la Nouvelle-France (1626-1634)," *Cahiers de la Société historique acadienne*, XVIII, No. 4 (janvier-mars 1987), 5-34; Robert Le Blant, "Les compagnies du Cap-Breton (1629-1647)," *Revue d'histoire de l'Amérique française*, XVI (1962), 86; Archives départementales de la Charente-Maritime (ADCM), minutes of various notaries such as one of maître Cousseau of La Rochelle (LR), 18 March 1630. See also ADCM, Gouin (Brouage), 19 November 1630; Tongrelon (LR), 26 November 1632.

[2]Massé, "Jean Tuffet."

Figure 1

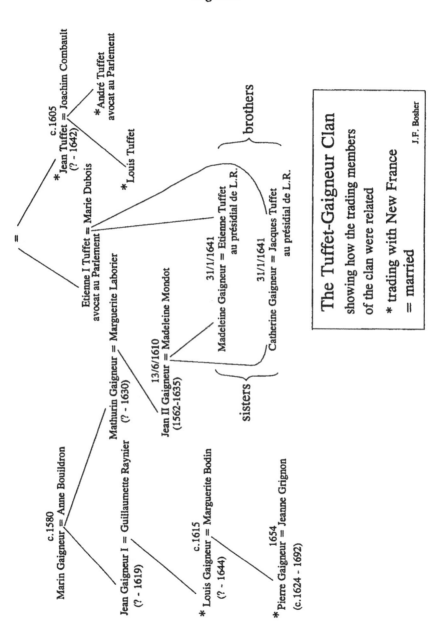

The Tuffet-Gaigneur Clan
showing how the trading members
of the clan were related

* trading with New France
= married

J.F. Bosher

J.F. Bosher

Figure 2

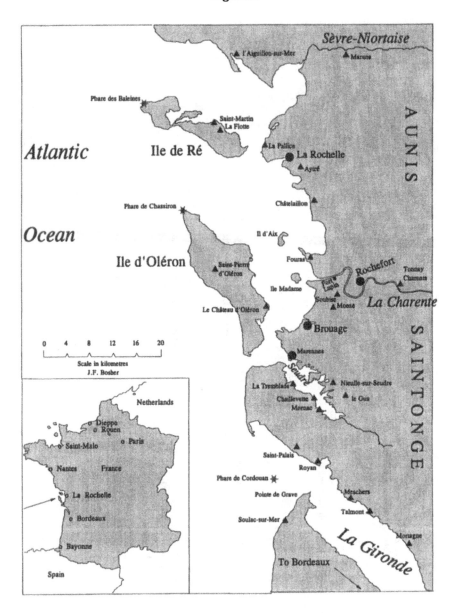

Figure 3

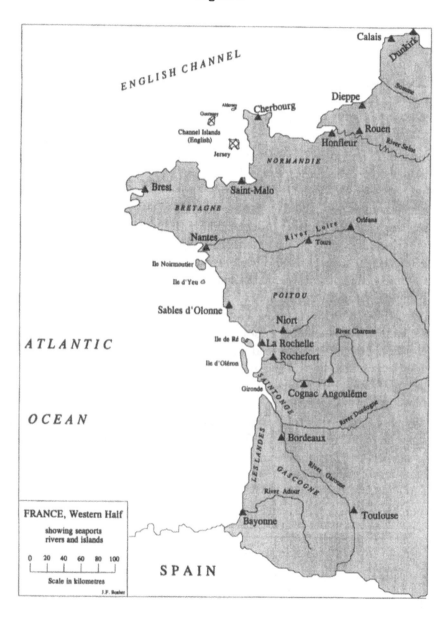

FRANCE, Western Half

showing seaports
rivers and islands

0 20 40 60 80 100

Scale in kilometres

J.F. Booker

Any Roman Catholic merchant of La Rochelle who began trading with the colonies of New France in the years 1628-1632, as Tuffet did, owed his position to circumstances created by the triumphant siege and conquest of the town. When the Rochelais surrendered on 28 October 1628, Louis XIII and Richelieu drew up a *Déclaration*, published three weeks later, that laid down the terms of a new order.[3] It guaranteed, in a brief sentence, freedom of worship for the surviving Huguenot population, but only in one place to be specified by the government. It explained in several pages of detail how the town was to be catholicized. The huge octagonal Calvinist Church was to be confiscated to serve henceforth as a Catholic cathedral; the secular clergy were to be restored to the parishes, from which the Huguenot régime had driven them out two generations earlier, and they were to be paid out of crown and municipal revenues; many religious orders, notably the Jesuits, the Capucins, and the Recollets were to be established (and they soon acquired much property); the hospices and hospitals were to be entrusted to specified Catholic orders; the town council and the entire governing structure of the Huguenot period were declared abolished; a new court of justice was to be established and, as Kevin Robbins tells us in detail, it was immediately packed with the members of several Catholic families who proceeded to collaborate with the clergy and with officials of the Crown in a policy of catholicizing the town.[4] One of these was the Gaigneur family in which there were magistrates as well as merchants. Finally, some two-thirds or four-fifths of the population having died during the siege by starvation, disease or violence, it was expected that new citizens would come from other parts of France, but the *Déclaration* expressly forbade Huguenots, or anyone but Catholics, to move into La Rochelle henceforth. It was in these conditions that Jean Tuffet returned to La Rochelle from Bordeaux where he had taken refuge. He was only one of several Roman Catholic merchants who moved in after the siege. Another such was Emmanuel Le

---

[3]The text is printed in full in P-S. Callot, *Jean Guiton, Maire de La Rochelle et le siège de 1628* (reprint, La Rochelle, 1967), 123–134; and in François Moisy, *Le rétablissement des structures catholiques après le siège de La Rochelle (1628-1648)* (Fontenay-le-Comte, 1973), 76–81.

[4]Kevin C. Robbins, "Municipal Justice, Urban Police and the Tactics of Counter-Reformation in La Rochelle, 1618-1650," *French History*, IX (1995), 273–293. See also Robbins, "The Families and Politics of La Rochelle, 1550-1650" (Unpublished PhD thesis, Johns Hopkins University, 1991).

Borgne who was soon busy trading, like Tuffet, with the trans-Atlantic missions and other settlements that made up the colony of New France.[5]

As French Catholic merchants, the Le Borgnes, Tuffets and Gaigneurs were men of their age. In the reign of Louis XIII, seaborne trade became a vehicle for the missionary work of the French Counter-Reformation. In the ideology of Bourbon France at that time, trade and religion were to be promoted as complementary activities, and the usual profit motive of the merchant was thus to be sublimated in the missionary endeavours of the clergy. Used in this way, the trade with New France came to be what one recent student of the subject calls *le négoce dévot*. "The discourse of *négoce dévot*," he writes, "treated as metaphysical that which we might regard as secular and concrete. Notably it endowed the concept of *navigation* with transcendant power."[6] This idea was developed in several serious books of that time written by Antoyne de Montchrétien in 1615, Pierre Bergeron in 1629, Jean Éon in 1646 and Jacques Savary in 1675. These all saw a Christianizing and civilizing mission (the two being seen as one and the same) as the main objective of overseas colonial enterprise. "According to Éon, Jesus himself intimated a link between grand commerce and civilizing functions."[7] In the seventeenth century, then, the public duty of a French merchant was to promote the missionary cause, and those who did so were favoured by Church and State. In France, the power of Church and State over merchants was very much greater than in Holland, where merchants were strongly represented in the Estates, or in England where merchants had voices in Parliament. Only in the municipal government of his town did a French merchant normally have a political voice, but in La Rochelle the power of Church and State was almost total after the conquest of 1628.

In the meantime, however, Tuffet had joined the new *Compagnie des Cents-associés*, the Company of New France that Richelieu and Louis XIII had founded during the siege. It was, indeed, while living at the siege headquarters outside La Rochelle in 1627-1628 that Richelieu and Louis

---

[5]J.F. Bosher, "The Lyon and Bordeaux Connections of Émmanuel Le Borgne (ca. 1605-1681)," *Acadiensis*, XXIII, No. 1 (Fall 1993), 128–145.

[6]Peter Allan Goddard, "Christianization and Civilization in Seventeenth-Century French Colonial Thought" (Unpublished DPhil thesis, Oxford University, 1990), 278.

[7]*Ibid.*, 293–294.

XIII had worked out the terms of this new company and decided to award it a monopoly of trade and settlement in the French colonies of North America. Its origins linked this Company with La Rochelle and in the period immediately following the siege Jean Tuffet was to be the Company's agent there. He was appointed almost immediately as one of its directors and was ready to promote its shipping to New France. But as close study of the Company makes clear, and indeed its founding act states explicitly, it was not primarily a trading firm: the main purpose of the Company of New France was to establish French Roman Catholic colonies in North America.[8] The fur trade was envisaged only as a way of paying for this process.

The Company of New France, like the Tuffet-Gaigneur clan, was evidently intended to supplant the Huguenot and foreign interests that had been trading with North America out of La Rochelle. What were these? Prominent among the Huguenot interests was a trading firm consisting of two brothers-in-law, Samuel Georges and Jean Macain, and their nephew, David Lomeron. These three had been fitting out ships for Acadia continually since about 1613, which was soon after the two older men had brought Lomeron to La Rochelle from his home town, Chinon in the Loire Valley. Earlier, Georges and Macain had been shipping to North America in partnership with the Huguenot *lieutenant pour le Roy en Nouvelle-France*, Pierre Dugua de Mons, whom Henri IV had appointed to govern New France by a commission of 8 November 1603.[9] Beginning about 1613, Georges, Macain and Lomeron fitted out at least thirty-two vessels for Acadia during the next quarter-century, often in partnership with other Huguenot merchants of the town. Some of their ships carried supplies and colonists for Charles de Saint-Étienne de La Tour, who was established at Port-Royal as *Lieutenant pour le Roy en Acadie,* and who

[8]*Collection de manuscrits contenant lettres, mémoires et autres documents historiques relatifs à la Nouvelle-France...* (4 vols., Québec, 1883), I, 62–75.

[9]W.I. Morse, *Pierre Du Gua, sieur de Monts, Records Colonial and `Saintongeois' Collected and Edited by...* (London, 1939); and Jean Liebel, *Pierre Dugua, sieur de Mons, fondateur de l'Acadie et de Québec* (reprographié en 1988 par les services techniques de l'Université de Bordeaux III, ADCM 6823).

had engaged them as his French agents.[10] Others went over to fish off the coasts of Nova Scotia or in the Gulf of Saint Lawrence and to trade at various points on the coast: a place on the south bank of the Saint Lawrence they called "Mentane," Tadoussac at the mouth of the Saguenay River, and elsewhere.[11]

The siege interrupted their trade with New France and, as a Huguenot firm, Georges, Macain and Lomeron found it extremely hard to recover, not least because the new *Compagnie des Cents-associés* now had an official monopoly of all French trade with North America. The firm sent out half a dozen ships in the early 1630s, but then, in June 1637, David Lomeron gave up the struggle. Leaving his wife in charge of his affairs, he went to Dublin where in April 1639 she was preparing to join him. The Lomerons were evidently emigrating like hundreds of Huguenots in earlier and later years. On 9 December 1639 by an official act of Parliament in London, "David Lomeron, merchant of the town of Chinon in the province of Touraine in France" was naturalized as an English subject of Charles I.[12] Meanwhile, his uncle Jean Macain had died in 1626, and Samuel Georges had dropped out of the trans-Atlantic trades about 1635 at the same time as Lomeron.[13] This old Huguenot firm moved out of the trade with New France at about the same time that the Tuffet-Gaigneur clan was moving into it. In short, the trans-Atlantic links with

[10]Robert Le Blant, "La première bataille pour Québec en 1608," *Buletin philologique et histoire du comité des travaux histoire et scientifiques (jusqu'en 1610)* (1971), 123-125; and Le Blant and Marcel Delafosse, "Les rochelais dans la vallée du Saint-Laurent (1599-1618)," *Revue d'histoire de l'Amérique française*, X (1956), 333–363.

[11]ADCM, passim in the minutes of Maîtres Chesneau, Cousseau, Gouin and Teuleron, notaries of La Rochelle, for example Chesneau (LR), 5 and 16 January 1616; 15 March and 10 October 1616; and 11 February, 13 and 14 March, 29 May and 6 June 1617; Teuleron (LR), 12 January 1633; 5, 10 and 12 April 1636; and 21 February, 13 and 16 April 1637; Cousseau (LR), 31 March and 16 April 1633; Gouin (LR), 27 October 1633; ADCM, B 5654, Samuel Georges and David Lomeron to Admiralty (LR), 28 April 1633.

[12]ADCM, Chesneau (LR), 12 May 1622, folios 28-29v, reg. 14 and 26 April 1639; Langlois (LR), 29 June 1637, proc. (missing); W.A. Shaw (ed.), *Denizations and Naturalizations of Aliens in England and Ireland, 1603-1700* (London, 1911), 336.

[13]*Archives historiques de la Saintonge et de l'Aunis*, XXXVIII (1908), 327: Monsieur Macqain, *pair de La Rochelle*, died 29 May 1626.

New France were being catholicized as was La Rochelle itself. Jean Tuffet and Louis Gaigneur were drawn into the Canada trade in these circumstances and were evidently part of the catholicizing process.

That process had another aspect. The siege of La Rochelle and the Company of New France were intended to oppose the foreign Protestant interests that had been so strong in French Atlantic ports. Dutch and English merchants in particular had long been prominent at La Rochelle and its satellite ports exporting salt, brandy and wine, managing the companies that Henri IV had invited to drain the swamps of Aunis, Saintonge and southern Poitou, and manufacturing paper on a large scale in the nearby province of Angoumois. Being nearly all Protestant, these foreigners had intermarried with Huguenot merchant families. Ships, goods and people moved easily between Holland, England, northern Germany, and the Huguenot parts of the French Atlantic coast; sons and nephews were commonly exchanged to learn foreign languages; persecution had driven many Huguenots to take refuge in the Netherlands and in England, notably after the Massacre of Saint Bartholomew's Day (24 August 1572) in Paris and the many massacres in other French towns during the next two months. The result was that a cosmopolitan society of Protestant trading families had been growing around the North Sea. By the 1620s it was also flourishing around the Baltic Sea and the Atlantic Ocean, increasing with the Dutch maritime empire that was the economic miracle of that age. But the "Protestant international" thus developing had also a political aspect. For more than half a century the Dutch and English governments had occasionally taken sides with the Huguenots, and the latest example of this was the Duke of Buckingham's expeditionary force that had tried to relieve La Rochelle in 1627-1628. A recent scholarly analysis of English foreign policy shows that it was driven during the years 1625-1629 by "a vital concern for 'those of the religion' in France."[14] Louis XIII's government was sensitive to this as can be seen in the royal *Déclaration* that followed the siege: only those Huguenots who had lived at La Rochelle before the "descente des Anglois" in 1628 were

---

[14]Thomas Cogswell, "Prelude to Ré: the Anglo-French Struggle over La Rochelle, 1624-7," *History*, LXXI (1986), 18. See also Cogswell, "Foreign Policy and Parliament: the Case of La Rochelle, 1625-6," *English Historical Review*, XCIX (1984), 241–267.

to be allowed to settle in the town.[15] These conflicts and tensions resembled many others throughout Europe at that time, the 1620s being the opening years of the Thirty Years' War when religious hostilities between governments as well as peoples were at fever pitch. In France, Church and State saw La Rochelle as an intrusion of hostile forces that were foreign as well as heretical.

French colonial trade was affected by this state of affairs. Throughout the first quarter of the seventeenth century, shipping to French North America had been part of a cosmopolitan trading system in which Huguenot and foreign merchants had been prominent. The posts being established in the new French colonies, Port-Royal and even Québec, were soon linked in trade with the Dutch and English colonies to the south and with many European ports. This did not disturb the French ruling authorities until the beginning of the French Counter-Reformation early in the reign of Louis XIII. His father Henri IV, until his death in 1610, maintained friendly relations with most of the Protestant countries of northern Europe which had, after all, been his allies earlier during his long struggle against the Catholic League. For example, a French East India Company formed in 1604 called upon Dutch mariners and shipping merchants, many recruited in the Netherlands by Peter Lintgens. In 1608, Henri IV was still interested in forming a Franco-Dutch trading company.[16] Again, on 10 January 1604 a patent was issued in the French king's name for two English vessels, the *Castor and Pollux* and her pinnace, the *Pollux and Castor*, to explore the North American coast as far north as Cape Breton. Financed mainly in London, they sailed under French captains with mixed Anglo-French crews.[17] Foreign merchants at La Rochelle and Rouen were in the early Canada trade and they show how cosmopolitan it was. One of the first was Corneille de Bellois, a Dutchman who had settled at Rouen and gallicized his name. As early as

---

[15]Moisy, *Le rétablissement*, 81.

[16]Gustave Fagniez, *L'économie sociale de la France sous Henri IV (1589–1610)* (Paris, 1897), 279–300; and Robert Le Blant and René Baudry (eds.), *Nouveau documents sur Champlain et son époque (1560–1622)* (2 vols., Ottawa, 1967), I, 162.

[17]David B. Quinn, "An Anglo-French 'Voyage of Discovery' to North America in 1604–1605, and its Sequel," *Bulletin de l'Institut Historique Belge de Rome*, XLIV (1974), 513–534, reprinted in Quinn (ed.), *Explorers and Colonies: America, 1500–1625* (London, 1990), 341–362.

1570 he had joined a French company formed to fish off Newfoundland. From 1604 to 1608 Corneille de Bellois was a member of Pierre du Gua de Mons's fur trading company, helping to fit out two ships in most years. He was one of the "Flamands" in Pierre du Gua's expedition of 1608. Later, from 1613 to 1620, he was a member of Champlain's *Compagnie du Canada.*[18]

Throughout the first quarter of the seventeenth century, merchants and sailors from the Netherlands, often with strong Huguenot connections, had explored and traded, occasionally raided, on the coasts of New France. For instance, in 1606 eight Amsterdam merchants sent a Dutch ship, the *Witte Leeuw*, to fish and trade in New France and she caused a furor by behaving like a privateer, seizing two French vessels and being aggressive in other ways.[19] The supercargo on that expedition was a certain Nicolas de Bauquemare, a Netherlander who had settled at Rouen in the large community of merchants there.[20]

Men from the British Isles were also active in early expeditions to New France and sometimes in partnership with Huguenot merchants. In 1593 a certain Steven de Bocall, a Basque Huguenot with considerable experience of the gulf of St. Lawrence, worked for Peter Hill and Thomas James of Bristol on the two ships they sent to fish for walrus near

---

[18]Bellois was related by marriage to Daniel Boyer, who was active in the Canada trade at Rouen during the first quarter of the century. See Le Blant and Baudry (eds.), *Nouveaux documents*, 82, 133, 214, 256, 403 and 418 note; Charles and Paul Bréard, *Documents relatifs à la marine normande et à ses armements aux XVIe et XVIIe siècles pour le Canada, l'Afrique, les Antilles, le Brésil et les Indes* (Rouen, 1889), 50 and 102.

[19]Thomas J. Condon, *New York Beginnings: the Commercial Origins of New Netherlands* (New York, 1968), 8.

[20]In 1606 and 1608 Bauquemare assisted Pierre Gua de Monts in expeditions in *Le Lion Blanc* to trade for furs in Canada. At Amsterdam on 1 January 1606 he hired the ship's captain, Hendrick Cornelisz Lonck (alias Henry Corneillessen Long), and two other Dutchmen, Jan Cupper and Bannes Heusen. In 1608 he engaged several "Flamands" and a certain "Mathieu de Coste, nègre." In 1611-1612, the Commissioners of the Amsterdam Admiralty sent out two ships, *Craen* and *Vos*, under captain Jan Cornelisz May to explore the coasts of New France. In 1613, an Amsterdam merchant with family connections in Rouen, Arnout Van Liebergen, originally a Protestant refugee from Bois-le-Duc, invested in Dutch expeditions to the Hudson River (Le Blant and Baudry, *Nouveaux documents*, 194, 196, 212, 226 and 388; and Condon, *New York Beginnings* [eds.], 7, 12 and 14-15).

Newfoundland and the Magdalen Islands.[21] In 1594, Bocall piloted a ship from Bristol to Newfoundland and Anticosti Island. He left England after that, but remained in touch with his English friends. A generation later, in 1629, the famous Kirke family, of Anglo-French origin, captured Québec and other French bases in North America. David Kirke (later Sir David Kirke) and his brothers had grown up in Dieppe where their father, Gervase Kirke, had been in the North American trades.[22] David Kirke traded with La Rochelle during the early 1620s.[23] In the cosmopolitan world of trans-Atlantic trade at that time he and his family thought nothing of joining a company of London merchants who were planning to seize the French bases in New France.

The first French merchants trading with Québec were in touch with foreign markets as well as French ones. Not unnaturally, much of the French fur trade was in foreign hands. Here is another aspect of the international or cosmopolitan trade which the Company of New France was intended to oppose. The Kirke family traded in furs with Mediterranean ports, but the principal fur markets were in northern Europe. Jean Macain of La Rochelle was sending beaver to Koenigsberg in 1603.[24] Furs brought to La Rochelle were often sold to merchants of Cologne, Amsterdam and other towns in Germany and Holland. Du Gua de Mons was doing business in Amsterdam easily and frequently even before he founded Québec.[25] Dutch and German merchants who had settled in Paris continued to buy much of the Canadian and Acadian fur landed at French ports. On 1 January 1606 Nicolas de Bauquemaure of Rouen engaged

---

[21]Gillian Cell, *English Enterprise in Newfoundland, 1577–1660* (Toronto, 1969), 49.

[22]*Ibid.*, 113. "Gervase Kyrke" was christened on 16 April 1568 at Norton, Derbyshire, son of Thurston Kyrke (parish registers at the Derbyshire Record Office).

[23]ADCM, Juppin (LR), 30 January 1624, a notarial minute signed at La Rochelle by David Kirke (alias Quercq) showing that he had several business contracts with Nicolas Reveillaud, a merchant of Saintes, who shipped wine to London for him from La Rochelle and Tonnay-Charente.

[24]Le Blant and Delafosse, "Les Rochelais dans la vallée", 334, 336; Cell, *English Enterprise in Newfoundland*, 113–114.

[25]Le Blant and Baudry (eds.), *Nouveaux documents*, 194.

three Amsterdam merchants to send a vessel to find furs in Canada.[26] German and Dutch interests in the Canadian fur trade were to be maintained throughout the age of New France, but they were especially prominent in the early seventeenth century.[27]

Among the biggest fur traders in the early years were members of a German-Dutch clan, scattered but working closely together. This clan included the Jabach, Hunthum (alias Hontom), Vogels, and Duysterloo families linked together by marriage alliances as well as business partnerships.[28] Their business headquarters were at Cologne, though the all-important Jabach family seems to have come from Antwerp.

Mathias Duysterloo (1548-1602) lived at Cologne where he was a native and senator of the city as well as a fur trader. It was the Duysterloo family that worked most closely with the French-Canadian fur trade. Henrick Duysterloo (1569-1615) traded at Middelburg from 1593 to 1600 and then at Amsterdam where he died in 1615. His son, Henrick II went to join a cousin in Paris and there became naturalized French in 1615. This cousin, himself naturalized French in 1607, was Mathias (alias Mathijs and Mathieu) Duysterloo, born at Cologne c. 1569, but he had been buying and selling Canadian furs in Paris since 1607, if not earlier, living at various addresses in the parish of Saint-Leu-et-Saint-Gilles. He was the clan's most prominent fur trader, at least from the French and Canadian point of view, and went on in the trade until 1648, perhaps later. He dealt with many agents, some of them relatives and most of them Dutch or German, in nearly every big town in western Europe. His

---

[26]Le Blant and Delafosse, "Le rochelais dans la vallée," 388.

[27]Lionel La Berge, *Rouen et le commerce du Canada de 1650 à 1670* (L'Ange-Gardien, 1972), 11; and E.E. Rich, *The Hudson's Bay Company, 1670-1870* (2 vols., London, 1958), I, ch. 5.

[28]Information about this clan comes from Simon Hart, *The Pre-History of the New Netherland Company: Amsterdam Notarial Records of the First Dutch Voyages to the Hudson* (Amsterdam, 1959), 41; and Robert Le Blant, "Un commerce international des pelleteries à Paris au début du dix-septième siècle," *Actes du 92ᵉ congrès national des sociétés savantes, Strasbourg, 1967, section histoire moderne*, II (1968), 9-23; see 10-15.

principal partners in the fur trade were, of course, his relatives, Jean Hontom, Evrard Jabach and Co.[29]

Also prominent among the Amsterdam merchants intruding in French colonial trade was a rich Lutheran, Lambert Van Tweenhuysen, born at Zwolle in 1564. He owned a soap factory, dealt in pearls, and traded with Istanbul, Africa, Norway and other parts of Europe as well as with North America. He traded in Canadian furs in association with Jean Macain and Samuel Georges of La Rochelle, when they were in Pierre Dugua de Mons's trading firm based at Rouen.[30] He also chartered ships for Baltic voyages on behalf of Macain and Georges. In 1613, Van Tweenhuysen et Cie sent ships to the Hudson River, and they were one of the strongest groups in the founding of the New Netherlands Company in 1614 to exploit the lands between Virginia and New England, a company regarded with the greatest suspicion in the French circles that were hoping to develop New France.

It was this complex of Huguenot and foreign Protestant business interests that was the principal target of the French campaign to crush La Rochelle and to control the North American colonies through the Company of New France. To the French clergy, who contributed three

---

[29]On their behalf he lent 1190 *livres* in 1608 to François Gravé du Pont, who was sending two ships to trade for furs at Tadoussac and Canso; Le Blant and Baudry, *Nouveaux documents*, 83. This was a bottomry loan at twenty-five percent premium. On 25 February 1609, Duysterloo lent du Pont 1000 *livres* to send *Le François* to trade for furs at Tadoussac, again on behalf of Jean Honton, Jabach and Cie., and on 23 December he bought 100 beaver skins from Gravé du Pont for 772 *livres*, these furs to be brought from Tadoussac to Honfleur by the Scottish captain William Douglas. (Le Blant, "Un commerce internationale," 11-12). Earlier that year Duysterloo had bought 200 Canadian beaver furs from Jean Sarcel of Saint Malo. In 1620 Duysterloo was a member of the Compagnie du Canada and in 1622 of the Compagnie de Montmorency. (Le Blant and Baudry [eds.], *Nouveaux documents*, 182, 418, 419, 432, 466 and 468). Another "Flamand," Lodewicz Vermeulen (alias Louis Vermeulles), had settled at Rouen and taken up the Canada trade. For five years beginning about 1607, Vermeulen and another merchant at Rouen, Jehan Andries, traded in Canadian furs in partnership with Arnout Vogels of the Jabach clan, who lived at Amsterdam. Serving this company as a supercargo on at least one early expedition to New France was François Gravé, Sieur du Pont. Later, from 1613 to about 1625, du Pont sent ships to Canada from Rouen. In those years, Lodewiscz Vermeullen, like Corneille de Bellois, was in Pierre du Gua's Compagnie du Canada. In 1622 he, like Duisterlo and others in the Compagnie du Canada, was admitted into the Compagnie de Montmorency.

[30]Condon, *New York Beginnings*, 14, 20 and 23; and Hart, *Pre-History*, 9.

million *livres* to the royal forces besieging La Rochelle, the purpose of the
struggle was to root out heresy; to the Jesuits and Recollets whom the
Kirke brothers deported from Québec and Acadia in 1629 the Company
of New France was a French endeavour to oppose heresy in North
America; but to Samuel Champlain, whom they also deported, and to the
government of Louis XIII and Cardinal Richelieu, the struggle against
heresy was also a struggle against foreign business interests and imperial
powers. French Catholic merchants, such as the Tuffet-Gaigneur clan,
were encouraged to trade with New France in the course of that struggle.
Assisting them was a way of promoting native French enterprise.

The growth of the trading families in the Gaigneur clan occurred
in the most propitious circumstances. In the reign of Louis XIII (1610-
1642) and the regency that followed (1642-1661) Church and State took
the initiative in founding an empire in North America for religious,
commercial and imperial reasons that can scarcely be separated. The
semi-official printing and publishing enterprises of the *Gazette* were used
by Cardinals Richelieu and Mazarin for a vigorous publicity campaign to
win support for the overseas missions in the Far East, Persia, the Levant,
Africa, the West Indies and not least in Canada. By a concerted effort of
the *dévots* (Catholic zealots) and the crown, the French reading public was
urged to take an interest in Canada through the *Jesuit Relations*, published
as a kind of annual report from 1632 to 1673.[31] In 1633, the editor of the
Jesuit Relations, a Paris bookseller named Sébastien Cramoisy, was a
procureur of the Company of New France as well as an *homme de
confiance* of Richelieu and several bishops; furthermore, it was he who
received and forwarded the large sums of money the Duchesse d'Aiguillon
donated to the hospital nuns of Québec.[32] As a result of this great
propaganda campaign by Church and State, a widespread missionary

---

[31]Charles Frostin, "Vogue canadienne et milieu métropolitain de soutien à la
mission lointaine au XVIIᵉ siècle: l'épopée mystique de la Nouvelle-France," in Joseph Goy
and Jean-Pierre Wallot, *Évolution et éclatement du monde rural: structures, fonctionnement
et évolution différentielle des sociétés rurales françaises et québecoises XVIIᵉ-XXᵉ siècles*
(Paris, 1986), 418–420.

[32]Françoise Bayard, *Le monde des financiers au xviie siècle* (Paris, 1988),
passim; Daniel Dessert, *Argent, pouvoir et société au grand siècle* (Paris, 1984), *passim.*;
and Louis Châtellier, *L'Europe des dévots* (Paris, 1987), 117.

impulse attracted funds from enthusiastic and generous donors.[33] Thanks to the *Jesuit Relations* the Canadian missions had a tremendous vogue in the forty years after the siege of La Rochelle; the Jesuit martyrs and the female missionaries to Canada became heroes and heroines to many. Meanwhile, the Vatican was promoting missionary campaigns through an organization intended to concert efforts to catholicize the world, the Congregation of the *Propagande Fide* founded by Gregory XV on 22 June 1622. In France, Louis XIII and Richelieu responded vigorously to this papal initiative, for instance, by founding the *Congrégation de l'Exaltation de la Sainte Croix* under the auspices of the famous Capuchin, Father Joseph, to support Catholic missions overseas and in France.[34] It would be difficult to exaggerate the ferment of the French Counter-Reformation, and it was driven by a desire to convert Protestant heretics as well as heathen tribes. In a second phase of French imperial endeavour, Louis XIV (1661-1715) and his minister Jean-Baptiste Colbert (1661-1683) began to sponsor overseas trade and colonial development in the 1660s.[35] This, too, was an aggressively Roman Catholic phase notwithstanding the "mercantilism" too often cited as if it were the only driving force in French imperial policies at that time. "Seventeenth-century 'mercantilist' discourse," Goddard reminds us in conclusion to his research, "was pervaded by notions of Christianization and civilization."[36] The Gaigneur clan were among the principal beneficiaries of this state of affairs.

Catholic merchants such as the Gaigneurs, though not high in the social pyramid, were part of the fabric of Bourbon French society. The Huguenot merchants were not. At La Rochelle they suffered the effects

---

[33]Claude Lessard, "L'aide financière de l'Église de France à l'Église naissante du Canada," in *Mélanges d'histoire du Canada français offerts au professeur Marcel Trudel* (Ottawa, 1978), 163–182. Many of the donations appear in Marie-Claire Daveluy, *La Société de Notre-Dame de Montréal, 1639–1663* (Montréal, 1965), deuxième partie, "Bio-Bibliographie des associés de Montréal."

[34]Bernard Jacqueline, "La sacrée congrégation *De Propagande Fide* et la France sous le pontificat de Grégoire XV," *Revue d'histoire écclésiastique*, LXVI (1971), 46–82; and Frostin, "Vogue canadienne," 421.

[35]J.F. Bosher, "The Imperial Environment of French Trade with Canada, 1660-1685," *English Historical Review*, CVIII (1993), 50–81.

[36]Goddard, "Christianization and Civilization," 304.

of the siege in 1627-1628, reinforced by the exile of more than two thousand Huguenots from the town in 1660-1661, and even more by the Revocation of the Edict of Nantes in October 1685. After 1685, indeed, they were outlawed unless they converted, or pretended to convert, to Catholicism. Even when they abjured and became "new Catholics," they suffered a number of disabilities. As a result, Huguenots trading with New France were restricted to trading as *marchands-forains* without a secure place, and they were socially insecure in old France also. As heretics they were normally prevented from buying venal offices that were open only to Catholics, and they were excluded from certain key institutions. At La Rochelle, the *Juridiction consulaire* (commercial tribunal), the *Présidial* (local law court), the *corps de ville* (municipal government), and the *Parlement* of Paris were all closed to Huguenots, but members of the Gaigneur clan appeared in all of them. When these are counted together with family members in the ranks of the clergy, the political strength of the Gaigneur clan becomes apparent, though in the nature of the case it cannot be exactly calculated.

In that age of the Catholic Counter-Reformation the Gaigneur family and its relatives were serving the Church as well as the Crown in their shipping to Canada. They were actively and intimately connected with the clergy, the life of the Church, and the official milieu of La Rochelle and nearby towns that had been Catholic since the siege. In 1630, Pierre Gaigneur's father, Louis Gaigneur, was a *syndic* representing the inhabitants of the parish of Saint Jean-du-Perot and ex-officio on the Catholic *Commission administrative* then established to govern the conquered town. Already Pierre Gaigneur's brother Thomas was a member of the Assembly of Notables which in 1629 established that *Commission administrative*.[37] It was one or the other of these who signed a letter to Louis XIII in 1629 requesting the foundation of a Jesuit College, which the king immediately granted and financed out of

---

[37]ADCM, notes Garnault.

municipal revenues.[38] Later, one of Thomas Gaigneur's sons, Georges Gaigneur, became a *conseiller au Présidial* and *Garde des sceau*.[39]

The family had close relations with the clergy. About 1641 Louis Gaigneur leased the "yield and fruits" of ecclesiastical seigneurial estates from Jehan François de la Tour, "prestre chanoine et archidiacre en l'Église cathédrale de Saint-Pierre de Xaintes, prieur & seigneur du prieuré & seigneurie de la Fondelay," for six years at a price of 1000 *livres* for each of the first three years and 1200 *livres* for each of the last three years.[40] About twenty years later, in 1661, Louis Pérouas tells us, "certain judges such as Le Gaigneur and Voyneau appeared to be fiercely against the Protestants."[41] It is therefore no surprise to find that the principal Canada merchant of the family, Pierre Gaigneur, like his father and brother, was a leading parishioner of Saint Jean-du-Perot: in the 1660s he served as a warden (*marguillier*); over several years he built the west wing of the church at his own expense and was therefore entitled to be buried in it; in 1668 the *fabriquants* and *marguilliers* granted him, his children and descendants, a tomb in the church.[42] His daughter Jeanne was schooled by the nuns of the Providence of St. Joseph and when she

---

[38]Jean Flouret, *Cinq siècles d'enseignement secondaire à la Rochelle (1504–1972)* (La Rochelle, 1973), 35.

[39]ADCM, 4J 996; Rivière (LR), 12 August 1677, *mariage*. In 1635 another merchant in the family, André Gaigneur, son of Pierre and of Jeanne Bouildron, was still living as a Catholic refugee at Bordeaux with one of those rare Bordelais members of the Company of New France, Emmanuel Hucgla.

[40]ADCM, Teuleron (LR) 25 Aug. 1645, fo 102, *transaction*. Louis Gaigneur died in 1642, but his widow carried on this lease until 1645 when she too died, leaving the contract for their children.

[41]Louis Pérouas, *Le diocèse de La Rochelle de 1648 à 1724: sociologie et pastorale* (Paris, 1964), 301n.

[42]ADCM, Teuleron (LR), 13 May 1668; Berthelot (LR), *liasses*, 3 January 1684, *association de Saint Jean;* Teuleron (LR), reg. 20 December 1667 [3 E 1306]: Pierre Gaigneur is a "fabriqueur de l'église Saint-Jean," and he hereby gives 300 *livres* to enlarge the church, "agissant en cette rencontre pour un motif de charité."

decided to become a nun herself he put up 2500 *livres* as a dowry for her.[43]

This was a family that was the beneficiary of official favour during the 1660s and 1670s. The Gaigneur clan was then employed in the maritime trade needed to sustain the French empire. Pierre Gaigneur had contracts with the Crown to transport soldiers to Canada and also to recruit and transport indentured servants (*engagés*). When these contracts began and ended is uncertain, but in April 1667 Colbert wrote to the intendant at Québec, Jean Talon, to say that he had chosen Pierre Gaigneur and some partners at Rouen to recruit 400 men and fifty women as emigrants to Canada. His letter shows the existence of earlier contracts:

> Le Roy fait passer encore cette année en Canada par les soins de la Compagnie ensuite du traité qu'elle a fait avec Sa Majesté quatre cens bons hommes, cinquante filles, douze cavales et deux estalons, et comme le Sieur Le Gaigneur de Rouen et les autres marchands qui sont associez avec luy se sont bien acquitez les années précédentes de tout ce qui a regardé la levée et le passage d'un pareil nombre d'hommes, de filles et de chevaux, je m'asseure que vous en aurez aussi une pareille satisfaction pour cette année, et la prochaine je feray en sorte qu'elle y fasse passer un plus grand nombre de filles afin que les soldats qui se seront habituez dans le pays et les nouveaux colons puissent se marier, et ainsy donner lieu à la multiplication du peuple. [you must arrange to have more habitations to receive them] ...et mesme une levée de deux ou trois cens suisses qu'elle pourra faire dans les Cantons Catholiques pour les y envoyer en mesmes temps....[44]

---

[43]ADCM, Nicolas (LR), 15 June 1680, folio 426.

[44]*Rapport de l'archiviste de la province de Québec* (1930–1931), 67ff., Colbert to Talon, 5 April 1667.

Official correspondence mentions a similar contract for the year 1670.[45] During the same period Gaigneur was also entrusted with sending shiploads of indentured servants for the *Compagnie des Indes* and for the Society of Jesus. With all these official and semi-official orders, he was managing a considerable shipping business, finding, fitting out, and dispatching at least six or seven ships in each of the peak years, 1662, 1666 and 1667.[46] This busy period came to an end in 1672 when Louis XIV and Colbert launched their assault on the Dutch Republic, but in that year Gaigneur was honoured for his services by an official order granting him rank and precedence ("il aura rang et séance") immediately after three other distinguished men at La Rochelle, "[*Messieurs*] Duval, juge magistrat de la police, Garbuzat et de Roy."[47] He seems to have been prosperous in that period, if buying houses and owning two black slaves is any indication.[48] And he was able to make generous contributions to the parish church of Saint-Jean-du-Perot.[49] All this circumstantial evidence points to a religious and political basis for the success of the Gaigneur family in trading with New France.

---

[45]National Archives of Canada, A.N. Colonies, C11A, III, folios 116–118 (bobine F–3), "A Monsieur Colbert, *Mémoire sur le Canada*," February 1670.

[46]ADCM, Teuleron (LR), *liasse* 16 January and 26 February 1666; 9 and 30 June 1667 [3 E 1306]; 12 April, 2 May, and 1 and 4 June 1668. There are also many notarial minutes in the *études* of *maîtres* Moreau (LR), Cherbonnier (LR), Demontreau (LR), Drouyneau (LR), and Savin (LR), Filion (Qc), Romain Becquet (Qc); and admiralty records at La Rochelle beginning with ADCM, B5663.

[47]ADCM, Es. 322, 176, 27 January 1672, Ordonnance of the intendant, Charles Colbert du Terron.

[48]ADCM, Teuleron (LR), 30 May 1668: Pierre Gaigneur buys a house next to his own, parish of Saint-Jean, between the *quai* and the ramparts; La Rochelle Town Library (LRTL), Saint-Jean du Perrot (LR), 24 November 1682, folio 18, *mariage*: of two black slaves from Guinée belonging to Pierre Gaigneur of this parish, Jean *dit sans soucy*, aged about eighteen, and Marie, aged about thirty-eight, neither one able to sign.

[49]ADCM, Teuleron (LR), reg. 20 December 1667 [3 E 1306]: Pierre Gaigneur is a "*fabriqueur de l'église Saint-Jean*," and he hereby gives 300 *livres* to enlarge the church, "*agissant en cette rencontre pour un motif de charité;*" Teuleron (LR), 30 May 1668: Pierre Gaigneur buys a house next to his own, parish of Saint-Jean, between the *quai* and the ramparts.

Signs of Religious Compromise under Business Pressures

The favour of Church and State is not, however, a full explanation for this clan's success. There is evidence of business arrangements in which they collaborated with Huguenot and Dutch heretics, presumably under the pressures of economic circumstances. Although they were strongly Roman Catholic they were also traders struggling for every profitable advantage in business. Wealthy Huguenot merchant families offered opportunities that were apparently too promising to forgo. This is the best explanation, at any rate, for the charters, loans and partnerships which the Gaigneur family contracted with Huguenots. Table 1 shows that Pierre Gaigneur and occasionally one of his forebears, chartered a total of at least twelve Dutch vessels, three others registered at Hamburg, one at Glasgow, six owned by Huguenot merchants of La Rochelle, and three registered at one of the Huguenot satellite ports on the Seudre River estuary. In addition, Pierre Gaigneur and his trading relatives hired Huguenot captains from time to time and entrusted their ships to them for voyages to New France: for example, Mathurin Fory and Tharé Chaillaud, both of La Tremblade, in 1666; André Pasquier, Jacques Chaillé and Pierre Gentet, all of La Tremblade, in 1667. In these arrangements they were making use of that complex of Protestant interests, foreign and native Huguenot, that dominated most of the ocean-going shipping of the seventeenth century. But the French government set itself against these interests more and more as the century wore on. In 1672 Louis XIV launched a war against the Netherlands, its shipping and its religion. In the next few years, Church and State began a campaign of persecution, at home and abroad, that reached a climax with the revocation of the Edict of Nantes in 1685.[50]

Gaigneur borrowed funds from Huguenot or foreign Protestant merchants as well. Table 2 lists some of his loan contracts. It is true that he and his family owed other large sums to Catholic lenders, especially an Irish immigrant, Richard Creagh.[51] But they apparently did not scruple to borrow from Huguenots. It might be argued that borrowing was merely a transaction and did not imply any closer relations than did buying and

---

[50]J.F. Bosher, "The Franco-Catholic Danger, 1660-1715," *History*, LXXIX (February 1994), 5–30.

[51]ADCM, Teuleron (LR), 20 April 1663, 19 April 1664 and 1 June 1665; Moreau (LR), 20 April 1663, showing at least 4000 *livres* owning to Creagh.

selling. A much stronger commitment, however, was Pierre Gaigneur's partnership with Jean Le Royer (died c. 1667), a Huguenot merchant active in the Canada trade and the Newfoundland fishery. In 1660 they both sailed to Canada, in a mixed group of Catholic and Huguenot merchants, at a time when Le Royer had just signed a partnership with another Huguenot in the Canada trade, Jacques Massé.[52] Then, in spring 1666 Gaigneur and Le Royer signed a partnership (*société*) of their own by which they agreed to trade as joint proprietors of *La Paix* of La Rochelle, a ship of 180 *tonneaux*, and to dispatch her to fish on the Newfoundland banks under Captain Mathurin Fory of La Tremblade.[53] Partnerships of Huguenot and Catholic merchants in business, though not so rare as partnerships in marriage, were by no means common in the seventeenth century. Gaigneur seems to have been drawn to cross the religious barrier for business reasons.

Table 1
Ships Chartered at Dutch and Huguenot Ports

Source and Date	Ship	Port	Owner	Captain
Teuleron (LR) 10/4/1636	*Don-de-Dieu*	Chaillevette	J. Derideau	J. Vignaud
Teuleron (LR) 8 and 20/4/ 1638	*Petit Saint-Jean*	Marennes		Jean Coupereau
Teuleron (LR) 23/4/1638	*Marie-Marthe*	Chaillevette	Pierre de Rideau	Nicolas Escubard

---

[52]Marcel Trudel, *Catalogue des immigrants, 1632–1662* (Montréal, 1983), 376 and 430; and ADCM, Cherbonnier (LR), 3 April 1660, *société Le Royer–Massé*. After Jean Le Royer's death, about 1667, his widow, Judith Tharay, and their son (of the same name) carried on the family's trade.

[53]ADCM, Teuleron (LR), reg. 24 April 1666 folio 75, *institution*; 4 May 1666, *société*.

Source and Date	Ship	Port	Owner	Captain
Savin (LR) 9/3/ 1657; Moreau (LR) 20/1/1657	*Armes d' Amsterdam*	Amsterdam		Jean Guyonneau
Moreau (LR) 9/1/1662	*Armes de Zélande*	Zeeland		Janvier de Combes
	Phénix [sic]	Vlissengen		
Cherbonnier (LR) 20/5/1662	*Saint-Jean-Baptiste*	Vlissengen		Guillaume Hurtin
Moreau (LR) 20/4/1663	*Phénix*	Vlissengen		Guillaume Hurtin
Teuleron (LR) 11/2/1664	*Aigle Blanc*	Vlissengen		André Chaviteau
Teuleron (LR) 28/2/1665	*Vieux Siméon*	Durkerdam		
Teuleron (LR) 6/4/1666	*Catherine*	La Rochelle	Jean Depont and Pierre Faneuil	
Savin (LR) 17/5/1666	*Paon*	Holland		André Chaviteau
Teuleron (LR) 24/4/1666, *institution*; 4/5/1666, *société*.	*Paix*	La Rochelle	Gaigneur and Jean Le Royer in partnership	Mathurin Fory of La Tremblade
Teuleron (LR) 2/2/1666	*Constance*	Cadiz	"des Flamands"	Jean Brower of Dorck, Holland
Teuleron (LR) 27/5/1666	*Fortune Blanche*	Amster-dam	C.C. de Vick of Amsterdam	V. de Neuville
Teuleron (LR) 30/4/1667	*Orange*	Nieudam		
Teuleron (LR) 20/5/1667	*Prophète Élie*	La Rochelle	Élie de Baussay	

Source and Date	Ship	Port	Owner	Captain
Teuleron (LR) 16/5/1667	*Petit Agneau*	Hoorn	Jacob Veen de Noornen	
Teuleron (LR) 13/4/1667	*Sainte-Philippe*	La Rochelle	Pagès, Paul Thévenin & Jean Depont	Pierre Gentet
Teuleron (LR) 1/7/1667	*Catherine*	La Rochelle	Jean Depont and Pierre Faneuil	
Teuleron (LR) 5/4/1667 & 5/5/1667	*Nouvelle-France*	La Rochelle	Dutch owners	André Chaviteau
Teuleron (LR) 6 and 18/6/ 1668	*Sainte-Anne de Holstein*	Hamburg		André Réunis
Drouyneau (LR) 8/6/1669	*Saint-Pierre*	Hamburg		Jacob Heull
Teuleron (LR) 6/4/1669	*Pot-de-Beurre*	Hoorn		
Teuleron (LR) 23/2/1669	*Saint-Hubert*	La Rochelle	Depont family	
Teuleron (LR) 8/5/1669	*Saint-Pierre*	Hamburg	Jacob Heuschel	J. Boutin
Teuleron (LR) 5/2/1671	*Saumon Doré*	Glasgow	5 Glasgow merchants	
ADCM no 376 2/9/1684	*Belle Madelon*	La Rochelle	Louis Allaire	

Sources: The information in Table 1 was collected from a number of sources, of which the principal source were the minutes of notaries at La Rochelle (LR) kept at the Archives de la Charente-Maritime, La Rochelle. The sources and their uses are explained in the introduction to J.F. Bosher, *Men and Ships in the Canada Trade, 1660-1760: A Biographical Dictionary* (Ottawa: Historic Sites & Monuments, Department of Environment, Parks Division, 1992).

Credit and Marketing Networks: Trade Organization

It is certain that Pierre Gaigneur did not dispose of much capital of his own, for he often borrowed for his Canadian ventures. Table 3 shows what we know of his borrowing, probably only a sample as our evidence is inevitably incomplete:

Table 2
Huguenot or Foreign Protestant Loans to
Members of the Gaigneur Clan

Source and Date	Sum in *livres*	Lender	Type of Loan	Interest or Premium
Moreau (LR) 3/4/1658	2000	Jacques Bardet	bottomry	30%
Teuleron (LR) 20/5/1662	1416	Antoine Dioré		
Teuleron (LR) 23/4/1663	440	Jean Massiot	bottomry	24%
Teuleron (LR) 23/4/1663	600	Élie or Ézechial Dioré		
Teuleron (LR) 3/4/1663	1250	Paul and Arnaud Walrauen for Abraham Chapman of Amsterdam	bottomry	24%
Teuleron (LR) 21/3/1663	2000	Paul and Arnaud Walrauen		

Source: See table 1.

These formal contracts are misleading, however, as they only hint occasionally at the credit and other benefits that Gaigneur and his many relatives afforded one another in their business activities as a clan. In some ways they worked as a kind of family mutual or co-operative. Gaigneur was seldom alone in his trans-Atlantic enterprises for the circle of his trading relatives was extensive. Various members of the clan had, indeed, been called upon from the very beginning of the family's trans-Atlantic trade. It is important to establish these people's genealogical details because they have commercial as well as personal significance, and so have a place in French imperial history.

Table 3
Pierre Gaigneur's Borrowing

Cherbonnier (LR) 14/3/1659	Pierre Gaigneur borrows 500 *livres* à la grosse from Boursault for use in sending goods to Canada on *Le Sacrifice d'Abraham* going to Canada.
Cherbonnier (LR) 20/5/1662	Pierre Gaigneur and wife borrow 170 *livres* at 24% from Daniel Goizin, md. for goods on *Le Saint Jean Baptiste* sailing to Canada where Pierre Gaigneur is going to trade.
Teuleron (LR) 20/5/1662	Pierre Gaigneur "advictuailleur en entier" of *Les Armes de Zélande* and *Le St. Jean Baptiste*, borrows 1416 *livres* from Antoine Dioré of LR for voyage to Québec.
Moreau (LR) 20/4/1663; Moreau (LR) 20/4/1663	Pierre Gaigneur renewed a bottomry loan passed in 1662 on *Armes de Zélande* and *Saint-Jean-Baptiste* going to Canada, an obligation not reimbursed then because the goods in Canada had not yet been sold. This loan amounted to about 18,000 *livres* and at the same time Grignon incurred an obligation of 4000 *livres* to Richard Creagh.
Teuleron (LR) 23/4/1663	Pierre Gaigneur borrowed 440 *livres* at 24% from Jean Massiot *père* and *fils* to fit out *Le Phénix de Zélande* for Canada and Newfoundland fishing.
Teuleron (LR) 23/4/1663; 22/4/1664	Pierre Gaigneur borrowed 600 *livres* from Élie Dioré.
Bagard (LR) *liasse* 1/5/1663 (*a Teuleron *acte* here filed)	Pierre Gaigneur borrowed 450 *livres* from Claude Torillon, sieur de la Garderie, *Receveur Général des Cinq Grosses Fermes en Poitou et des Aides de La Rochelle*.
Teuleron (LR) 3/4/1664:	as part of a sale of skins, Pierre Gaigneur borrowed 1250 *livres* at 24% from Walrauen on goods and victuals loaded in *Ange Blanc* of Vlissengen.
Teuleron (LR) 15/5/1664; Teuleron (LR) 10/4/1665; Lefebvre (LR) 10/4/1665:	Antoine Grignon and his wife together with Arnaud Peré borrowed 600 *livres* for Pierre Gaigneur from Jean Tausiède in their own names but, in fact, the money was for Pierre Gaigneur, who so certified in an acte of Bagard (LR) *liasse*, 1/5/1679, and then promised to repay Grignon's widow in six months.

Michelon (LR) 14/4/1674 *Obligation*	Pierre Gaigneur borrowed 1500 *livres* from Antoine Bouchel at five percent per month for six months or more of a voyage of *La Nouvelle France*, 250 *tonneaux*, of which he is sole *advictuailleur* for a voyage to Lisbon, Madeira, the WI and back to Nantes or Bordeaux
Bagard (LR) *liasses* 20/3/1689 *venthe de meubles*	Pierre Gaigneur owed Antoine Bouchel 2000 *livres* and offered furniture from his house in repayment of 1500 *livres* of it.
Bagard (LR) 28/2/1690 *sommation*	Guilhen and others of Pierre Gaigneur's creditors have seized this furniture.
Bagard (LR) reg. 6/5/1691	Pierre Gaigneur and his wife have paid 705 *livres* owing to Pierre Cousard, *marchand apothicaire,* by *acte* of Teuleron (LR) 26/8/1675 *obligation*.

Source: Minutes of notaries at la Rochelle, kept at the Archives de la Charente-Maritime, La Rochelle.

Jean Tuffet, the first member of the clan to send ships to New France, organized and managed his trading business almost entirely as a family enterprise and this was typical at that time. We do not know, of course, what he thought about these matters, but the steps he took are eloquent. His son André Tuffet was soon brought into the firm and was ready to step in when his father died in 1642. Almost from the beginning, Jean Tuffet had brought in his nephew, André's cousin, Louis Gaigneur: early in 1630 he engaged Louis Gaigneur to victual the *Petit Saint-Jean,* a ship of fifty *tonneaux* he was sending with supplies to Acadia that year. And in 1632 when *L'Espérance-en-Dieu*, 300 *tonneaux*, returned from Acadia that year, the captain, Charles Menou d'Aulnay, was expected to report to Louis's brother, Jean Gaigneur, a *procureur au présidial* who was active in the family's Canada trade thereafter.[54]

From these beginnings in the 1630s, the family trading circle widened. Already the Gaigneur family had married daughters to merchants in other families who were then drawn into the trade with New France. Indeed, some of them were already in it. And most of them had useful connections with other commercial centres. For instance, a new

---

[54]ADCM, Tongrelon (LR), 26 November 1632; and Teuleron (LR), 12 January 1633.

branch of the clan had developed from the marriage in 1615 of Françoise Gaigneur, Louis's sister, with Guillaume Feniou who traded in brandy and wine at the town of Cognac on the Charente River.[55] He died at some time before March 1656, but his son, also called Guillaume Feniou (1631–c. 1672), travelled to Québec in spring 1656, soon after his father's death, settled there as a merchant, and eventually married into a Québec family.[56] In France meanwhile, two of Feniou's sisters, both named Marguerite, married other merchants who were likewise drawn into the Canada trade. One of these was Léonard Compain, a merchant from Angoulême, with whom Guillaume Feniou *fils* signed a partnership on 4 February 1656 before sailing to Canada; *autre* Marguerite Feniou had married him five years before on 12 February 1651.[57] The other was Jean Chanjon, a merchant of Rodez (Aveyron) whom her sister Marguerite Feniou married in 1637.[58] This link with the Chanjon family was renewed in the next generation when, in 1668, Guillaume Chanjon married Catherine Roy, daughter of Jean Roy and Jeanne Truchot, for Jean Roy's first wife had been Marie Gaigneur, Pierre Gaigneur's sister, daughter of the Canada merchant, Louis Gaigneur.[59] And Jean Roy, a merchant from the Agenais, another region within the orbit of La Rochelle trade, had arranged a partnership with Jean Chanjon and the notary, Pierre Teuleron, on 20 March 1633, to trade together for fifteen years.[60] The partnership contracts and the marriage contracts were both ways of extending the family's trading circle.

The central figure in the history of this clan, as we have seen, was Louis Gaigneur's son, Pierre (c. 1624–1692), the most active merchant of

---

[55]ADCM, Combault (LR), reg. 17 May 1615 (3 E 1251), *mariage*.

[56]See J.F. Bosher, *Men and Trade* (Ottawa, 1992), 64–65.

[57]ADCM, Teuleron (LR), 12 February 1651, *mariage*; Teuleron (LR), 4 February 1656, folio 15, *association*; and A. Godbout, "Familles venues de La Rochelle," *Rapport de l'archiviste de la province de Québec*, XLVIII (1970), 95.

[58]ADCM, Teuleron (LR), 4 May 1637, *mariage*.

[59]*Ibid.*, liasses, 6 May 1634, *mariage* (also in reg., 14 May 1634).

[60]*Ibid.*, liasses, 23 March 1637, *transaction* concerning the partnership signed privately on 20 March 1633.

them all. The family took the biggest step in their development when Pierre Gaigneur contracted to marry Jeanne Grignon on 14 February 1654, a contract signed by a great many family members.[61] The bride was the daughter of an illiterate but capable businessman, Antoine Grignon (c.1612-1675), who was drawn into the Gaigneurs's trans-Atlantic trade almost immediately, and Grignon was to become Pierre Gaigneur's principal partner as well as a shipping merchant in his own right. From this marriage of his daughter, Grignon sent at least one ship to Canada almost every year until he died in 1675, and he died in Gaigneur's house. When he made his will in 1675 he counted an *habitation* at Québec and its furnishings in the account of what he had already given to his son Jean, as well as the interest on several loans and 400 *livres*, "the remainder of a greater sum for moose hides (*orignaux*) which he [Jean] sold for me in Holland."[62] Among the assets counted in Antoine Grignon's postmortem inventory were outstanding claims in Canada totalling 11,246 *livres* and unspecified sums for cargoes of goods left there, some in Eustache Lambert's care.[63] By the time of Antoine Grignon's death his son, Jean Grignon (1639-1703) was also in the Canada trade, and he fitted out *L'Honoré* (150–200 *tonneaux*) for Canada many times in the years from 1678 to 1692, an exceptionally long series of trans-Atlantic voyages for one vessel owned by one merchant.[64] This steady trading may have been due to a relationship with the clergy. In February 1657, for instance, he was fulfilling an order from the Ursulines of Québec, signed on 20 September 1656 by Marie de l'Incarnation, for whom he dispatched "a bale encased, covered with straw, trimmed and roped in several places; on the top and on one end there is written in large letters, *To the Reverend Mothers, Ursulines at Québecq*, and then is written three hundred and fifty and marked with this mark in the margin [of this present document], with which bale the said Grignon is satis-

---

[61]ADCM, Moreau (LR), 14 February 1654, folios 46–47.

[62]ADCM, Teuleron (LR), *liasses*, 9 December 1675, *testament*.

[63]*Ibid.*, *liasses*, 18 December 1673, *inventaire*.

[64]Bosher, *Men and Ships*, 155–156.

fied...."[65] This notarial act was signed "AG" by Grignon, who declared that he could not write, and it was witnessed by Pierre Gaigneur. The Grignon family formed an active branch of the Gaigneur clan.

When Pierre Gaigneur married Jeanne Grignon in 1654 he acquired three more brothers-in-law, besides Jean Grignon, all of whom went into the Canada trade: Auger Grignon (1645-?) who settled in Canada and was still trading there in 1670; and somewhat later, Suzanne Grignon's husband, Arnaud Peré (c. 1640-1695), and his brother Jean. The Peré brothers probably came from Arthez-en-Béarn, but when Arnaud married into the Grignon family he had been trading at La Rochelle for twelve or thirteen years.[66] After several voyages to Canada in the 1650s and in 1660, Arnaud Peré remained at La Rochelle, bought a house in the rue de Saint-Jean-du-Perot and a pew in the church of that name, and went on trading on a considerable scale.[67] Much of his business was with his brother Jean who spent years as a fur trader and explorer in Canada but married and died at La Rochelle. An interesting glimpse of Jean Peré's activities in Canada may be gleaned in a will he made in January 1666, aged twenty-three, when he seems to have thought he was dying.[68] Even at that young age he owned a house at Trois Rivières and another at Cap de la Madeleine, and he already had six godchildren in Canada to whom he wished to leave twenty *livres* apiece. Among his assets he listed two bills of exchange drawn on the Indies Company (545 *livres* and 205 *livres*); several packets of beaverskins left in various places; claims for about sixty moose hides owed to him by Indians whose

---

[65]ADCM, Teuleron (LR), *liasses*, 18 December 1675 (3 E 1364), *inventaire*; and Cherbonnier (LR), *liasses*, 20 February 1657.

[66]LRTL, Saint-Jean du Perrot (LR), 1 August 1661, *mariage*; and ADCM, Moreau (LR), 31 July 1661, folio 161, *mariage* contract. The Peré family's origins remain obscure because the seventeenth-century parish registers for Arthez-en-Béarn have disappeared. Yet this must have been their native town because there is no sign of the Peré family in the registers for the parish of St. Pierre the only seventeenth-century parish in the nearby town of Orthez (which too many authors have cited, without investigating, as the home of the Peré family).

[67]ADCM, Teuleron (LR), reg. 6 March 1669, *transport*, 13 January 1680, folio 27; Trudel, *Catalogue*, 319, 330, 344, 392 and 430.

[68]ADCM, Teuleron (LR), 3 January 1666, folio 2v, *testament*. He signed "Jean Peray" with the usual seventeenth-century indifference to spelling.

names and debts were recorded in a notebook he had left in Canada with
a Jesuit priest, R.P. Harbanel; other claims "of which I know not the
number" in the hands of a Canadian surgeon named Gamelin; and
"something from Sieur Boucher" the amount of which he left to Boucher's
conscience. The debts included seventy-six *livres* owed to Pierre Gaigneur
and to be paid in beaver pelts at the rate of a pound of pelts per *livre*; 500
to 600 *livres* owing to Sieur Petit; and other sums owning to Simon
Baston, these last two being Huguenot merchants.

    None of these other families that were drawn into the Gaigneur
trade were Huguenots or foreign Protestants. All were Catholic and
involved with the clergy no less than the Gaigneurs. As we have seen,
Antoine Grignon was supplying the Ursulines of Québec in 1657 on the
orders of Marie de l'Incarnation. His post-mortem inventory shows six
religious pictures hanging in his rooms in Pierre Gaigneur's house, and
four more in his house at the village of Chagnollet. Jean Grignon
eventually bought a tomb in the Saint-Pierre chapel next to Pierre
Gaigneur's tomb.[69] The Peré family lived in the same parish, rue Saint-
Jean-du-Perot, and Arnauld Peré became a warden (*fabriquant*) of that
church; he and his wife eventually bought a pew in it near the Saint-Pierre
Chapel where they were buried later.[70] In April 1667 Peré hired *engagés*
for the Jesuits of Québec, and twenty years later he was described as
"Merchant, Secretary of the large congregation of men established in the
house of the reverend Jesuit fathers of this town."[71] Their son, Jean-
Arnauld Peré, became a Jesuit priest who served at La Rochelle from
1688 to 1711, perhaps even longer.[72] In 1688 he, like Pierre Gaigneur
earlier, was engaging indentured servants for the Jesuits at Québec and

---

[69]*Ibid.*, 2 January 1680. He paid twenty-two *livres* for it.

[70]ADCM, Berthelot (LR), *liasses*, 3 January 1684, *association de Saint Jean*.

[71]ADCM, Masson (LR), 20 June 1688 folio 57, *engagement* of Jacques
Delouche, a twenty-one-year-old surgeon, and René de Bissay, both from Clermont;
Teuleron (LR), 12 April 1667, *engagement*; Berthelot (LR), 1 and 19 February 1682;
Micheau (LR), 16 September 1686, folio 57, *marché*.

[72]ADCM, Masson (LR), reg. 20 June 1688, folio 57; Marchand (LR), reg. 22
June 1711, folio 100.

sending them across the Atlantic.[73] Other families linked with the clan by earlier marriages were similarly Roman Catholic. The Chanjon family, for instance, were active in the parish of Saint Barthélemy where Jean Chanjon was a *syndic* in 1651; in 1663 their daughter Marguerite became a hospital nun at the age of sixteen on the same day (and in the same notarial act) as her cousin Marguerite Roy, aged twenty, daughter of Jean Roy and of Marguerite Chanjon; a son Auger Chanjon became a priest and was serving at Saint-Martin-de-Ré in 1671.[74] Nothing leads us to doubt that in their attachment to the Catholic cause this clan of La Rochelle merchants matched the Québec community they traded with.

Pierre Gaigneur was in close touch with all these other branches of his family; indeed, he was even present at the double marriage of two lady cousins with two Tuffet magistrates in 1641. And all of Pierre Gaigneur's trading relatives appear to have played parts in his trade with New France, which was extensive. Between 1657 and 1680 he was the manager (*armateur*) or the owner, sometimes both, of at least thirty-four ships sailing to Canada, more than any other individual according to our records, but as these are inevitably incomplete the figure was probably even higher. Some of these ships were jointly owned or chartered with partners and many were instructed to fish for cod after delivering their cargoes at Québec. Gaigneur was not merely an investor in the Canada trade: he chartered or purchased ships, appointed captains and pilots, borrowed funds when necessary, bought ships biscuit (*pain bis cuit*) in large quantities from local bakers, assembled cargoes, and received what his ships brought back across the Atlantic.[75] Now and then he sailed to Canada on one of his vessels, as in 1659 on *Le Sacrifice d'Abraham*, in

---

[73]*Ibid.*, reg. 20 June 1688, folio 57, *engagement*. On this occasion Peré sent René de Bissary and Jacques Delouche, both from the diocese of Clermont.

[74]ADCM, Lefebvre (LR), reg. 19 November 1651 and 30 January 1653; and Teuleron (LR), reg.16 June 1663, folio 205, *liasses*, 25 September 1669 and 4 September 1667, *acte*.

[75]An example of biscuit purchasing is a contract of 12 January 1662 with Moïse Mouhé, who undertook to deliver 100 quintals of biscuit, half at the end of that month and the rest in February, at a price of 13 *livres* 5s per quintal, and Gaigneur paid him 600 *livres* in advance. By 18 March, however, Mouhé had delivered only twenty-seven quintals and so released Gaigneur from the contract so that he could legally buy biscuit elsewhere (ADCM, Demontreau (LR), 18 March 1662, *accord*).

1660 on an unidentified ship and in 1664 on *L'Ange Blanc*.[76] Furs, skins and fish products were, of course, the principal return cargoes, continually mentioned in notarial contracts but difficult or impossible to measure by these occasional brief references. As well as the ships and cargoes, Gaigneur engaged and sent off many indentured servants (*engagés*), at least thirty of them in February and March 1657 alone, several for the Jesuits of Québec and the Indies Company in 1667 and 1668.[77] The West India trade also attracted Pierre Gaigneur: in December 1645, only ten years after France had occupied Martinique, he took a one-eighth share in a plantation (*habitation*) there.[78] But Canada was his principal overseas destination.

Pierre Gaigneur's children were among the next generation of Canada merchants. Gaigneur himself never matched the flourishing decade of the 1660s in his shipping business, and indeed our knowledge of maritime life in Bourbon France leads us to suspect that the Crown probably failed to pay its debts to him. At any rate, he was evidently in financial difficulties in 1689 because he invited Antoine Bouchel, another Canada merchant to whom he owed 2000 *livres*, to choose furniture in his house to the value of 1500 *livres*.[79] When he died on 11 November 1692 his heirs renounced the inheritance as unprofitable.[80] Already a new generation of merchants had been founded in 1685 when his daughter, Marie-Anne Gaigneur, had married one François Viennay Pachot (1658-

[76]ADCM, Cherbonnier (LR), *liasses*, 14 March 1659; Teuleron (LR), 25 April 1664, *vente d'orignaux;* Trudel, *Catalogue*, 349, 392 and 430.

[77]ADCM, Moreau (LR), 3 February and 13 March 1657; and Teuleron (LR), 4 and 12 April and 9 and 30 June 1667, and 12 April, 2 May and 4 June 1668.

[78]ADCM, Teuleron (LR), 30 December 1645, folio 143, *société*. Gaigneur joined with Anthoine Jousset, sieur de la Varennes, living at Brest, Brittany, in taking a quarter-share. The biggest shareholder seems to have been Benoist Baudoin. In 1645 Jousset's plan was to fit out *Le Rochelais* of La Rochelle (100 *tonneaux*) for Martinique.

[79]ADCM, Bagard (LR), *liasses,* 20 February 1689, *venthe de meubles*. Pierre Gaigneur sent few ships to Canada after about 1670 and his last venture seems to have been as ship's captain (!!) of *Le Soleil Couronné*, sailing from Bordeaux, where Jean Jung signed the official papers for the voyage.

[80]ADCM, Rivière & Soulard (LR), 17 May 1700, folio 141.

1719), another merchant trading with New France.[81] By this marriage, the Gaigneurs formed an alliance with what was already a considerable circle of French and colonial traders. Until 1698, Pachot himself traded at Québec, exchanging cargoes with his father, François Viennay Pachot *père* (c. 1628-1698), a merchant at La Rochelle. Their relationship coloured even their bills of exchange: a typical one drawn by the father on the son, and which was preserved only because the son refused to pay (!), begins: "My son, God having conducted Captain Pierre Moizan and the *Saint François Xavier*, of about 40 tons burden, which he commanded after God, you will pay him the sum of 525 *livres* at four days sight [of this bill]."[82] After the father's death, the son went bankrupt in 1705 as a result of wartime losses.[83]

The Pachot family had, as one might expect, formed relationships not only with the Gaigneurs but with other families in the trans-Atlantic trades, thus adding to this great clan in their own way. One of these was the family of Mathias Aramy, a curious figure who lived in Beauvais-sur-Matha, a village at the centre of a wine-producing district southeast of La Rochelle, where he described himself as a "restorateur du corps humain."[84] Whatever it was that he did, Mathias Aramy had brought up several children, four of whom became involved in the colonial trade. Jehan Aramy (1634-?) worked in La Rochelle as a master hatter (*maître chapellier*) and his sister, Marie Aramy (1621-?) married another in the

---

[81]LRTL, St. Jean du Perrot (LR), 29 January 1685, *mariage*; and ADCM, Grozé (LR), 28 January 1685, *mariage* contract.

[82]ADCM, Hirvoix (LR), *liasses*, 27 June 1690, *protest*.

[83]Michel Bégon, letter of 21 March 1705, in L. Delavaud (ed.), *Archives historiques de la Saintonge et de l'Aunis*, XLIX (1935), 78; and ADCM, Cherbonnier (LR), *liasses*, 13 March 1657.

[84]Beauvais-sur-Matha Town Hall, parish register; ADCM, Teuleron (LR), *liasses*, 21 December 1667, *inventaire*; Cherbonnier (LR), reg. 15 August 1655, *mariage*; Grozé (LR), reg. 17 May 1683, *quittance*, 16 September 1686, *quittance*; Berthellot (LR), reg. 8 March 1690, *testament*; and LRTL, Moreau (LR), ms. 1852, folio 46, 18 February 1662, *mariage*, ms. 1844, folios 8-9, January 1655, *mariage*. See also Godbout, "Familles venues de La Rochelle," 133-134, for more details.

same trade, both of them using beaver imported from Canada.[85] Indeed, Jehan Aramy visited Québec in 1683.[86] More important, another sister, Jeanne Aramy (1625-1678) was François Viennay Pachot's mother, having married his father in 1655 and so brought these two families together.[87] And the fourth was Thomas Aramy (1630-80) who emigrated to Québec, became a fur trader there, and had children of whom at least two traded at La Rochelle in the next generation.[88] These were Marie Aramy who in 1681 married Jean-Blaise Busquet (1641-1705) from Dusme (Landes) and Jeanne Aramy who in 1702 married André Estournel, originally from Saint-Étienne-en-Forêt, a well-known trans-Atlantic trader.[89] It should be added that Busquet's children by Marie Aramy were in the next generation of merchants, for two of his daughters married Pierre Charly (1672-1726) of Montréal, who settled at La Rochelle, and Jean Jacques Catignon, who traded across the Atlantic with Estournal early in the eighteenth century.[90]

Thus, the Gaigneur clan had linked itself with at least a dozen other merchant families, many of whom it had introduced into the Canada trade: Aramy, Busquet, Catignon, Charly, Chanjon, Compain, Estournel, Feniou, Grignon, Juchereau, Roy and Viennay Pachot. These formed almost as many different branches of the clan. They lived mainly at La Rochelle but some settled in Canada. Among the lot of them, and including the Tuffet family earlier, they sent at least eighty ships to New France in the years 1630 to 1700, but the identification of ships being so incomplete it seems certain that the total was even greater. In addition, the clan dispatched many cargoes on ships owned or managed by others. All

---

[85]ADCM, Moreau (LR), 18 February 1662, folio 46, *mariage* contract; and Dougnet (LR), 8 November 1643, *mariage* contract, cited in Teuleron (LR), *liasses*, 21 December 1667, *inventaire*.

[86]ADCM, Grozé (LR), 17 May 1683, folio 203, *quittance*.

[87]ADCM, Cherbonnier (LR), 15 August 1655, folio 262, *mariage*.

[88]ADCM, Moreau (LR), 28 November 1755, folio 320, *mariage*.

[89]LRTL, St. Jean du Perrot (LR), 12 November 1681, folio 16, *mariage*; and 13 February 1702, *mariage*.

[90]Bosher, *Men and Ships*, s.v. *Catignon, Charly* and *Estournel*.

of these families did not, of course, work as one business firm but they collaborated in their trade with Canada and Acadia. They were evidently ready to trade, and even occasionally to form a partnership, with a Huguenot merchant, but circumstantial evidence points to the support of Church and State as the basis for their success. It was when that support weakened in Louis XIV's wars that they began to suffer bankruptcies. In the context of the seventeenth century, their activities and success for two generations are best explained as the result of collaboration among an expanding network of relatives that was blessed with the support of Church and State.

Credit, Risk and Reputation
in Late Seventeenth-Century Colonial Trade

Nuala Zahedieh

"Credit is the value raised by opinion," observed Nicholas Barbon, "it buys goods as money does; and in all trading cities there's more wares sold upon credit than for present money."[1] Credit in the sense of belief, confidence, faith, trust, the estimate in which a character is held, reputation, was the elusive but fundamental key to success in early modern commerce. A brief look at the intricate workings of seventeenth-century colonial trade, the nature of the risks involved, and the role of reputation in risk reduction strategies show the overwhelming importance of "credit" and suggest ways in which it shaped the structure of the enterprise.

England's colonial trade was well established by 1660, by which time its people had settled permanent plantations on the American mainland in the Chesapeake and New England and, in the Caribbean, in St. Christophers, Barbados, Nevis, Antigua, Montserrat and (as yet precariously) in Jamaica which had been seized from the Spaniards in 1655. The southern plantations produced valuable cash crops for exchange including tobacco, sugar, indigo, ginger, cotton, and dyewoods; New Englanders provided fish, timber, ships, and shipping services to the southerners; the mother country provided the colonists with manufactured goods, food, and labour (first white but, increasingly, black slaves taken in Africa). In the period down to the Glorious Revolution in 1688 England consolidated and extended settlement in the middle colonies and the lower south and, with the aid of the Navigation Acts streamlined after the Restoration, ensured that an increasing share of the expanding commerce remained in its hands, concentrated on London which emerged as the hub of the system.[2] The precarious figures which survive suggest that the value of

---

[1]Nicholas Barbon, *A Discourse of Trade* (London, 1690), 27.

[2]L.A. Harper, *The English Navigation Laws: Seventeenth Century Experiment in Social Engineering* (New York, 1939); and Nuala Zahedieh, "London and the Colonial Consumer in the Late Seventeenth Century," *Economic History Review*, XLVII, No. 2 (1994), 242.

London's imports from the colonies more than doubled between the 1660s and the end of the century, with similar growth in exports (table 1). Colonial trade accounted for about twenty percent of London's overseas trade but, on account of the long distances involved, a far higher proportion of the shipping and related services.[3] Trade was particularly buoyant in the peace years between 1674 and 1689 with a reported peak in 1686 and many of the figures given here are taken from a computerized survey of the port books for that year.[4]

Table 1
London's Plantation Trade (£ Sterl.)

	1663	1669	1686	1699-1701
Imports	334915	413022	881649	863000
Exports	105910	107792	211868	410000

Sources: 1663 and 1669: British Library (BL), Add. Ms. 36,785; 1686: Great Britain, Public Record Office (PRO), E/190, 139/1, 141/5, 136/4, 143/1 and 137/2, London Port Books (values for 1686 are taken from official valuations assembled by D.W. Jones from the Inspector General's Ledgers, 1696-1698); 1699-1701: R. Davis, "English Foreign Trade," *Economic History Review*, 2nd ser., VI (1954), 150-166.

Organizing the despatch and distribution of goods in colonial trade was a complex and cumbersome process which required trust and credit at every stage. The merchant's first task was to assemble an outward cargo of miscellaneous merchandize on his own or his colonial correspondent's behalf. Information about taste, purchasing power, and seasonality in overseas markets was eagerly sought and willingly supplied but instructions were on the whole fairly general, leaving the London

---

[3]According to Ralph Davis, *The Rise of the English Shipping Industry in the Seventeenth and Eighteenth Centuries* (Newton Abbot, 1962), 306-310, merchant shipping tonnage increased from a pre-Civil War peak of about 150,000 tons in 1640 to about 340,000 tons in 1686. The North Atlantic trades played a major role in this expansion, increasing from virtually nothing in the early seventeenth century to almost forty percent of the total in 1686.

[4]For more comprehensive discussion, see N. Zahedieh, *The Capital and Colonial Commerce in the Late Seventeenth Century* (forthcoming).

merchant to employ his skill and discretion in assembling the most appropriate cargo from goods available.[5] Thus, Walter Mico ignored Waldron's advice to send narrow coloured calicoes and Bengalls to Boston in 1680 and substituted speckled calicoes "which are a better commodity and as I am informed will double my money."[6] Goods were ordered from a variety of suppliers in the provinces as well as in London and usually paid for on delivery, being placed in the debtor column if purchased on behalf of the colonial correspondent. It was impossible to check every parcel of goods and the merchant needed to rely on the skill and honesty of the supplier in providing the quality and quantity specified.[7]

The merchant then needed to arrange specialist packing, of vital importance if the goods were to arrive safe and sound and requiring vast quantities of materials and ingenuity. Hats and books were packed in casks or boxes; Cheshire cheeses were sewn in canvas and tarred to protect them from rats; packing a coach in the 1690s took almost thirty yards of flannel and abundant haircloth.[8] Meanwhile the merchant made enquiries and looked at bills posted in the Exchange to find a ship ready to sail to the intended destination with space for his goods.[9] Needless to say it was important to freight on a stout, sea-worthy vessel with an honest

---

[5]For example, in 1674 Henry Blake of Montserrat advised John Bawden that "those goods most fitting for middle and common planters, them being most the tobacco and indigo makers, will sell well, as canvas, ozenbrigs, blue linen, hats, hoes not broad and other iron wares, with such other as you think best for them and their families. And likewise a parcel of fine goods; few pieces of fashionable stuffs with all trimmings, some ribbons and some other fine goods as you will think good, a parcel of haberdashery will not go amiss. I need not go to particulars being assured of your knowledge in goods needful in those parts." Great Britain, Public Record Office (PRO), High Court of Admiralty (HCA) 15/10, Henry Blake to John Bawden, 4 November 1674.

[6]Massachusetts Historical Society (MHS), Jeffries Family Papers (JFP), VII, folio 12, Walter Mico to Isaac Waldron, August 1680.

[7]*Ibid.* Barbon, *Discourse*, 12, puts the case succinctly: "Because the difference in quality of wares are so difficultly understood it is that the trader serves an apprenticeship to learn them; and the knowledge of them is called the mystery of trade; and in common dealing the buyer is forced to rely on the skill and honesty of the seller to deliver wares with such qualities as he affirms them to have."

[8]MHS, JFP, VII, folio 124, Account, 8 August 1698.

[9]*Ibid.*, II, folio 101.

and competent master who could be trusted to stow the goods with skill and care; make the long Atlantic crossing as quickly and safely as possible; and deliver the entire consignment to the colonial correspondent.[10] It was also important to try and time departure so that the goods would arrive in a favourable market, maximizing prices and minimizing turnaround time in the colonies. The merchant's last task before embarking the goods was to deal with various formalities at the Custom House and, although the author of *The Compleat Tradesman* claimed these were conducted "with all order imaginable," the merchants were vociferous in their complaints about time-wasting and venal officers.[11] John Ive exclaimed in 1683 that "a porter in London is paid better for his time" than he was and the custom house was so troublesome that he "dearly earns" the 2.5 percent commission for goods outwards.[12]

When the cargo arrived at its destination the colonial merchant collected the goods, dealt with legal formalities, and settled with the ship's master for freight and damage. If the goods were spoiled he was expected to do all he could to ensure they were in merchantable condition so, for example, in 1674 £5 was paid to two women to wash and dry John Bawden's goods after they were swept overboard in a storm at Antigua.[13] But at times merchants employed more dubious practices: for example the Halls added molasses to sweeten sour beer in 1688 and in engaging in such activities agents needed to strike a balance between loyalty to their English correspondent and their customers. The English principle would trust the balance lay in his favour. The colonial agent also had to be trusted to employ shrewdness and honesty in selling the goods for the best price obtainable to people who could be judged likely to pay as quickly as

---

[10]The shortest passage was to New England, which was reached in seven or eight weeks and from where it took half as long to return. The longest passage was to Jamaica which took ten weeks out and twelve to return. See Zahedieh, *The Capital and Colonial Commerce*, ch. 2.

[11]H.N., *The Compleat Tradesman* (1684), 6.

[12]MHS, JFP, II, folio 109, John Ive to John Usher, 1 March 1683.

[13]PRO, HCA 15/10, Deposition of Robert Shorton, 19 April 1675.

possible.[14] He also needed to assemble returns in the form of commodities and bills of exchange engaging in a similar round of activities as the merchant shipping outwards.

When the goods arrived back in London the merchant collected them and dealt with customs, damage (picking out dry ginger from wet, or washing and drying damaged molasses) and warehoused them before sale.[15] There was no central market place for selling colonial imports. The Royal African Company, which was the largest single importer from the West Indies, did hold six auctions a year at Africa House in the 1680s but this accounted for only five percent of total imports in 1686.[16] The remaining ninety-five percent of West Indian and all North American goods were sold privately with much haggling and bargaining.

In 1678 William Freeman importing from Nevis described his transactions with John Fleet, a major re-exporter of sugar. Fleet had offered the top price of 25/3 per 100 lbs. for nineteen hogsheads of sugar unseen. When the sugars were viewed they

> proved such goods that I never before have seen indeed they could not bear the name of sugars which occasioned the party to refuse his bargain and not without just cause but however I contested it with him and referred it to honest men who were of the opinion they could not bear the name of sugars so that the bargain was void in itself...I believe the worst trash that ever the island of Barbados made could not be so bad. However, Mr Fleet was so fair in a proposal he made me that no man in justice could refuse. That was that I should try the market

---

[14]Efforts to ensure the best price could involve some very dubious practices. For example, the Halls reported in 1689 that "the beer that came out next and so to the end proved bad that we were forced to strengthen it with molasses and rum etc., and sell for £12 per ton. Some of it was quite sour. We have sold about 20 pipes from £13 to £14.10s. We hope they will rise but however the charges of keeping them is great and a good customer is better than a bad." PRO, C110/152, Brailsford Papers (BP), Halls to Brailsford, 20 June 1689.

[15]H.N., *Compleat Merchant*, 149-150; M. Balderston (ed.), *James Claypoole's Letter Book London and Philadelphia, 1681-1684* (San Marino, 1967).

[16]K.G. Davies, *The Royal African Company* (London, 1957), 179-181.

and whatever any man bid for them he would give 12d per cent more in conformity to his bargain which I did and brought several sugar bakers to look upon them, some whereof would not bid any money for them others bid 19 shillings and 20 shillings the highest bid 20/6 per cent forced to sell them to the said Mr Fleet at 21/6 per cent.[17]

Once again the merchant needed considerable skill to judge the state of the market in terms of quantity and quality of goods available so that he could squeeze the last penny from his purchaser, negotiating not only over the basic price, but over charges such as warehousing and wastage. It was also important to judge the depth of the purchaser's pocket, as Claypoole retorted on being told he was outsold by another merchant, "as to the man he then sold to he broke twice if not thrice and I would not have trusted him [even] if he would have given me six shillings per cent more than I sold for....I think I know how to sell sugar as well as he or any man."[18]

The merchant who had despatched goods to the colonies on his own account could now judge whether he had made a profitable bargain by reckoning what he had made over and above "prime cost, charges and interest" or the time he had been out of his money.[19] A ship would make the return voyage within a year but, of course, the merchant's money was tied up much longer. The months taken to assemble the cargo, the months to obtain sale and payment in the colonies and the months to receive payment at home extended transactions to years. Much depended on the skill, judgement, and assiduity of the agents at each stage.

Misfortune had ample opportunity to reduce or wipe-out profit. Bad weather, fire, piratical attack, were only some of the common hazards facing trans-Atlantic traders. But these accidents could be insured against and the fact that premiums were as low as three to seven percent in peace time and that merchants like the Halls in Port Royal insured only half their ventures suggests that these were not perceived as major

---

[17]Institute of Jamaica (IJ), Ms. 134, "William Freeman's letter book," folio 3.

[18]Balderston (ed.), *Claypoole*, 149.

[19]Barbon, *Discourse*, 2 and 12.

threats.[20] In fact all but one of twenty-one ships leaving London for Jamaica in 1686 arrived safely and the island's naval officer's returns for the same year indicate only five examples of misadventure among 152 ships entering the port. Three vessels were plundered by the pirate Bannister and two Spanish masters claimed they were "forced in by stress of weather," a usual excuse for illegal entry.[21] In a sample of 172 court cases culled from late seventeenth-century Admiralty, Chancery and Exchequer proceedings it is striking that defendants frequently blame loss on some accident but, in most cases, the protestations might easily be a disguise for poor judgement or, worse, perfidy. For example, one captain who entered London with a fraction of the expected cargo claimed that he had been forced into Kinsale (a notorious "back-door" for evasion of the Navigation Acts) by bad weather and was forced to sell goods to purchase provisions.[22] Others claimed goods were thrown overboard in a storm; cargoes were damaged, even entirely devoured by rats; fire was caused by women Negroes smoking tobacco between the decks; pirates plundered entire vessels; gluts and scarcities explained extremely high and low prices as well as long turnaround times. Not surprisingly merchants often suspected the defendants' veracity. At each stage of the lengthy, complex, and unpredictable process involved in colonial exchange the merchant needed to trust the "fidelity, diligence, and honesty" of others.[23] Suppliers, packers, captains, colonial correspondents or purchasers were all in a position to undo him and as misplaced trust was the major source of loss, fraud limitation was the main preoccupation of the players in the game.

The long distances involved in Atlantic commerce and its unpredictability meant it was impractical to try to tie down agents with rigid instructions and a principal usually confined himself to vague exhortations to his agent to "carefully, diligently, and faithfully imploy and apply, use, and exercise himself according to the best and utmost of

---

[20]PRO, BP.

[21]PRO, Colonial Office (CO) 142/13, Naval Officers' Returns, Jamaica, 1682-1705.

[22]PRO, HCA 13/131, Hopewell deposition.

[23]*Ibid.*, HCA 13/79, 13/131 and 13/132; and H.N., *Compleat Tradesman*, 155.

his power, knowledge, skill, and experience."[24] Of necessity much was left to the agent's discretion.

Various incentives were offered for good behaviour. Remunerations were higher in colonial commerce than other branches of overseas trade. Captains were paid twenty percent more than those engaged on European voyages.[25] Factors were paid eight to ten percent commission in America compared to two to three percent in France, Spain, and Portugal and as low as 1.5 percent in Holland.[26] Every effort was made to ensure loyalty through offering repeat business, and exclusive agency as in the case of Henry Ashurst writing to Hampden in 1684 promising "if I can get more ready I intend to ship more of this kind of cloth. I can buy as well or better than any other and if you sell them well I design to send what I do wholly to you."[27] Undertaking reciprocal services which ensured that your agent was as dependent on you as you on him was an obvious strategy for promoting good behaviour. Finally every effort was made to create goodwill through gift exchange, sponsorship of drinking of health, and general expressions of friendship and exchange of family news.[28]

Unfortunately for many disappointed merchants the returns to cheating were so high, the risks of quick discovery so low, that high commissions and mutuality often weighed relatively little. It took William Freeman years to realize the full extent of his losses in Montserrat at the hands of

> a crafty undermining sophister who would not fail to make use of all opportunities to deceive me and abuse my interest as he hath done for these eight years last past by

---

[24]Oxford University, Bodleian Library (OUBL), Ms. Aubrey 4 (SC 25279), folio 1, Indenture between William Paggen and John Hardmian, 1684.

[25]Masters in the West India trade were paid £6 per month in the 1680s and given the benefit of carrying a venture of £200 or £300 freight free; PRO, HCA 13/79.

[26]H.N., *Compleat Tradesman*, 155.

[27]OUBL, Ashurst Letter Book.

[28]PRO, BP, Halls to Brailsford, 4 October 1688.

meanes whereof he hath raised to himself a very considerable estate.[29]

Although late seventeenth-century businessmen mainly subscribed to the view that they were privileged to live in a country where their liberties and properties were secured by "a gracious prince and most wholesome laws" they did, nonetheless, find the law more useful as a threat than in reality; litigation was a last resort to be avoided if at all possible.[30] But, if the law was a blunt instrument at home it was an even blunter instrument for preventing or punishing crime across the Atlantic. This was well illustrated in 1685 in the case of William Smith who claimed John Thornberry had embezzled proceeds of eight jars of oil sold on his behalf in Jamaica. It was impossible even to prove Thornberry's precise whereabouts, whether in Jamaica or Spanish America as he claimed. Thornberry asserted that all his papers had perished at sea and "witnesses that should testifie the truth of all and singular the promises are in Jamaica and in other places beyond the seas....not able to appear on the behalf of your orator at any trial at law, your orator must necessarily be remediless according to the strict rules of common law."[31]

With relatively little effective protection from the law merchants relied heavily on "reputation" and "credit" as tools for building essential networks of tried and trusted agents. Reputation was built on a code of conduct which bound rules of reason and religion; honour and interest: a neat blend of pragmatism and idealism which promised deviants punishment in the form of divine wrath, a stinging conscience and, above all, public shame alongside damage to pocket and pride. The prototype

---

[29]IJ, Ms. 134, "Letterbook Of William Freeman," folio 387, letter, 14 September 1682.

[30]*The Character and Quality of an Honest, Loyal Merchant* (1686); and *The Art of Thriving* (1674); "Then again if you would grow rich be not given to law, for the quarreling dog hath a tattered skin; and men of strife, like too sharp a sword, cut their own scabbard. And truly, what our Lord saith, is prudently practicable: he that sueth thee at law for any cloak, let him take thy coat also: for it is much better to sit down with some manifest loss, than to recover any right by a trial at law, unless the matter be of very great moment is the lawyer alone goes away with the gain." H.N., *The Pleasant Art of Money-Catching* (1686), 134.

[31]PRO, E 112/475/2127.

"merchant of reputation" appears in contemporary advice books, pamphlets, broadsheets, and ballads.[32] He was a paragon of prudence, wisdom, and justice. He was knowledgeable about his business (familiar with countries, ports, shipping routes, commodities, financial and legal instruments, and much else). He knew, understood, and abided by merchant custom. He was diligent, but careful not to overburden his mental or physical resources. He was cautious in extending and taking credit. He regulated his domestic expenses for "expensive living is a kind of slow fever that preys upon the spirits and vitals of the tradesman, and when it is considerably increased it is fatal and as sure to kill: it feeds upon the two most essential branches of his trade, his credit and his cash; whereby the languishing tradesman is overwhelmed."[33] He kept careful accounts and often inspected his affairs; "hence his books are allowed evidence and looked upon as a kind of records."[34] He displayed "justice" or fairness in his dealings; performed his promises, paid and demanded a fair price for his goods, was exact about weights and measures, and ensured good quality goods. He paid his bills and debts promptly for "a small script of two or three lines only under his hand, without either witness or seal, passes over the world for thousands of pounds."[35] He took particular care not to go bankrupt "upon design" in order to defraud creditors of their dues and enrich himself with their spoils. According to Richard Steele the last was the most inexcusable violation of justice:

> Such iniquity can have no refuge to screen itself from confusion and remorse, but a feared conscience, or direct atheism: how many heinous sins dost thou wilfully and deliberately commit, for a little momentary gain. Here are repeated lies, if not perjury; stealing, notorious

---

[32]Examples include R. Steele, *A Tradesman's Calling* (1686); *Character and Qualifications of an Honest, Loyal Merchant* (1686); *A Description of Plain-dealing, Time, and Death, Which all Men Ought to Mind Whilst They Do Live on Earth* (1686).

[33]*The Religious Tradesman* (new edition; London, 1802), 31.

[34]*Character and Qualifications*, 5.

[35]*Ibid.*

hypocrisy and dissimulation; contempt of God's law and justice and injury to men."[36]

The first task for a young man embarking on a career in trade was to establish his own reputation in order to attract custom. In a very real sense a merchant's reputation was his capital: "wealth is the result of credit and credit the natural effect of fair-dealing."[37] When Claypoole recommended business with John Bawden, London's leading West-India merchant, he pointed to his having "as great estate *and* repute as few beyond him in the city."[38] Both were essential: business with a poor man was risky but business with a dishonest man was simple foolishness.

A merchant needed to advertise his credit and reputation and since little store could be placed on the self-puffery and assertions of personal "integrity and honesty" common in commercial correspondence more convincing evidence was required. Willingness to take occasional losses was one ploy to demonstrate "uniformly upright conduct...whether it meets with present applause or not, or even though it should sometimes thwart his present interest."[39] As Francis Hall complained in 1688 when selling for low prices, "its nonsense to trade at such vast disadvantages and really what we do now is with an ill-will, but must do it that may not lose the reputation that have gained amongst my friends of selling cheap."[40] Claypoole often felt obliged to share a loss or bear partial costs of damage even though not compelled by "law, custom or equity."[41] Similarly, Freeman's account of his transaction with Fleet underlines the importance attached to "justice" and "square-dealing." Although the sugars were pronounced substandard by "honest" arbitrators, Fleet felt an obligation having made a prior bargain and "was so *fair* in a proposal he made me that no man in *justice* could refuse." A mutually acceptable

---

[36]*Religious Tradesman*, 58.

[37]*Case of the Fair Trader*.

[38]Balderston (ed.), *Claypoole*, 173 and 183.

[39]*Religious Tradesman*, 50.

[40]PRO, BP, Halls to Brailsford, 20 June 1689.

[41]Balderston (ed.), *Claypoole*, 88.

compromise was worked out using the "honest men" as brokers which spread the loss resulting from inferior goods being delivered and preserved business reputations and a good relationship.[42]

In addition to establishing his own reputation an intending merchant faced the more taxing task of deciding who to trust. As the advice manuals warned this was where the real difficulties lay for although men were not created in order to "prey upon and devour one another" and both interest and conscience required that everyone should deal with others as they wished to be dealt with themselves, nonetheless "their vicious inclinations prevail with them to act contrary to it."[43] As Richard Steele warned:

> Great prudence is necessary in the choice of...whom to trust; for it is not always the metal that glitters most, that is always the richest; men are often deceitful, and too many make it their business to deceive, and enrich themselves with the spoils of the unwary and credulous. It is better, therefore, to be at the pains of a diligent inquiry after their abilities for the trust that we repose in them; than endure the grief of sad experience that we were mistaken in our apprehensions concerning them. Certain it is that there is prudence in trusting some, and charity in trusting others; so there are many whom it is neither prudence nor charity to trust at all.[44]

Information about character and reputation was eagerly sought. The *Lex Mercatoria* noted that each man's credit was determined by talk at the merchant's London meeting place – the Royal Exchange. Claypoole visited daily and was scathing about the less conscientious:

> I suppose Dr. Harding has advised thee to deal with Thomas Hinchman who is his friend...but if thou does I am sure thy business will be neglected and thy sugars ill-

---

[42]IJ, Ms. 134, "William Freeman's Letter Book," folio 3.

[43]*Religious Tradesman*, 50.

[44]*Ibid.*, 28.

sold and possibly a bad debt, for he dwells in the country and has only a lodging in London and is seldom seen at the Exchange.[45]

Malicious gossip and defamatory rumours could do immense damage to a man's business and were actionable at common law. But although accusations of dishonesty and bankruptcy were actionable in themselves the courts became so overloaded that they construed words like "bankrupt" and "knave" as innocent when used adjectivally or in the heat of passion and insisted on proof of financial damage as distinct from insult. Many cases were handled by municipal and guild courts or by arbitration but the law could seldom provide adequate repair to damage.[46]

Table 2
Merchants in London's Colonial Export Trade, 1686

Value of trade £ sterling	0-99	100-999	1000-4999	5000-9999	Total
West Indies					
Number of merchants	521	166	20	2	702
Value of trade, £	14355	54393	31303	11341	113392
Percent of total	13	49	28	10	100
North America					
Number of merchants	476	176	18	1	691
Value of trade, £	13379	51500	29780	5881	100541
Percent of total	13	51	30	6	100

Source: PRO, E190/139/1; 141/5 and 136/4. Values are taken from official valuations assembled by D.W. Jones from the Inspector General's Ledgers.

---

[45]Balderston (ed.), *Claypoole*, 183.

[46]R. Grassby, *The Business Community of Seventeenth Century England* (Cambridge, 1995), 299-300.

Merchant correspondence is full of requests for information about others and what amounts to informal character references. But information travelled slowly and was only as good as the provider who was often as distant from retribution as the subject of enquiry. Given these difficulties in obtaining accurate information, the very high levels of risk and dependence on others requiring careful nurturing of personal contacts it is perhaps unsurprising that, despite it's openness, celebrated by contemporaries and historians, colonial trade was, in fact, quickly concentrated into relatively few hands.[47] It is true that large numbers participated in the trade. The London port books of 1686 list 1283 merchants importing from the West Indies and 626 from North America; these were high numbers in a period when a London Directory lists a total of 1953 overseas merchants.[48] But most of the entrants participated in a small way. About sixty percent of those people consigning goods to either North America or the West Indies exported goods worth less than £50 and over forty percent imported less than £50 worth. Small and first-time investors were particularly vulnerable to loss through fraud or incompetence, having less leverage over their correspondents, and as Price and Clements have shown for the Chesapeake trade, a small number of merchants quickly came to dominate the whole colonial trade.[49] In 1686, twenty-two merchants exported English goods over the value of £1000 to the West

---

[47]A report to the Council of trade in 1686 pointed out the advantages of plantation trade: "Neither is this trade stinted To any company but all His Majestie's subjects whether in England or Ireland may without any special license trade thither if they will so that the trade of our plantations doth not as some other trades swell one part of the Kingdom and make all the rest feeble and lean; but is a trade that far more equally distributes itself into all parts of these nations, that any, or all the trades that we have besides." OUBL, Ms. Rawl A 478. On the political implications of open access to the trade see R. Brenner, *Merchants and Revolutionaries: Commercial Change, Political Conflict and London's Overseas Traders, 1550-1653* (Cambridge, 1993). Claypoole indicates the reluctance to risk new relationships in a letter to a friend in New England: "I have spoken to some of my friends to correspond with thee, but at present they are fixed and loath to alter, but be sure I shall make use of every opportunity of recommending thee to such as I know to be fair-dealing men." Balderston (ed.), *Claypoole*, 63.

[48]*The Little London Directory of 1677* (1878).

[49]J.M. Price and P.G.E. Clemens, "A Revolution of Scale in Overseas Trade: British Firms in the Chesapeake Trade, 1675-1775," *Journal of Economic History*, XLVII (1987), 1-43.

Indies accounting for about forty percent of the total value and nineteen merchants exported over £1000 value to North America comprising thirty-five percent of the total. In the import trade twenty-eight merchants imported over £5000 value from the West Indies (accounting for almost half of total value) and seven from North America added nearly thirty percent (see tables 2 and 3).

Table 3
Merchants in London's Colonial Import Trade, 1686

Value of trade £ sterling	0-99	100-999	1000-4999	5000-9000	+10,000	Total
West Indies						
Number of merchants	742	427	86	15	13	1283
Value of trade, £	25845	101847	187533	118104	217186	674518
Percent of total	3.5	20	28	17.5	32	100
North America						
Number of merchants	339	172	38	5	2	626
Value of trade, £	10972	57923	77078	32992	28166	207131
Percent of total	5	28	37	16	14	100

Source: PRO, E190/143/1 and 137/2. Values as in table 2.

The importance of personal connections and the difficulty in building more than a few solid relationships is further reflected in high levels of specialization by destination. Taking the twenty-eight largest importers from the West Indies only, seven imported significant amounts from more than one island, including the Royal Africa Company and the King who received a 4.5 percent tax on output in Barbados and the Leewards (see table 4).[50] Similarly all but one of the top twenty importers from North America specialized by destination. There was some overlap

---

[50]PRO, CO 1/19, folios 47-51, "Act for Settling an Imposition...," 12 September 1663. For a discussion of the duty, see A.P. Thornton, *West-India Policy under the Restoration* (Oxford, 1956), 22-38.

between the two trades — sixty percent of New England traders with over five consignments also recorded entries from the Caribbean, reflecting the mutual dependence of the two regions. For example, John Ive, London agent of various leading Boston merchants including David Jeffries and John Usher, imported goods worth £3179 from Jamaica. Although there was considerable specialization by destination there was little specialization by commodity other than that dictated by the economies from which the goods were shipped. Agents and planters aspired to remit whatever goods seemed likely to be more advantageous and engaged in long discussion of local availability and prices versus the expected price in Europe.[51] But their information was patchy, partial, and out of date and anyway they had less autonomy than they cared to imagine and usually had to make up cargoes as best they could from what was offered locally and the resources at their disposal at the time. Furthermore, as the Royal African Company's factors often complained, the presence of many small traders foiled attempts to rig markets.[52]

By the 1680s most merchants involved in Atlantic trade in a substantial way seem to have established a high degree of regional specialization stemming from the overwhelming necessity of firm, reliable credit networks dependent on little more than the fragile ties of reciprocity and reputation and the difficulty of maintaining more than very few such relationships. Ready-made trust networks were clearly important tools for the aspiring merchant but, for most people, these were confined to kin networks. Many merchants echoed Ashurst's pleadings to his cousin Hampden that "upon the score of relation as well as your own interest you will do what you can in the sales."[53] And there were cases such as the Heathcotes where kin networks were very effective. However, cousins, nephews, siblings, even fathers and sons often proved disappointing;

---

[51]The theme of prices is prominent in all merchant correspondence. An example is the discussion of pimento prices in PRO CO 110/52, Brailsford Papers, Halls to Brailsford, 28 September 1689.

[52]In November 1681 the African Company's Jamaican factors reported that they had agreed with the most considerable merchants to lower the price of sugar by resisting from buying. But in March 1684 they reported that the prices of sugars were kept up "by little traders." In February 1686 they reported another attempt to reduce sugar prices, again to no avail. PRO, T70/10, folio 28; and T70/12, folios 63, 71 and 75.

[53]OUBL, Ashurst Letter Book, folio 35.

presumably this was because exclusion from the family circle was not always viewed with horror.

Table 4
Merchant Consignments from the West Indies to London, 1686

	Barbados	Jamaica	Leewards	Total
Royal African Company	85	88	26	198
John Gardner	242	13	16	271
Francis Eyles	256	13		269
King James II	128	-	43	171
John Harwood	247	1	2	250
Thomas Tryon	174	4	1	179
Paul Allestree	151	-	-	151
Joseph Perkins	143	4	1	148
Thomas Clarke				
Christopher Fowler	130	4	2	136
Stephen Skinner	126	3	2	131
Richard Tilden	147	-	2	149
Thomas Elliot	-	-	31	31
Bartholomew Gracedieu	2	57	-	59
William Wrayford	4	1	42	47
Richard Cary	1	5	31	37
Thomas Hunt	99	12	14	125
William Barnes	-	3	18	21
Joseph Martin	2	-	42	43
Henry Hale	112	5	2	119

Source: PRO, E190/143/1; 137/2.

Religious networks proved more robust, being able to provide reliable information about individuals, support in crisis and powerful disciplinary measures to deter wrong-doing. Shame or, in extreme cases, exclusion from the community mattered. The importance of Quakers in colonial commerce is well established but the secular explanation is probably more important than the usual emphasis on the content of their code of conduct, which differed very little from that exhorted in all contemporary advice manuals.[54] What set the Quakers apart was their ability to enforce the code and transmit information about character and wrong-doing.

Table 5
Exports from London to the West Indies, 1686 (£ Sterling)

	Barbados	Jamaica	Leewards
Anthony Gomezsera	759	138	136
Gilbert Heathcote	-	1034	-
Thomas Tryon	1023	-	14
Anthony Lauzado	1125	-	-
John Eston	1141	-	-
Peter and Pier			
Henriques	896	257	-
John Pitt	1174	-	-
Richard Goodall	560	-	53
Francis Eyles	1275	35	-
Stephen Jermyn	1407	20	-
Moses Barrow	-	1443	-
William Coward	-	1446	-
Joseph Bueno	1031	452	9
John Hill	1514	-	57
Emanuel Perara	332	-	1255
John Harwood	1715	-	8
John Gardner	1953	8	40
William Wrayford	35	23	2092
Robert Curtis	1112	-	-
Thomas Hunt and Co.	3345	-	-
Manuel Mendez	5001	-	-
Thomas Hunt	5837	502	-

Source: See table 2.

---

[54]F.B. Tolles, *Meeting House and Counting House. The Quaker Merchants of Colonial Philadelphia, 1682-1763* (Chapel Hill, 1948).

By the late seventeenth century there was a Quaker meeting in almost every colony as well as in every county of England with a yearly meeting in London acting as the hub for both information and regulation. Meetings sent regular communications and when the yearly meeting compiled a code of conduct it was copied out and sent to meetings everywhere.[55] Friends were instructed to watch over one another and ensure adherence to rules against over-trading, or breaking trust in any way and were notoriously hard on those who failed in business. Bankruptcy was ground for disownment, that is expulsion from the meeting, which was a powerful deterrent to men like Claypoole who participated in the total Quaker lifestyle. Monthly and quarterly meetings were not taken up with unfocused generalities about sin and forgiveness: members delivered detailed criticism of individual personal, social or business behaviour, followed up by visits to miscreants and systematic reports on the restitution they were required to make. It is not surprising that Quakers became attractive to deal with outside their own community.

The discipline of the meeting was reinforced by the communication networks between meetings. Distant Quakers would not only provide detailed business information about their own members but also good general intelligence.[56] Friends needed to carry certificates of clearance and introduction when they travelled between meetings.[57] Finally they provided solid support to all members whether familiar or strangers, helping friends to get apprenticeships, set up in business, providing custom and financial assistance at time of crisis.[58] All in all Quakers were equipped to do relatively well in colonial commerce.

Jewish success was even more striking and again may be attributed to effective communication and trust networks based on an enforceable code of conduct. In 1686, although there were fewer than 1000 Jews in London all told, there were seven among the twenty-two

---

[55]Friends House, Yearly Meeting Minutes, I, 19-20, 27 March 1675.

[56]Friends House, Epistles Received, Vol. I (1683-1706); Minutes of Yearly Meeting.

[57]American Philosophical Society Library, Ms. 917, 29/W455, George Welch, "A Journal of My Voyage," 1671.

[58]T. Story, *A Journal of the Life of Thomas Story* (Newcastle, 1747).

largest exporters from London to the West Indies.[59] The well-established
Sephardi transit trade between Europe and Iberian America had taken new
shape following the collapse of Dutch Brazil in 1645-1654, for this had
led to the expulsion of the Jews and the spread of sugar cultivation in the
Caribbean islands.[60] The Jews, whose commercial success in Europe
rested on importing and processing colonial products, together with the
bullion and jewel trade, fanned out all over the Caribbean, numbering
about 4000 in the 1680s living in various small, close-knit communities
including about 300 in both Barbados and Jamaica.[61] All were linked, not
only by religion, but also by kinship, language, culture, and commercial
interest across boundaries between different empires and all, to some
extent, revolved around the hub of Sephardim in Amsterdam.

The universal and long-standing precariousness of Jewish life
militated strongly in favour of subjection to discipline and authority.
Boards of Elders nominated each year from among a congregation's
wealthiest members could exert authoritarian, even despotic rule. It was
not simply a question of upholding the Torah and pursuing the moral
ideals of Judaism. Anything likely to disrupt the unity of the congregation
or to exacerbate the ever present reality of popular hatred was deemed a
threat to the community. Boards of Elders controlled charity, sick care
and education, exercised moral and intellectual censorship, arbitrated in
business disputes, suppressed anything which could be viewed as
provocative behaviour and maintained a generally formidable grip over
every aspect of the Jewish way of life. Isaac Cordosa claimed that "the
Jews are not the Serfs of other nations but a Republic apart which lives
and governs itself by its laws and precepts which God gave them at Sinai."
Congregants, unless they wished to be cast adrift among the gentiles, had

---

[59]Maurice Woolf, "Foreign Trade of London Jews in the Seventeenth Century,"
Jewish Historical Society of England Transactions, XXIV (1974), 38-58.

[60]J.I. Israel, *European Jewry in the Age of Mercantilism, 1550-1750* (Oxford,
1985), 154-158.

[61]PRO, CO 1/44, folio 1420379, Census of Barbados, 1680; W. Samuel, "A
Review of the Jewish Colonists in Barbados in the Year 1680," *Jewish Historical Society
of England Transactions*, XIII (1932-1935), 1-97. On the rapid penetration of Jews into
Jamaica's contraband trade, see Nuala Zahedieh, "The Capture of the Blue Dove, 1664.
Policy, Profits and Protection in Early English Jamaica," in R. McDonald (ed.), *West
Indies Accounts* (Kingston, Jamaica, 1996), 34-35.

little choice but to comply.[62] Evidence that the Jews were successful in enforcing discipline and promoting mutual trust is seen in the pattern of their trade which is significantly different from that of gentile merchants. Although the latter concentrated on their trade in one destination Jewish activity was often evenly divided between different destinations. Access to reliable information about reputation backed by strong guarantees of good behaviour provided the Jews with a strong competitive advantage which underpinned their substantial role in Atlantic commerce.

Table 6
Value of Goods Imported by Major Jewish merchants, 1686 (£ Sterling)

	Barbados	Jamaica	Leewards	Total Value
Emanuel Perara	431	-	-	431
Joseph Bueno	845	-	-	845
Peter/Pierre Henriques	1358	1851	-	3209
Manuel Mendez	2075	-	-	2075
Anthony Lauzado	2045	1	367	2423
Anthony Gomezsera	1286	206	1702	3194

Source: See table 3.

England's westward expansion in the seventeenth century provided a wide range of opportunities to manufacturers, merchants and shippers. The vigour and enthusiasm with which these were exploited was reflected in the rapid rise of colonial commerce after the Restoration and contributed to a substantial restructuring of the national economy which brought accelerated growth in the eighteenth century. However, the expansion was attended by very high risks. The commerce was based on a long chain of promises: promises to provide goods, promises to pay, promises to deliver and so on. Those on either side of the bargain relied largely on trust and inevitably a merchant needed to pay careful attention to promoting and publicizing his own probity and justice while taking adequate steps to ensure the good character of others. The preoccupation

---

[62]This paragraph draws heavily on Israel, *European Jewry.*

with fraud as the major source of loss and the pivotal role of trust and reputation in risk reduction strategies was reflected in the structure of the trade which, despite being celebrated as open to all, quickly became concentrated in relatively few hands with high levels of regional special-ization. Merchants reduced risks, not by spreading business between as many agents as possible, but by confining themselves to a few well-tried and trusted correspondents with whom a standing relationship was reinforced, where possible, by mutuality and the promise of repeat business. Furthermore, the nature of risk in colonial commerce placed groups such as Quakers or Jews in a strong position which no doubt explains their levels of participation, (well above what would be predicted from their total numbers in the population) and the more dispersed nature of their trade. Their strength drew partly on their "awe of God and con-science" but, perhaps even more, on the community leaders' ability to enforce good conduct and information flows. The paper thus ends with a somewhat revised and secularized version of the theses propounded by Weber and Tawney, reinstating the importance of discipline and integrity achieved by some religious groups in the forefront of explanations of economic change.

The Huguenot Diaspora and the Development of the Atlantic Economy: Huguenots and the Growth of the South Carolina Economy, 1680-1775[1]

R.C. Nash

In the late seventeenth century, Louis XIV's persecution of French Protestants or Huguenots, culminating in the Revocation of the Edict of Nantes of 1685, led to a massive flight of Huguenots from France and their diaspora among a number of neighbouring countries, including Holland, Prussia, Switzerland and England. The vast majority of the 50,000 Huguenots who went to England settled permanently in the country but about 2000 moved on to British America in the late seventeenth and early eighteenth centuries.[2] These transatlantic migrants established substantial communities in three colonies — South Carolina, Massachusetts and New York — but it was in South Carolina that they had their greatest effect on the economic and social evolution of British America. The great majority of migrants to South Carolina arrived in the years 1680-1695, shortly after "Carolina" was founded in 1670. Most of the Huguenots who fled from France to England in the late seventeenth century were middle-aged or elderly, but the migrants to South Carolina were predominantly young, single or married adults, as older refugees were not generally prepared to suffer the hardships involved in crossing

[1]The research in South Carolina, upon which this paper is partly based, was made possible by grants from the British Economic and Social Research Council and the University of Manchester. I would also like to thank my colleague Steve Rigby and my good friend Hilary Wood for their excellent comments on earlier drafts of this paper.

[2]Robin D. Gwynn, *Huguenot Heritage: The History and Contribution of the Huguenots in Britain* (London, 1985), 35-36; and Jon Butler, *The Huguenots in America: A Refugee People in New World Society* (Cambridge, 1983), 27-28 and 47-49.

the Atlantic and settling in a new colony.[3] By c. 1700, there were 400-500 migrants in the colony and some 100 children born to Huguenot parents in America, comprising about fifteen to eighteen percent of South Carolina's white population of 3250.[4]

Jon Butler has provided the most compelling thesis on the character of the Huguenot migration to South Carolina and its impact on the colony's economic and social development. He argues that Huguenot migrants to America were generally poor and that many had spent several years in England living wholly or partly on charity before migrating overseas. He also shows that migrants were rich in human capital, bringing with them a wide range of artisanal and industrial skills, but that in practice these skills were of scant value in a frontier colony like South Carolina, where the population's small size and limited wealth produced little demand for specialised craftsmen. Besides, the future of the colony lay not in sericulture, linen weaving or in the dozens of other crafts practised by the Huguenots but in the slave-plantation production of naval stores, rice, and indigo – the export staples that dominated the South Carolina economy from 1700 to the Revolution. Butler argues that the principal theme of the history of South Carolina's Huguenots is their success in integrating themselves into the mainstream of the colony's evolving agricultural economy and in shaping its evolution. The majority of the migrants settled in a small number of compact agricultural settlements and, taking advantage of the generous land grants made by the

---

[3]The rigours faced by migrants are described in the celebrated letter by Judith Giton, who migrated to South Carolina in 1685, aged about twenty; see, Slann Legare Simmons, "Early Manigault Records," *Transactions of the Huguenot Society of South Carolina (THSSC)*, LIX (1954), 25-27.

[4]Butler, *Huguenots in America*, 27-30, 50-52 and 56-60; Butler, "The Revocation of the Edict of Nantes and Huguenot Migration to South Carolina," in R.M. Golden, *The Huguenot Connection: The Edict of Nantes, Its Revocation and Early French Migration to South Carolina* (Dordrecht, 1988), 64-67; Amy E. Friedlander, "Carolina Huguenots: A Study in Cultural Pluralism in the Low Country, 1679-1768" (Unpublished PhD thesis, Emory University, 1979), 86-102; and Bertrand Van Ruymbeke, "L'Émigration Huguenote en Caroline du Sud sous le Régime des Seigneurs Propriétaires: Étude d'une Communauté du Refuge dans une province Britannique d'Amérique du Nord (1680-1720)" (Unpublished PhD thesis, Université La Sorbonne Nouvelle, 2 vols., Paris, 1995), I, 357-358. For population estimates for South Carolina, see Peter A. Coclanis, *The Shadow of a Dream: Economic Life and Death in the South Carolina Low Country, 1670-1920* (New York, 1989), 64-66.

South Carolina proprietors to migrants, channelled their energies and ambitions into slave-plantation agriculture. Indeed, until the 1750s, their accumulation of land and slaves outpaced that of non-Huguenot colonists, although thereafter the Huguenots' lead over other colonists evaporated. Butler further argues that the Huguenots' successful assimilation into South Carolina's economic life was matched by their social assimilation, by their absorption into the mainstream of the colony's religious, political and cultural life. The Huguenot churches, first in the rural areas and then in Charleston, conformed to Anglican practices or ceased to exist. The Huguenots inter-married with non-French colonists to the point where, by the mid-eighteenth century, marriages purely between individuals of French descent were rare. Finally, in South Carolinian politics, the Huguenots acted not as the delegates of French-populated areas, but as non-partisan representatives of the wider population. The conclusion to Butler's powerfully argued thesis is that the Huguenots arrived in the late seventeenth century as French-speaking, Calvinist exiles, but that by 1750 they had become simply South Carolinians. They had French surnames, but in every other way, "they were indistinguishable from all other settlers in the colony, except of course slaves."[5]

Butler's thesis has been challenged in some respects by J.F. Bosher's recent work on Huguenot merchants in Boston and New York and Bertrand Van Ruymbeke's dissertation on the Huguenot migration to South Carolina. Bosher argues that research on the Huguenot emigration to America has neglected the fact that the Huguenot diaspora strengthened and extended the international trading networks which French Huguenots had formed since the late sixteenth century. The great success of the Huguenot merchants in America is explained not by their rapid and complete assimilation into local societies but by the opposite, by their continuing membership of a distinctive, separatist and international trading culture, which was organised through family-based Huguenot trading networks. The considerable achievements of Huguenot merchants in America are partly explained by their adaptation to local economic

---

[5]Butler, *Huguenots in America*, 91-143; the quotation is from 92. Friedlander, "Huguenots and the Historians," *THSSC*, XCIV (1989), 5, also stresses the Huguenots' preoccupation with agriculture: "many of the skilled artisans must have come to terms with the economic reality of the colony, namely, that acquisition of land was the name of the game." For an earlier view that the Huguenots assimilated rapidly, see Arthur H. Hirsch, *The Huguenots of Colonial South Carolina* (Durham, NC, 1928), 90-102 and 165-195.

conditions, but mainly by their exploitation of their transatlantic mercantile connections. Van Ruymbeke's exhaustive study of the first generation
of Huguenots in South Carolina also emphasises that the Huguenots'
success as agriculturalists should not overshadow the powerful contribution they made to Charleston's early urban and mercantile development.[6]

This paper takes up Bosher's and Van Ruymbeke's theme and
considers the South Carolina Huguenots in the colonial period not, in
Butler's terms, as planters and slave-owners but rather as merchants and
traders. The paper is divided into three sections. The initial section asks
two questions. First, what contribution did the South Carolina Huguenots
make to the development of the colony's mercantile economy and how did
this contribution compare with their impact on slave-plantation agriculture? Second, to what extent was the success of Huguenot merchants in
South Carolina based on their connections to prominent circles of
European-based Huguenot merchants, in the way suggested by Bosher?
The next section focuses on the Huguenot merchants' social behaviour in
Charleston and asks whether the merchants sustained their position in
South Carolina's commercial economy through a high degree of mutuality
and collaboration based on their common ethnic background. The final
part concludes by asking what light does the study of South Carolina's
Huguenot merchants throw on recent debates about the Huguenots in
British America?

I

From the late 1680s to 1775 three generations of Huguenot merchants
traded in South Carolina. The first, the immigrant group, was active in
trade from c. 1680-c. 1720 and included eighteen Huguenot migrants who
became major merchants in Charleston (see table 1). This is not a
complete listing of Huguenot merchants of the first generation, but does
include all the leading merchants who were active in trade for ten or more
years. There were also forty English migrants who were merchants for ten
years or more, indicating that Huguenots made up about thirty percent of
the first generation of major South Carolina merchants. For the second

---

[6]J.F. Bosher, "Huguenot Merchants and the Protestant International in the
Seventeenth Century," *William and Mary Quarterly*, Third Series, LII (1995), 77-102;
Bosher, "The Imperial Environment of French Trade with Canada, 1660-1685," *English
Historical Review*, CXIII (1993), 50-82; and Van Ruymbeke, "L'Émigration Huguenote."

and and third generations, those merchants who traded from 1720 to 1775, I have focussed on two sets of sample years – 1738-1743 (second generation) and 1762-1767 (third generation.) There were twenty-four Huguenots who were leading Charleston merchants in the years 1738-1743, comprising twenty-three percent of a Charleston merchant community that numbered 104 merchants in these years (see table 2.) The third generation, identified here as those active in trade from 1762-1767 (see table 3), consisted of thirty-seven merchants, twenty-two percent of a Charleston merchant community of 170 merchants.[7] The share of trade controlled by Huguenot merchants was more or less equivalent to their proportion of the merchant population as a whole. For example, twenty-two percent of the import trade in slaves in 1735-1775, and twenty-one percent of the import trade in general merchandise in 1735-1765, was handled by Huguenot merchants or by firms with Huguenot partners.[8]

Huguenot merchants thus played a major part in South Carolina's commercial economy in the colonial period. Indeed, they made a greater relative contribution in this sphere than in slave-plantation agriculture. Butler has shown that Huguenots and their descendants made up six to ten percent of slaveholders in colonial South Carolina in the years between 1736 and 1765; the evidence presented here indicates that they provided

---

[7]Data on Charleston merchants are taken from my wider research project on the Charleston business community. See R.C. Nash, "Urbanization in the Colonial South: Charleston, South Carolina, as a Case Study," *Journal of Urban History*, XIX (1992), 12 and 19-23; and Nash, "The Organisation of Trade and Finance in the Atlantic Economy: Britain and South Carolina, 1670-1775," in Rosemary Brana-Shute and Randy Sparks (eds.), *New Directions in the History of the South Carolina Lowcountry* (Columbia, SC, forthcoming). Huguenot merchants had an even more prominent role in the trade of South Carolina's second and third ports, Georgetown and Beaufort. This, in part, reflected the nearness of the ports to areas of French settlement, such as Purrysburg and the Santee. See South Carolina Department of Archives and History (SCDAH), Records of the South Carolina Court of Common Pleas, Judgment Rolls, 1773, 26A; Lawrence S. Rowland, "The Purrysburg Swiss in the Beaufort District," *THSSC*, XCVIII (1993), 20-26; Philip M. Hamer, *et al.* (eds.), *The Papers of Henry Laurens* (12 vols., Columbia, SC, 1968-90), VI, 434n; and George C. Rogers, Jr., *The History of George Town County, South Carolina* (Columbia, SC, 1970), 47-52.

[8]Data based on firms paying £500 or more in import duties on slaves and £200 or more in import duties on general merchandise; see W. Robert Higgins, "Charles Town Merchants and Factors Dealing in the External Slave Trade 1735-1775," *South Carolina Historical Magazine (SCHM)*, LXV (1964), 205-217; and Stumpf, "South Carolina Importers of General Merchandise, 1735-1765," *SCHM*, LXXXIV (1983), 1-10.

a much higher proportion (twenty-two to thirty percent) of Charleston's merchant community in the same period.[9] Of course, the great majority of successful Huguenot merchants, like their English counterparts, went on to acquire land and slaves, but their fortunes were founded in trade and shipping, not in agriculture.[10]

Given that the Huguenots and their descendants represented only a small and declining proportion of South Carolina's population, how can we account for their central and sustained role in South Carolina's commercial economy?[11] To a large extent, the Huguenots' success in business reflected the fact that they arrived in South Carolina very soon after its foundation in 1670, at a time when the colony's trading and commercial system was taking shape. In the late seventeenth century four significant groups of Huguenot immigrants were established in the colony. The first large group of Huguenots arrived in South Carolina under the leadership of René Petit and Jacob Guerard in 1680. They formed a French agricultural colony in the area which became known as the Orange Quarter, which in 1700 had a French population of about a hundred. In the next fifteen years 300 or so more Huguenot migrants settled in three locations. By 1690, a number of families had settled on the Santee, about sixty miles north of Charleston, which in 1700 had a French population of about 110. A small group settled in Goose Creek, close to Charleston, which numbered about thirty in 1700. Finally, Huguenots settled in the town of Charleston, which had a French population of 200 in 1700, or about a quarter of Charleston's white population.[12] Thus, although the Huguenot agricultural communities have attracted the greatest attention from historians, the main Huguenot migration was to Charleston.

---

[9]See Butler, *Huguenots in America*, 123-124, tables 1-3, for data on slaveholding by Huguenots and non-Huguenots.

[10]See Nash, "Organisation of Trade and Finance."

[11]Huguenots made up about fifteen percent of the white population about 1700 but only three percent in c. 1770; see Friedlander, "Carolina Huguenots," 5.

[12]SCDAH, Records in the British Public Record Office Relating to South Carolina, 1663-1782 (36 vols., microcopy), IV, 1698-1700, Memorandum of Peter Girard, 14 March 1699; Hirsch, *Huguenots of Colonial South Carolina*, 14-26; and Van Ruymbeke, "L'Émigration Huguenote," II, 663-664.

Table 1
French Huguenot Migrants to South Carolina
Who Became Leading First-Generation Merchants

Pierre Buretel	John LaRoche	Lewis Pasquereau
Benj. De La Conseillere**	Francis LeBrasseur	Pierre Pasquereau
James Du Poids D'Or	Jacques LeSerrurier	Henry Peronneau I
Paul Douxsaint**	Pierre Manigault	Pierre St. Julien
Benjamin Godin**	Issac Mazyck I	Abraham Satur
John Guerard I	John A. Motte**	Jacob Satur

Notes: ** = arrived after 1700. The others arrived before 1700, or at a time which is unknown. Merchants listed traded in South Carolina for ten years or more in the period 1685-1730.

Sources: South Carolina Department of Archives and History (SCDAH), Records of the Secretary of the Province (21 vols., 1675-1731); Records of the South Carolina Court of Common Pleas, Judgment Rolls, 1703-1730; Court of Chancery, Oversize (1736-1760), no. 3, Samuel Wragg versus Joseph Wragg, 4 June 1749; SCDAH, Records in the British Public Record Office Relating to South Carolina, 1663-1782 (36 vols., microcopy), I-XVI; PRO, Colonial Office (CO), 5/509, Naval Office, Port of Charles Town (1717-1724); Guildhall Library, London, Account Book of Alexander Baily and Nathanial Lewis, Ms. 11,096 (1711-1712); Alex S. Salley (ed.), *Journal of the Commons House of Assembly of South Carolina, 1692-1735* (22 vols., Columbia, SC, 1907-1947); Stuart O. Stumpf, "The Merchants of Colonial Charleston, 1680-1756" (Unpublished PhD thesis, Michigan State University, 1971), 6-7 and 18-20; Anne K. Gregorie (ed.), *Records of the Court of Chancery of South Carolina, 1671-1779* (Washington, DC, 1950); William L. McDowell (ed.), *Journals of the Commissioners of the Indian Trade, 1710-1718* (Columbia, SC, 1955); bibliographical essays and notes in *Transactions of the Huguenot Society of South Carolina*, cited below in notes 37 and 46; Caroline T. Moore (ed.), *Records of the Secretary of the Province, 1692-1721* (Columbia, SC, 1978); Caroline T. Moore and Agatha A. Simmons (eds.), *Abstracts of the Wills of the State of South Carolina, 1670-1740* (Columbia, SC, 1960); Walter B. Edgar and N. Louise Bailey (eds.), *Directory of the South Carolina House of Representatives. II: The Commons House of Biographical Assembly, 1692-1775* (Columbia, SC, 1977); R.C. Nash "Trade and Business in Eighteenth-Century South Carolina: The Career of John Guerard, Merchant and Planter," *South Carolina Historical Magazine (SCHM)*, XCVI (1995); and Van Ruymbeke, "L'Émigration Huguenote."

Table 2
Second-Generation Major Huguenot Merchants
Active in Trade, 1738-1742

Peter Benoist	[A]	Paul Labilliere	[P]	Henry Peronneau II	[M]
David Dalbiac	[P]	William Lasserre	[I]	Arthur Peronneau	[M]
Peter Delemestre	[I]	Peter Leger	[A]	Samuel Peronneau I	[M]
Paul Douxsaint*	[M]	Gabriel Manigault	[M]	Samuel Prioleau	[P]
Benj Godin*	[M]	Issac Mazyck II	[M]	Philip Prioleau	[P]
John Guerard II	[M]	Samuel Montaigut	[P]	Matthew Roche	[I]
Gab Guignard	[I]	Jacob Motte	[M]	John Royer	[M]
Benj. D'Harriette	[I]	John Mayrant	[P]		
Peter Horry I	[P]	John Neufville I	[P]		

Notes: * = a merchant of the first generation who continued to trade in the second generation.

Social origins of merchants indicated by:
[I] = immigrant   [M] = Merchant   [P] = Planter   [A] = Artisan
[I] = 5 (20%)   [M] = 10 (40%)   [P] = 8 (32%) [A] = 2 (8%)

Sources: See table 3.

These migrants reached Charleston at a critical point in its development. Charleston was only relocated from its original site – Old Charles Town on the Ashley River – to its present location in 1680. In the 1680s and early 1690s, Charleston was a village surrounded by a wilderness, a point of entry for immigrants rather than a trading port. South Carolina had almost no exports other than a few deerskins and some provisions, and these minor trades were run by planter-merchants from their plantations as a professional merchant class had not materialized in the port.[13] In the next twenty-five years, Charleston, with the rise of its export trades in deer skins, rice and naval stores, became a significant

---

[13]See SCDAH., Records in the British Public Record Office Relating to South Carolina, 1663-1782, II, 199 and 218-220; IV, 88; V, 150-155; Verner W. Crane, *The Southern Frontier, 1670-1732* (Durham, NC, 1928), 108-136; Stumpf, "Merchants of Colonial Charleston," 6-7 and 18-20; and Carville V. Earle, "The First English Towns of North America," *Geographical Review*, LXVII (1977), 41-44.

commercial and shipping centre in the English transatlantic trading system.[14] The Huguenots fortuitously reached Charleston at exactly the right time; at the point when the city was undergoing rapid development, yet lacked an established merchant community, thus allowing the newly-arrived to have their greatest impact. The Huguenots were present at the birth of Charleston's commercial economy, and they played a major part in shaping the city's subsequent economic evolution.

The Huguenot migrants to South Carolina were very largely of urban origin and many of them came from a bourgeois and trading culture. Van Ruymbeke has shown that eighty percent of the migrants came from French towns and cities, with nearly half of them coming from La Rochelle and the lesser ports in its vicinity. A high percentage of the male migrants (nearly a quarter) were merchants and another eleven percent were drawn from the ranks of the minor gentry or *écuyers* of western France, a class which had close links with the urban bourgeoisie. The proportion of merchants in the French migration was much higher than amongst the English migrants to South Carolina or, indeed, amongst the French Protestant migrations to the Caribbean and to Canada.[15] It is therefore not surprising that many of the French migrants to South Carolina became merchants, retailers and shipowners in Charleston. We can trace the origins of sixteen of the eighteen first-generation Huguenot merchants (table 1). Of these, twelve were descended from merchant families of towns in western France, principally Bordeaux, La Rochelle, Rouen, and Tours, two were the sons of Normandy noblemen, and two were the sons of a Calvinist minister.[16] To give examples. Issac Chardon

---

[14]Nash, "Urbanization in the Colonial South," 3-6.

[15]Van Ruymbeke, "L'Émigration Huguenote," I, 296-310 and 323-324.

[16]Information on the origins of first-generation Huguenot merchants comes mainly from SCDAH, Records of the Secretary of the Province (21 vols., 1675-1731); Records in the British Public Record Office Relating to South Carolina, 1663-1782; Van Ruymbeke, "L'Émigration Huguenote;" Edgar and Bailey (eds.), *Biographical Directory*; Hirsch, *Huguenots of Colonial South Carolina*; Butler, *Huguenots in America*; Louis Manigault, "The Manigault Family of South Carolina," *THSSC*, IV (1897), 48-57; Katharine B. Mazyck, "Notes on the Mazyck Family," *THSSC*, XXXVII (1932), 43-53; Myrta J. Hutson, "Early Generations of the Motte Family of South Carolina," *THSSC*, LVI (1951), 57-63; and Virginia Gourdin, "Madeleine Chardon, of Tours, Touraine and Her Family," *THSSC*, XCI (1986), 64-104.

was descended from a family which had been important Protestant merchants of Tours for several generations. Louis Pasquereau Sr., a merchant in Tours who originated from an Angers merchant family, migrated to South Carolina with his wife Madeleine Chardon, who was probably Issac Chardon's cousin, and their two sons, Louis and Pierre Pasquereau, who both became first-generation merchants in Charleston.[17]

However, while we can establish the impeccable merchant pedigree of the majority of Charleston's first-generation Huguenot merchants, can we show that their success in Charleston was founded on the exploitation of their international trading connections, in the manner suggested by Bosher? Certainly, it is possible that those migrants who arrived before 1700, and who were descendants of mercantile families of western France (the Pasquereaus, Pierre Buretel, Jacques LeSerrurier, Pierre Manigault, Henry Peronneau etc.) succeeded in transferring merchant capital from France to England and then to South Carolina. However, we have almost no evidence to prove this and the frequent claims made by historians about the supposed funds brought by Huguenot merchants to America are speculative.[18] Indeed, the fact that many Huguenots who arrived before 1700 only became merchants after some years in the colony, that is after having tried their hands at non-mercantile occupations, suggests that they lacked the trading capital and the European connections which would have given them a more ready entry into foreign trade. For example, John Guerard Sr., the son of the Normandy noblemen Jacob Guerard, who co-founded the Petit-Guerard colony, occupied himself for nearly a decade as a weaver and planter before entering trade. Similarly, Pierre Manigault, who was of a La Rochelle mercantile family, was for some time a planter and then rum distiller, and only began trading with the West Indies many years after his arrival in South Carolina.[19]

---

[17]Gourdin, "Madeleine Chardon," 68-73; and Van Ruymbeke, "L'Émigration Huguenote," I, 95-96 and 334.

[18]For examples of such speculation, see Manigault, "The Manigault Family," 54; Hirsch, *Huguenots of Colonial South Carolina*, 229 and 232; Gourdin, "Madeleine Chardon," 67 and 74; and Van Ruymbeke, "L'Émigration Huguenote," I, 308-309.

[19]Manigault, "The Manigault Family," 52-55; Simmons, "Early Manigault Records," 32-33; Stumpf, "Merchants of Colonial Charleston," 25, 42 and 49-50; Friedlander, "Carolina Huguenots," 110; Maurice A. Crouse, "Gabriel Manigault: Charleston Merchant," *SCHM*, LXVIII (1967), 221; Nash, "Trade and Business," 8-9; and

Moreover, while the evidence about the trading operations of these early Huguenot merchants is meagre, it suggests that their trading connections in England were mainly, although not exclusively, with merchants of English rather than of Huguenot descent.[20]

For the merchants who arrived after 1700, we find more concrete evidence that the success of Huguenot merchants in South Carolina was based on their connections to prominent networks of European-based Huguenot merchants. The Revocation of the Edict of Nantes strengthened Huguenot economic power by dispersing Huguenot merchants amongst the leading trading centres of Europe. The Huguenots were the most important element in the massive influx of foreign merchants into England (including also Dutch and German Protestants and Portuguese Jews) which itself was the most important change experienced in the organisation of English foreign trade in the late seventeenth and eighteenth centuries. Huguenot merchants had traded in London from the late sixteenth century, but the first major wave of Huguenot merchant-migrants to England came in the post-Revocation period, mainly from western France, from the ports and inland trading towns which had prospered in the seventeenth-century expansion of the Atlantic economy and which were dominated by Protestant merchants. These refugee merchants traded principally with northern Europe and the Mediterranean.[21] Their colonial interests were

---

Van Ruymbeke, "L'Émigration Huguenote," I, 355; and II, 584 and 662.

[20]See SCDAH, Records of the Secretary of the Province (1694-1705), 253; (1714-1717), 65; and (1711-1717), 8; Guildhall Library, Ms. 11,096, Account Book of Alexander Baily and Nathanial Lewis (1711-1712), which shows a number of accounts between Charleston Huguenot and Bristol merchants; "Will of Peter Pasquereaux," *THSSC*, XIII (1906), 15-17; "Will of Issac Chardon," *THSSC*, XLV (1940), 69-71; and "Will of Francis LeBrasseur," *THSSC*, XLVIII (1943), 50-53.

[21]Charles Wilson, *Anglo-Dutch Commerce and Finance in the Eighteenth Century* (Cambridge, 1941), 138-139, 160 and 203; Herbert Luthy, *La Banque Protestante en France de la Revocation de L'Édit de Nantes à la Révolution* (2 vols., Paris, 1959-1961), I, 78-84, and II, 81-83; Guy Chaussinand-Nogaret, *Les Financiers de Languedoc au XVIIIe Siècle* (Paris, 1970), 161-213; Jacob M. Price, *France and the Chesapeake: A History of the French Tobacco Monopoly, 1674-1791, and of Its Relationship to the British and American Tobacco Trades* (2 vols., Ann Arbor, 1973); Alice C. Carter, *Getting, Spending and Investment in Early Modern Times: Essays on Dutch, English and Huguenot Economic History* (Assen, 1975); D.W. Jones, *War and Economy in the Age of William III and Marlborough* (Oxford, 1988), 253-260; François Crouzet, "Walloons, Huguenots and the Bank of England," *Proceedings of the Huguenot Society of London*, XXV (1990), 167-178;

focused on the established trades to the West Indies and to Boston and New York; before 1700 these merchants took little interest in the insignificant Anglo-Carolinian trade.[22]

However, in the early eighteenth century, Charleston's growing importance as a trading port began to attract the attention of two sorts of Huguenot merchant firms in London. First, and most importantly, a number of Huguenot firms which originated in western France established family members in Charleston as resident agents in the Anglo-South Carolinian trade. For example, David Godin, a rich Rouen merchant, had been naturalised in London in 1690, where he traded in partnership with his elder son Stephen. In about 1700, his younger son Benjamin was dispatched to South Carolina where he formed what was probably, after the business of Joseph and Samuel Wragg, Charleston's most important merchant-firm of the early eighteenth century. Alongside the Godins there were a number of other prominent English-domiciled Huguenot mercantile families with representatives in Charleston and London in the early eighteenth century, including the Belins, Douxsaints, LeSerruriers and

---

François Crouzet, "The Huguenots and the English 'Financial Revolution,'" in P. Higonnet, D.S. Landes and H. Rosovsky (eds.), *Favorites of Fortune: Technology, Growth and Economic Development Since the Industrial Revolution* (Cambridge, MA, 1991), 221-266; Stanley Chapman, *Merchant Enterprise in Britain From the Industrial Revolution to World War I* (Cambridge, 1992), 29-35; David Ormrod, "The Atlantic Economy and the 'Protestant Capitalist International,' 1651-1775," *Historical Research*, LXVI (1993), 197-208; and J.F. Bosher, *Business and Religion in the Age of New France, 1600-1760: Twenty Two Studies* (Toronto, 1994), for example, 211-213.

[22]The rise of the Huguenot merchants of New York, for example, was very rapid; by 1703 there were thirty-one Huguenot merchants in the city compared with twenty-nine English and thirty-six Dutch merchants; see Butler, *Huguenots in America*, 85-87 and 150-154; and Bosher, "Huguenot Merchants and the Protestant International." On the other hand, almost no Huguenot merchants went to Philadelphia, founded in 1680, which was as commercially undeveloped at the time of the Huguenot migration as Charleston; see Gary B. Nash, "The Early Merchants of Philadelphia: The Formation and Disintegration of a Founding Elite," in Richard S. Dunn and Mary M. Dunn (eds.), *The World of William Penn* (Philadelphia, 1986), 354-362. For the minor late seventeenth-century trade organised by Huguenot refugees of western France from Plymouth, England, to South Carolina, see Alison Grant, "By Sea: Huguenot Maritime Links with Seventeenth-Century Devon," *Proceedings of the Huguenot Society of London*, XXV (1993), 451-463.

Saturs (table 1).[23] Second, a number of recently-arrived London Huguenot merchants traded with South Carolina's Huguenot merchants even though they lacked family connections in the colony. These included René Baudouin and Pierre Renew, formerly merchants of Tours and Bordeaux respectively, who traded mainly with Europe but who had subsidiary interests in the South Carolina trade.[24] However, despite this increased involvement of London Huguenot merchants in the Anglo-South Carolinian trade, the bulk of the commerce at the English end in the early eighteenth century was organised by English merchants. Thus, in 1719, the sole year in the eighteenth century for which we have detailed data, twenty-four percent of rice imports and seventeen percent of naval stores imports into London from South Carolina were handled by the Huguenot merchants of London; the remaining imports were dealt with by London merchants of English extraction. Similarly, in the years 1718-1720, of the 160 London-based individuals listed as owners of ships in the Charleston trade, only twenty-two (fourteen percent) were London Huguenots.[25]

---

[23]SCDAH, Court of Chancery, Oversize (1736-1760), no. 3, Samuel Wragg versus Joseph Wragg, 4 June 1749; Records of the Secretary of the Province (1711-1717), 42-46; vol. B (1722-1724), 176-177; and vol. F (1727-1729), 74-75; Records of the South Carolina Court of Common Pleas, Judgment Rolls (1720), 71A-1; Records in the British Public Record Office Relating to South Carolina (1663-1782), IX, 141; X, 91; XI, 111, 225-226 and 235; Leeds City Library , Sheepscar Branch (LCL), Archives Department (AD), Newby Hall Ms. (NH) 2440, London Port Book (Christmas 1718-Christmas 1719); Moore (ed.), *Records of the Secretary*, 227; "Peter Pasquereaux," 15-17; Edgar and Baily (eds.), *Biographical Directory*, II, 283-284, 403 and 591-592; Nash, "Trade and Business," 8-9; Gourdin, "Madeleine Chardon," 101-103; and Van Ruymbeke, "L'Emigration Huguenote," II, 592 and 669.

[24]The main sources for identifying London Huguenot merchants trading to South Carolina in the early eighteenth century are signed petitions, memoranda, and the like, submitted by London merchants to the Lords of Trade and other agencies recorded in SCDAH, Records in the British Public Record Office Relating to South Carolina (1663-1782), Records of the Secretary of the Province (1675-1731); Records of the South Carolina Court of Common Pleas, Judgment Rolls (1703-1720); lists of owners of ships in the Charleston trade, in PRO, CO 5/509, Naval Office, Port of Charles Town (1717-1732). For Baudouin and Renew, see also SCDAH, Records of the Secretary of the Province (1694-1705), 229-230; Jones, *War and Economy*, 254-256; Gourdin, "Madeleine Chardon," 76; and Armand Mauzey, "On to Glory," *THSSC*, LXXXII (1977), 119-123.

[25] LCL, AD, NH 2440, London Port Book (Christmas 1718-Christmas 1719). The port book is incomplete; see Jacob Price and Paul G.E. Clemens, "A Revolution of Scale in Overseas Trade: British Firms in the Chesapeake Trade, 1675-1775," *Journal of*

Table 3
Third-Generation Major Huguenot Merchants
Active in Trade, 1762-1767

Peter Bacot	[P]	William Guerin	[P]	John Neufville II	[M]
Peter Bochet	[P]	Peter Horry II	[M]	John Perdriau	[A]
Anthony Bonneau	[P]	Henry Laurens*	[A]	James Poyas	[M]
Daniel Bourdeau	[P]	James Laurens	[A]	John Poyas	[M]
Issac Bourdeau	[P]	Peter Leger*	[A]	Arthur Peronneau*	[M]
Samuel Chollet	[I]	Daniel Legare	[A]	Henry Peronneau III	[M]
Alex Chovin	[P]	Samuel Legare	[A]	Samuel Peronneau II	[M]
Paul Douxsaint II	[M]	Thomas Legare	[A]	Samuel Prioleau*	[M]
Gideon Dupont	[P]	Gabriel Manigault*	[M]	Philip Prioleau*	[M]
John Fabre	[A]	Peter Manigault	[M]	Edward Simons	[P]
John Lewis Gervais	[I]	Jacob Motte	[M]	Maurice Simons	[P]
John Guerard*	[M]	Peter Mazyck	[M]	Peter Villepontoux	[P]
Theodore Gaillard	[P]	Edward Neufville	[M]		

Notes: * = Merchant of the second generation who still traded in the third generation. [I] = 2 (5%), [M] = 16 (42%), [P] = 12 (32%), [A] = 8 (21%).

Sources: Merchants in tables 2 and 3 have been identified from: a) Lists of importers and exporters in: W. Robert Higgins, "Charles Town Merchants and Factors Dealing in the External Slave Trade, 1735-1775," *SCHM*, LXV (1964), 205-217; Stumpf, "South Carolina Importers of General Merchandise, 1735-1765," *ibid*., LXXXIV (1983), 1-10; W.O. Moore, Jr., "The Largest Exporters of Deerskins from Charles Town, 1735-1775," *ibid*., LXXIV (1973), 144-150; and J.A. Calhoun, M.A. Zierdan and E.A. Paysinger, "The Geographic Spread of Charleston's Merchant Community, 1732-1767," *ibid*., LXXXVI (1985), 207-220. (b) Lists of owners of ships clearing Charleston, 1738-1739 and 1762-1767; and ships' manifests showing consignors of rice and indigo on ships bound from Charleston, January to April 1764. It is assumed that owners of ships making two or more voyages carrying rice and indigo were traders in those commodities, PRO, CO 5/509, 511, Naval Office, Port of Charles Town, 1738-1739 and 1762-1767. (c) Business accounts and papers: Charleston Museum Archives, Merchant's Day Book [James Poyas], 1761-1764; South Carolina Historical Society, 34-325, Merchant's Day Book [James Poyas], 1764-1766; SCDAH, Inventories of Estates, 1736-1776; Records of the South Carolina Court of Common Pleas, Judgment Rolls, 1731-1775; Records of the Secretary of State, Miscellaneous Records, 1732-1776; New York Public Library, Transcripts of the Commission of Enquiry into Losses of American Loyalists Amongst the Audit Office Records, LII, 505-517, LIV, 266-274 and LVI, 576-595; and PRO, Treasury Office Papers, LXXIX, American Loyalist Claims Commission, V, XV, XXXVI and XLII.

Economic History, XLVII (1987), 18-20. For ship ownership, see PRO, CO 5/509, Naval Office, Port of Charles Town (1717-1720). In the early eighteenth century there was a close coincidence between the shipowning and trading groups; hence, the distribution of ship ownership is a useful guide to the pattern of trade organisation.

Nevertheless, the early eighteenth century marked the high-water mark of Huguenot involvement in the trade and in the later colonial period the dominance of English firms increased. First, the prominent, family-based connections between Huguenots in London and Charleston which had been established in the early eighteenth century did not survive after 1720, as merchant families in South Carolina became planters or died out and as Huguenot merchants in England turned to other trades and interests. For example, Benjamin Godin withdrew from trade and became a major planter and slave owner, as did his sons, while the London Godins withdrew from the South Carolina trade and concentrated their interests in the commerce with north Europe, Russia and the Mediterranean.[26] These family connections had provided the main trading links between Huguenot merchants in Europe and South Carolina; their disappearance meant that from 1720 the involvement of European Huguenots in the South Carolina trade depended on the extent to which the wider Huguenot merchant community in London participated in the trade. This community grew in size and wealth in the middle decades of the eighteenth century, but its character was changing in a way which reduced the links between London and Charleston Huguenot merchants. The first major wave of Huguenot merchant-migrants to England had come largely from western France, a region whose economy was based on Atlantic trade, and a few of these merchants, as we have seen, became important traders to South Carolina. However, the second major wave of Huguenot merchants, which arrived in England from the 1720s, came mainly from the Languedoc and Switzerland. These Anglo-Swiss and Anglo-Languedocian firms had vast commercial and financial interests, but they specialised in the major European and Mediterranean trades and they were as deeply or more involved in international banking and finance

---

[26]Among other Anglo-South Carolinian families, the Belins ceased to trade in South Carolina; the LeSerruriers, who had been engaged in trade left the colony; the Saturs died out in the male line; and the Douxsaints continued in trade in Charleston, although their contacts with the London Douxsaints ceased. On these families, see SCDAH, Records of the Secretary of the Province, vol. F (1727-1729), 74-75; Records of the Secretary of the State, Miscellaneous Records, Main Series (Miscellaneous Records), vol. KK (1754-1758), 110-111; Moore (ed.), *Records of the Secretary*, 227; Wilson, *Anglo-Dutch Trade*, 113-114; Price, *France and the Chesapeake*, I, 394 and 625; Edgar and Bailey (eds.), *Biographical Directory*, II, 283-285 and 403; Van Ruymbeke, "L'Émigration Huguenote," I, 352-354; Gourdin, "Madeleine Chardon," 101-103; and "Belin," *THSSC*, LXXXIX (1984), 153-154.

as in commodity trade. In so far as they had colonial interests these were in the Virginia and the West Indies trades and the great majority of these firms had no connections with South Carolina.[27]

There were of course exceptions, a small number of leading London Huguenot firms which traded to South Carolina as a subsidiary line of business. For example, Joseph and Henry Guinand, brothers born in Lunel in the Languedoc, formed one of the dozen most important firms of Languedoc merchant-bankers in London. Their main interests were in the financing of the Asian and Languedoc trades and in British government stocks. In c. 1750 the elder Guinands sent their younger brother Peter to Charleston, where he formed a firm with his fellow Huguenot Andrew Fesch, which, backed by his brothers, established a substantial trade in dry goods and slaves. Peter Guinand and Fesch moved into planting, again with London backing, but their deaths in South Carolina in the early 1760s left the firm heavily in debt to the London Guinands, who then took over and managed the Carolina estates. Another example is Peter Simond, born in the Huguenot settlement at the Cape of Good Hope in 1690, who received his commercial education in Amsterdam before moving to London in 1715, where he formed, with his brother, a leading firm trading to the West Indies. In the late 1720s and 1730s Simond developed major interests in the southern mainland colonies. He was the London commercial agent for the trustees of the new colony of Georgia, managed several ships in the South Carolina trade, specialising in the rice trade from Charleston and virtually monopolising the naval stores trade from Georgetown in the 1730s, and he acquired extensive lands in the Purrysburg area. From 1740, however, Simond withdrew from the South Carolina trade, concentrating instead on the West Indies trade, British government stocks and supplying the French tobacco monopoly.[28]

---

[27]See the sources cited in note 21. See also William A. Shaw (ed.), *Letters of Denization and Acts of Naturalization for Aliens in England and Ireland, 1701-1800* (London, 1923), which gives the origins of most London Huguenot merchants.

[28]Other notable London Huguenot merchant with minor interests in the South Carolina trade, c. 1720-c. 1770, include James Blaquiere, James Bourdieu and Samuel Chollet (see below, note 32), Pierre Cabibel, James Chalie, Charles, Elias and Noah de La Fontaine, Charles Noiray, Ciprieu Rondeau and Matthew Testas. For these merchants and the Guinands and Simonds see, South Carolinia Library, William Ancrum Account Book, 11163, 1757-1758, 1776-1782 [containing some accounts of Guinand and Fesch];

These post-1720 connections between Huguenots in England and South Carolina are of interest in themselves but they were only minor threads in a trade that was dominated by English merchants. In the decades before the American Revolution there were two main groups of London merchants trading to South Carolina. The most important group consisted of British merchants who had traded for long periods in Charleston and who then returned to London to set themselves up as "Carolina" merchants.[29] The second group, London merchants who traded to South Carolina but who had never resided there, were more varied. They included a number of English merchants with major interests in the slave and West Indies trade, but who also had connections with South Carolina, along with a wide circle of London wholesalers (linen drapers, ironmongers, etc.) types of businessmen who played a very significant part in financing the export trades to British America.[30] Charleston Huguenots wishing to enter international trade were required to forge connections with these English merchant groups rather than with London Huguenot merchants. For example, when the young Huguenot merchant Henry Laurens (tables 3 and 4) began trading in Charleston in the late 1740s he did so by ordering goods from wholesalers and merchants in London and a number of provincial ports, establishing his creditworthiness on the basis of his close connection with the Scot James Crokatt, the

---

SCDAH, Miscellaneous Records, Vol. BB (1732-1733), 27-38, October 1732 [Claims Against James Le Chantre]; PRO, CO 5/511, Naval Office, Port of Charles Town (1762-1767); LCL, AD, NH 2440, London Port Book (Christmas 1718-Christmas 1719); Price, *France and the Chesapeake*, I, 540, 543 and 564; II, 687-699, 738-741 and 1018-1019; Luthy, *La Banque Protestante*, I, 66, 231-232; II, 240 and 351; Chaussinand-Nogaret, *Les Financiers de Languedoc*, 182-183 and 188; Harriette Leiding, "Purrysburg, A Swiss-French Settlement of South Carolina, on the Savannah River," *THSSC*, XXXIX (1934), 31; Hamer, *et al.* (eds.), *Papers of Henry Laurens*, II, 155; III, 2-3, 49, 51, 81n, 120-122, 218, 229, 412 and 492; IV, 47-49 and 60-63; VII, 204 and 392n; VIII, 437 and 673-674; J.A. Lefroy, "The British Factory at Leghorn: Some Huguenot Associations," *Proceedings of the Huguenot Society of London*, XXII (1971-1972), 81-89; and Randolph Vigne, "The Killing of Jean Calas: Voltaire's First Huguenot Cause," *ibid.*, XXIII (1981-1982), 280-282.

[29] These firms included two with Huguenot partners, James Poyas and Co. and Neufville and Rolleston, firms founded by Carolina-born Huguenots who moved to London, not by established London Huguenot houses which had spawned connections in Charleston.

[30] See Nash, "Organization of Trade and Finance," and notes to table 4.

leading Carolina merchant in London at that time. None of the merchants he dealt with were Huguenots. Indeed, a close reading of his vast commercial correspondence for the period 1747-1775 reveals that Laurens seldom dealt with English-based Huguenot merchants and that such contacts were always incidental to his main business connections with English firms in London, Bristol and elsewhere.[31] The central nature of the connections between Charleston's Huguenot merchants and the core of *non*-Huguenot London merchants who controlled the South Carolina trade is shown in table 4, which lists the English agents and bankers for a large sample of Charleston Huguenot merchants in the period 1755-1775. In every case but one, the Charleston Huguenot merchants dealt with one or other of the elite London firms of English extraction which dominated the wider financial and commercial relations between London and South Carolina.[32]

To sum up: the majority of the migrants who made up the first generation of Huguenot merchants in South Carolina were descended from merchant families in western France. However, with the exception of a few prominent individuals who arrived after 1700, it appears that these merchants did not establish themselves in Charleston on the basis of their connections to international networks of Huguenot merchants. In any case, from ca.1720 the influence of English-based Huguenot merchants in the

---

[31]Hamer, *et al.* (eds.), *Papers of Henry Laurens*, especially citations in note 28; for Laurens' early career, see *ibid.*, I, 8-28, 56-58, 182-185, 200-212 and 230-232.

[32]The exception to this rule in table 4 was the short-lived Charleston firm of Chollet and Gervais, a migrant firm of recent creation, which drew on the credit of their London backers, the Anglo-Swiss Huguenot firm Bourdieu and Chollet and the Scot Richard Oswald. James Bourdieu was born in England of Huguenot parents and was a London merchant from the 1740s, first on his own account and then from 1769 in partnership with the Swiss-born Huguenot immigrant Samuel Chollet. The firm had vast trading and financial interests, especially with France. In the 1750s and 1760s the firm developed a small import trade in South Carolina indigo, and then in about 1770 Chollet's son, Samuel Chollet Jr., was sent to Charleston to establish a "very capital house in the Carolina trade." Backed by the London firm, Chollet, in partnership with another Huguenot migrant John Lewis Gervais, a protégé of Henry Laurens, traded in slaves and dry goods in the early 1770s, but he failed to establish a stable partnership with Gervais, and in 1774 he returned to London. Price, *France and the Chesapeake*, II, 687-699 and 738-741; Luthy, *La Banque Protestante*, II, 240 and 382-387; and Hamer, *et al.* (eds.), *Papers of Henry Laurens*, VIII, 496-498, 517, 546 and 636-638; IX, 127-128, 167 and 324-325. For Oswald, see table 4, notes.

Anglo-Carolina trade diminished. What then does explain the important and above all the sustained role that the South Carolina Huguenot merchants played in Charleston's trade from about 1720 to the American Revolution?

Table 4
South Carolina Merchants, 1750-1775: Trading Activities
and English Commercial And Financial Connections

Merchants born in South Carolina	Import Trades			Export Trades		Status of Trade*	British Agents-Bankers-Creditors
	Dry goods	Slave factors	Gen. merch.	Rice/ indigo	Deer skins		
Gideon Dupont		x				CA	John Nutt[a]
John Guerard	x	x	x	x	x	I	William Jolliffe[b]
William Guerin	x	x	x	x	x	CA	Greenwood and Higginson[c]
Henry Laurens	x	x	x	x	x	CA	Richard Oswald[d]; John Nutt
Peter Leger	x	x	x	x	x	I	Greenwood and Higginson
Gabriel Manigault	x	x	x	x	x	CA	Neufville & Rollestond
Samuel and Arthur Peronneau	x		x	x	x	I	John Beswicke and Co.[e]; Sarah Nickleson[f]
James Poyas	x		x	x		I CF	John Beswicke and Co.; Greenwood and Higginson

Merchants born in South Carolina	Import Trades			Export Trades		Status of Trade*	British Agents-Bankers-Creditors
	Dry goods	Slave factors	Gen. merch.	Rice/ indigo	Deer skins		
Maurice and Edward Simons	x	x	x	x	x	I CF	Davis Strachan and Co.ᵉ
(John Wagner) and Peter Bochet	x				x	I	Greenwood and Higginson
Immigrant Merchants							
Sam Chollett and John Gervais	x	x				CA	Bourdieu and Cholletʰ; Richard Oswald

ᵃJohn Nutt - The major merchant firm in the trade in the 1760s and 1770s after Greenwood and Higginson, see below. Had close connections to the Scot, James Crokatt (the preeminent British merchant in Charleston in the 1720s and 1730s, and who from 1737 was London's leading Carolina merchant and the colony's agent). Nutt's interests in South Carolina were handled by his brother Joseph, a merchant in Charleston in the 1750s and 1760s.

ᵇWilliam Jolliffe - Major merchant of Poole, Dorset, with mercantile and shipowning interests in South Carolina from c. 1720-c. 1760. John Guerard's partner from 1748-1760.

ᶜJohn Beswicke; Greenwood and Higginson - London firms trading to South Carolina. Original firm founded in London by John Beswicke (a major merchant in Charleston in the 1730s and 1740s), his nephew William Higginson and William Greenwood. Beswicke died in 1764. Greenwood's son, also William, was then sent to Charleston where he formed a partnership with the Huguenot-descended Peter Leger (see tables 2 and 3). Greenwood and Higginson was by far the leading London-Carolina firm on the eve of the Revolution.

ᵈRichard Oswald - A Scot who became a London merchant of great wealth and vast interests, with particular concerns in the West Indies and slave trades, although he also had important connections with South Carolina, and with the colonization of Georgia and Florida. Close associate of Henry Laurens.

ᵉNeufville and Rolleston - The Huguenot John Neufville and his sons John and Edward Neufville were Charleston merchants active in trade from the mid-1740s to the mid-1760s. Edward then moved to England where he traded in partnership with the English merchant Christopher Rolleston, first in Bristol and then in London.

^fSarah Nickleson - John Nickleson, Thomas and Richard Shubrick had migrated from England to Charleston where they established a major trading firm in the 1730s and early 1740s. Nickleson married the Shubricks's sister, Sarah. In the early 1740s Richard Shubrick and Nickleson moved to London where they set up major and separate houses in the Carolina trade. After Nickleson's death, c. 1760, his widow, Sarah, carried on the business for some years.

^gDavis, Strachan and Co. - Major firm in trade from c. 1769.

^hBourdieu and Chollet - See note 32.

*Status of trade refers to types of entrepreneurial activities carried on by Charleston merchants.

CA = Commission Agent; such a merchant mainly bought and sold slaves, dry goods and rice on commission for English and other principals.
I = Independent Trader; such a merchant acted as an independent entrepreneur, trading on his own account and risk.
CF = Country Factor; country factors acted for the South Carolina planters, selling their rice and other crops on commission in Charleston. Factors also imported dry goods and other commodities on their own accounts, which they sold on a retail and wholesale basis. The numbers of independent traders and country factors grew rapidly in the period from c. 1740 to the Revolution.

II

In other colonial cities, the replenishing and expansion of merchant communities was based to a large degree on migration. For example, Gary B. Nash has shown that in colonial Philadelphia there were 143 merchants in the city's second generation of merchants from 1711-1740, of whom fifty percent were migrants, only twenty percent were the sons of first-generation Philadelphia merchants, and thirty per cent were the sons of artisans, farmers, etc. Reviewing the evidence for Philadelphia and other colonial cities, he concluded that the economic and political power of first-generation merchants in new colonies rapidly disintegrated:

> the building of economic dynasties...proved to be unusu-
> ally difficult in the seaport towns of colonial America.
> Commercial centres were growth centres, always charac-
> terised by the arrival of new men on the make.[33]

---

[33]Nash, "Early Merchants of Philadelphia," 340-431, 350 and 359-362. The quotation is from 350. Nash was unable to identify the origins of forty-one of the 143 second-generation merchants. I have assumed that two-thirds of these unidentified merchants were migrants, given that it is much more difficult to trace the origins of migrants than of individuals born in America. Thomas M. Doerflinger, *A Vigorous Spirit*

Migration was also of great significance to the renewing and expansion of the English merchant community of Charleston. In the period 1750-1775, for example, between one third and one half of the merchants who sat as representatives in South Carolina's Commons House of Assembly were recent arrivals.[34] However, there was relatively little Huguenot migration to South Carolina after 1700, with the exception of the settlements at Purrysburg in the 1730s and at New Bordeaux in the early 1760s, neither of which made much impact on the Charleston business community: only five (twenty percent) of the second generation of South Carolina Huguenot merchants and only two (five percent) of the third generation were migrants.[35]

The later generations of Charleston Huguenot merchants therefore emerged from within South Carolina society itself. First, while many successful British merchants in Charleston returned to England, Huguenot merchants did not regard England as "home" and few of them returned to England to retire or to set themselves up as merchants. Consequently, the Huguenot merchant community did not suffer a serious loss of talent and capital in a reverse flow of migration to England. This meant that Huguenot merchants, unlike their English counterparts, created a number of trading dynasties in Charleston. This was all the more remarkable given that South Carolina's very high levels of mortality led to a high proportion of families dying out in the male line.[36] Thus, of the eighteen first-generation Huguenot merchants for whom information survives, only twelve had surviving sons while six had only daughters or no surviving children. But of the twelve, eight had one or more sons who followed them in trade, while three had sons who became planters and one had a

---

of Enterprise: Merchants and Economic Development in Revolutionary Philadelphia (Chapel Hill, 1986), 55-56, analyses a sample of ninety-one Philadelphia merchants for the colonial period as a whole, over one-third of whom were immigrants.

[34]Richard Waterhouse, *A New World Gentry: The Making of a Merchant and Planter Class in South Carolina, 1670-1770* (New York, 1989), 169-171.

[35]See tables 2 and 3. Only two Charleston merchants, James and John Poyas, were descended from a Purrysburg settler, John Lewis Poyas.

[36]On mortality rates see, Coclanis, *Shadow of a Dream*, 42-43; and Van Ruymbeke, "L'Émigration Huguenote," I, 93-95.

son who resided in the West Indies.[37] As late as the 1760s, nine (twenty-five percent) of the major Huguenot merchants of Charleston were the sons or grandsons of first-generation merchants. In contrast, only one of the 100 or so English merchants active in trade in the 1760s was descended in the male line from the first generation of Charleston merchants.[38] Second, the great success of the Huguenots as planters meant that they were well-positioned to place themselves, and especially their sons, in trade in Charleston so that planters or their descendants made up eight (thirty-three percent) of the second and twelve (thirty-two percent) of the third generation of merchants. Finally, Huguenots always made up a significant proportion of Charleston's artisan population, an occupational group which made a useful contribution to the formation of Charleston's merchant community, providing two (eight percent) of the second and eight (twenty-one percent) of the third generation of Huguenot merchants.

Given that the Huguenot merchant community in Charleston was replenished from within colonial society rather than by further migration from Europe, is it the case that Huguenots sustained their strong position in South Carolina's mercantile economy through a high degree of reciprocity and cooperation based on their common ethnic background? There were three main ways by which such "ethnic association" could have promoted economic success: shared religious and cultural activities, business partnerships and marriage alliances.[39] The highest incidence of

---

[37]See notes to table 1 and Manigault, "Manigault Family," 48-57; Simmons, "Early Manigault Records"; Mazyck, "Mazyck Family," 43-53; Hutson, "Motte Family," 57-63; Gourdin, "Madeleine Chardon," 64-104; [Notes on Will of Issac Mazyck], *THSSC*, XIV (1907), 39-41; Michael Jenkins Hutson, "Peronneau of South Carolina," *THSSC*, LXXXIX (1984), 49-58; "Will of Issac Chardon," *THSSC*, XLV (1940), 69-71; "Will of Francis LeBrasseur," 50-53; "Francis LeBrasseur," *THSSC*, LIX (1954), 39-42; Nash, "Trade and Business"; Van Ruymbeke, "L'Émigration Huguenote." Gary Nash, "Early Merchants of Philadelphia," 342-343, has shown that forty percent of the first generation of Philadelphia merchants "either had no sons or lost their sons before they reached adulthood."

[38]The most prolific Huguenot family was that of Peronneau, who produced at least eight leading merchants in the colonial period; see tables 1-4; SCDAH, Records of the Secretary of the Province, C (1722-1724), 11-12; and Hutson, "Peronneau of South Carolina," 49-58.

[39]One could add a fourth way, the residential clustering of French merchants in Charleston's business districts. However, the only substantial study of the spatial distribution of Charleston's merchants does not suggest that Huguenot merchants gathered

ethnic association is found, as one might expect, between the Huguenot merchants of the first generation. The French Church in Charleston remained a strong centre of Huguenot religious practice from its foundation in c. 1685 to 1720 and during this period many of its most prominent members and benefactors were leading Charleston merchants. For example, in 1693 three of the five elders of the Church were important traders.[40] With respect to marriage practices we have information about a total of nineteen first and second marriages contracted by first-generation Huguenot merchants; fifteen of these marriages were with French women and four with English women, although three of the English marriages were with second wives and took place after the French merchants in question had been in America for many years. The first-generation merchants also formed twelve business partnerships: ten of these involved solely French merchants, of which seven firms brought together partners who were closely related by blood or marriage. Two partnerships were formed between French and English merchants.[41] The "sociale endogamie" of the first-generation took a number of forms. For example, three of the daughters of first-generation merchant Jacques LeSerrurier married French merchants, including LeSerrurier's principal business associates, Issac Mazyck and Pierre de St Julien (table 1). An example of a different kind is provided by Elizabeth Buretel, the widow of the merchant Pierre Buretel. From her husband's death in 1703 to her own death in 1727, Madame Buretel lived on the interest drawn from loans she made to 110 South Carolina planters, merchants and artisans. Her debtors were mainly Huguenots, including a number of the merchants listed in table 1 as well as other less prominent Huguenot merchants.[42]

---

together in a distinctive quarter; see Calhoun, Zierdan and Paysinger, "Geographic Spread," 207-220.

[40]On Charleston's French Church, see Hirsch, *Huguenots of Colonial South Carolina*, 50-60; Ruymbeke, "L'Émigration Huguenote," II, 372-395, 421-423 and 450-460; and Butler, *Huguenots in America*, 107-120 and 134-143.

[41]See note 37.

[42]SCDAH, Records of the Secretary of the Province, Vol. F (1727-1729), Inventory of Elizabeth Buretel, 1727, 94-95; Elizabeth M. Pruden, "Investing Widows: Autonomy in a Nascent Capitalist Society," in Brana-Shute and Sparks (eds.), *New Directions*; [Notes on Will of Issac Mazyck], 39-41; and Van Ruymbeke, "L'Émigration Huguenote," I, 352-354 and 365. Pruden shows that the Widow Buretel was not unique;

But among the second and third generations of merchants there was a sharp decline in the high degree of religious, economic and marital cohesiveness which characterised the first generation of Huguenot migrants. Charleston's French Church was irretrievably damaged in 1719 by the departure for England of its long-serving pastor, Paul L'Escot, and subsequently the great majority of Huguenot merchants worshipped at the city's English Churches or ceased to engage in regular religious practice. Aside from the French Church there were no other French institutions in Charleston and consequently the full part that Huguenot merchants played in the city's eighteenth-century social and cultural life was achieved through membership of prestigious clubs and societies which were dominated by English members and officers.[43] After 1720, then, there is little evidence that Huguenot merchants participated in religious and cultural activities of a distinctively French character. With respect to business alliances, the great majority of Huguenot merchants of the second and third generations operated in partnerships for most of their careers in order to ease the problems of raising trading capital.[44] For the period 1740-1775 we have information about sixty-two mercantile partnerships entered into by fifty-four Huguenot merchants: twenty-two (thirty-five percent) of these partnerships involved solely French merchants, of which twelve involved fathers and sons, brothers or other close family relations. The other forty partnerships (sixty-five percent) were formed between French and non-French merchants. The pattern of trading partnerships therefore does show evidence of cooperation between Huguenots but, as in the first generation, these partnerships were based as much on family connections as on a common ethnic background.[45] For marriages, we have

---

over a third of her sample of eighty women who lived off money-lending in the period 1720-1770 were "affiliated with the French Huguenot community."

[43]For example, the Charles Town Library Society, founded in 1748, had 125 members in 1750, of whom ten were French, including eight merchants; see Hirsch, *Huguenots of Colonial South Carolina*, 161 and 164.

[44]On partnerships, see Nash, "Trade and Business," 9-11.

[45]Trading partnerships have been identified mainly from SCDAH, Records of the South Carolina Court of Common Pleas, Judgment Rolls (1730-1775), in which the most frequent litigants by far were merchant firms suing for the recovery of debts; see also miscellaneous business papers cited in table 3, note c; Hamer, *et al.* (eds.), *Papers of Henry Laurens*; and Edgar and Baily (eds.), *Biographical Directory*, II. If Charleston

information about sixty-two first and subsequent marriages contracted by fifty-one Huguenot merchants of the second and third generations: nineteen (thirty percent) of these marriages were with French-descended women and forty-three (seventy percent) with English women or those descended from other nationalities. Obviously, the stock of potential marriage partners was much larger than that of business partners and much less Huguenot in composition, as Huguenots made up about twenty-five percent of the merchant community but only about three percent of the population. Huguenot merchants therefore showed a clear but far from overwhelming preference for French wives.[46]

The generally exogamous nature of the marriages undertaken by Huguenot merchants of the second and third generations provides some support for Butler's view that Huguenots so frequently inter-married with non-Huguenots to the point, in the 1760s, when marriages between people of French descent were uncommon. But this is not surprising since Butler's evidence is drawn from St. Philip' Parish in Charleston, the city's main Anglican church, where many Charleston merchants were married.[47]

Huguenot merchants had chosen their business partners randomly from among the merchant community, then twenty-five percent of their selections in the 1760s would have been fellow Huguenots.

[46]Marriages have been traced mainly through Robert Wilson, "Prioleau Family," *THSSC*, VI (1899), 24-27; "Will of Gabriel Guignard," *THSSC*, XXXVIII (1933), 89-100; W. Allan Moore, Jr., "The Bonneau Family," *THSSC*, LII (1947), 38-39; Martha Burns, "Vincent Guerin of St. Thomas and St. Denis," *THSSC*, LXIX (1964), 37-43; "Bacot Records," *THSSC*, LXXVII (1972), 93-103; Edward Gaillard, "A Brief Outline of My Family Background," *THSSC*, LXXXII (1977), 85-93; Mazyck, "Notes on the Mazyck Family"; "Early Generations of the Legare Family in South Carolina," *THSSC*, XLVI (1941), 72-81; "Perdriau," *THSSC*, LXVIII (1963), 72-85; Hutson, "Peronneau of South Carolina," 49-58; Robert F. Clute (ed.), *The Annals and Parish Register of St. Thomas and St. Dennis Parish in South Carolina, from 1680-1884* (Baltimore, 1974); A.S. Salley, Jr., (ed.), *Register of St. Philip's Parish, 1720-1758* (Columbia, SC, 1971); D.E. Huger Smith and Salley (eds.), *Register of St. Philip's Parish, 1754-1810* (Columbia, SC, 1971); A.S. Salley, Jr. (ed.), *Marriage Notices in the South-Carolina Gazette and its Successors (1732-1801)* (Albany, NY, 1902); Moore and Simmons (eds.), *Abstracts of the Wills, 1670-1740*; Moore (ed.), *Abstracts of the Wills of the State of South Carolina. Vol. 2: 1740-60* and *Vol. 3: 1760-1784* (Columbia, SC, 1964, 1969).

[47]Butler, *Huguenots in America*, 132-134, His other evidence is taken from the Register of St. Thomas and St. Denis Parish, records which were kept by British ministers and which "probably exclude marriages performed by the French ministers at St. Denis." The quotation is from *ibid.*, 133, table 5, note b.

However, the marriage practices of Huguenot merchants differed from those of the Huguenots in the agricultural settlements who, as Friedlander shows, were much more likely to marry French spouses and to live out their lives in French neighbourhoods. Friedlander analyzed a large, colony-wide sample of 740 marriages involving one or two French partners. The majority of marriages were endogenous ones through the 1760s, and even for the fourth generation, for which the median date of marriage was as late as 1782, forty percent of marriages were endogenous. For the rural population, the consciousness of a common ethnic origin remained an important factor in the choice of a marriage partner throughout the colonial period.[48] By contrast, for the Huguenot merchants of Charleston, at least after the first generation, the ethnic origin of marriage partners was less important than their occupational status and wealth. Thus, of the sixty-two merchant marriages discussed above, twenty (thirty-two percent) were with women from mercantile families, while the great majority of the rest were with women from established planting families. In the major decisions about their careers, that is in decisions about the choice of business and marriage partners, Huguenot merchants acted as members of a close-knit and cosmopolitan English and French business community, with its distinctive "mercantile" patterns of marriage and business co-operation, rather than as members of an ethnic minority.[49]

Indeed, most Huguenot merchants of the second and third generations moved flexibly between the French and English groups within the wider Charleston business community, although Huguenot merchants did have a tendency to reaffirm their Huguenot connections in their later careers. For example, Jacob Motte, the son of the migrant merchant John Motte, was apprenticed in 1711 to a prominent Huguenot merchant of the first generation, Francis LeBrasseur. On the completion of his apprenticeship in 1720, Jacob Motte went into business with the English migrant Charles Hill, his father's former partner, and then in 1725 struck out on his own, becoming one of the major merchants in Charleston. At about

---

[48]Friedlander, "Carolina Huguenots," 252-266 and 278-281.

[49]Of course, while the urban and rural Huguenots had different social and marital patterns there were very important connections between the two groups. Many Huguenot merchants married planters' daughters or shifted from trade to the ownership of plantations and slaves, while the rural planters provided many recruits for the Charleston merchant community in the second and third generations.

the same time he married an English wife, Elizabeth Martin. In later years, however, Motte returned to his Huguenot roots. In the 1750s he formed a business partnership with James Laurens, Henry Laurens' brother and a major second-generation Huguenot merchant, and in 1763 he married Anne LeBrasseur, the daughter of the Huguenot merchant to whom Motte had been apprenticed exactly fifty years before! Similarly, John Guerard II, began his trading career in 1730 when he entered into a partnership with Benjamin Godin, his father's former partner. In 1735 he formed a major trading partnership with Richard Hill, Charles Hill's son, and he married Richard's sister, Elizabeth. When Hill died in 1746, Guerard formed a twenty-year partnership with the English merchant William Jolliffe. In this last phase of his career, however, Guerard rediscovered his Huguenot connections. First, he was linked in business with the planter David Godin, Benjamin Godin's son. Second, following the death of his first wife in 1744, he married Marrianne Godin, Benjamin Godin's daughter and his own cousin.[50] A final example is Henry Laurens, who married an English wife and whose partners were the English immigrants George Austin and George Appleby, and who mainly traded with English merchants. Yet from the 1760s, as Laurens moved from being a loyal British citizen to become one of South Carolina's leading patriots, we see the re-emergence of his Huguenot identity. First, Laurens gave a helping hand to a number of Huguenot migrants to America, including the young, poor Huguenot migrant John Lewis Gervais (tables 3 and 4), in whose plight Laurens clearly detected strong echoes of his own family's history. Second, in the early 1770s he travelled in Britain and on the continent of Europe. He was highly critical of many aspects of English and French life, although he did try to trace his ancestors in La Rochelle, and he reserved his greatest respect for Geneva, that "wonderful republic." As he wrote in Geneva in August, 1774:

> If the oppressions of America continue, and her efforts to get rid of them prove ineffectual, I shall not hesitate about settling in this part of the world. There are no nobility, no standing army, no taxes, no custom-house officers, and, above all, no King – the support of whose pride, pomp, and intolerable vanity by courtiers, called *necessary*

---

[50]Hutson, "Early Generations of the Motte Family," 57-63; Edgar and Baily (eds.), *Biographical Directory*, II, 478-480; Hamer, *et al.* (eds.), *Papers of Henry Laurens*, II, 285; and Nash, "Trade and Business," 6-29.

expenses, inevitably produces these, and a thousand other grievances.[51]

III

How does the evidence presented here reflect on recent debates on the Huguenots in South Carolina? First, while Butler and others have placed great emphasis on the Huguenots' contributions to the development of slave-plantation agriculture, this paper has shown that Huguenots throughout the colonial period played a very significant and hitherto unappreciated role in South Carolina's commercial economy. The Huguenots represented only a small and declining fraction of the colony's population, but from the 1680s to the 1770s they comprised an important component of the Charleston merchant community. Their decision to become merchants in late seventeenth-century Charleston was shaped by the experience and knowledge gained in the culture from which they fled, the commercial and bourgeois world of the French Atlantic ports. Nevertheless, Bosher's argument that the success of Huguenot merchants in America was based on their connections with prominent Huguenot merchants in Europe has only a limited application to the Charleston Huguenots. A few leading Huguenot firms in England did have interests in South Carolina, but none of them established major connections with Charleston Huguenots, other than with members of their own families. Huguenot merchants in England, insofar as they had colonial interests, participated far more in the trades to the West Indies and to the other mainland colonies than in the trade to Charleston. The success of the Huguenot merchants of Charleston was underpinned, as was that of the English merchants of Charleston, by their connections with the non-Huguenot circles of London and provincial merchants who controlled the Anglo-South Carolinian trade.

Second, Huguenot success was boosted by the cohesive economic and social behaviour of the first-generation Huguenot merchants, whose families were linked by numerous religious, business and marriage connections. But this ethnic cooperation declined amongst the merchants of the second and third generations, who did not engage in a distinctively

---

[51]Hamer, *et al.* (eds.), *Papers of Henry Laurens*, IV, 331-338; V, 33-34; VIII, 316, 496-498, 503, 517, 528, 546 and 636-637; and IX, 51-52, 56-57, 127-128, 294-295, 308-312, 324-325, 377-379 and 540-541 (from which the quotation is taken).

French religious and cultural life and who were more likely to take business partners from the English, rather than the Huguenot, merchant community and to marry English rather than French spouses. This appears to confirm Butler's view that "refugee cohesion had suffered serious erosion as early as 1710 and had then thoroughly shattered by 1750," but we need to make three qualifications to Butler's argument.[52] First, there was a very high degree of ethnic association between the Huguenot merchants of the first generation until c. 1720. Second, the awareness of a common French heritage and ethnicity did not disappear amongst the Charleston Huguenot merchants of the second and third generations, a number of whom rekindled their Huguenot connections in their later lives. Third, Butler fails to distinguish clearly between the behaviour of the Huguenots in the agricultural communities and those in Charleston. Amongst the rural Huguenots, French neighbourhood communities and endogenous marriage patterns survived far into the colonial period and beyond. The urban Huguenots, on the other hand, maintained a distinct identity, but as part of a cosmopolitan, Protestant trading community held together by innumerable business and marriage connections, connections which were based more on a communal sense of vocation or occupation, than on an awareness of shared ethnicity and origins.

Finally, were the Huguenot merchants integrated and absorbed into South Carolina culture and society, as Butler has suggested, or should we heed Bosher's argument that Huguenot merchants in America maintained a distinctive, commercial culture based on their links to international, Huguenot trading networks? The universal decision of South Carolina Huguenots to become naturalised English subjects shows that they had no desire, or at least expectation, of returning to their mother country. Nevertheless, the Huguenot merchants did not transfer their allegiance from France to England, nor did they focus their loyalties, as did refugee Huguenots in other societies, on their family ties to international clans of Huguenot merchants. Rather their allegiance appears to have been to South Carolina. Certainly, they assimilated themselves far more thoroughly into colonial society than did the British merchants, many of whom harboured long-term plans to return to Britain. This became clear at the Revolution, when numerous South Carolina merchants and storekeepers of British descent declared themselves Loyalists, whereas

---

[52]Butler, *Huguenots in America*, 92.

the overwhelming majority of merchants of French origins were ardent supporters of the Revolutionary cause.[53]

---

[53]Three Huguenot merchants who became loyalists were Gideon Dupont, Henry Peronneau III (see table 3), and Tacitus Gaillard, a minor merchant of the late colonial period; see, New York Public Library, Transcripts of the Commission of Enquiry into Losses of American Loyalists Amongst the Audit Office Records, LII, 505-517; LIV, 266-274; and Hutson, "Peronneau of South Carolina," 93.

Breaching the Mercantile Barriers of the Dutch Colonial Empire: North American Trade with Surinam during the Eighteenth Century

Johannes Postma

The Dutch Republic of the seventeenth and eighteenth centuries is often perceived as a bastion of free trade. No doubt, Hugo Grotius' celebrated publication *Mare liberum* (*The Open Seas*) has contributed to that image, although Grotius soon afterwards defended Dutch monopolistic practices.[1] As Immanuel Wallerstein has asserted, nations that enjoy a hegemony of world trade — as the Dutch "carriers of the world" did during the seventeenth century — have the advantage of supporting freedom from restrictions in international trade.[2] However, it has been well established that the Dutch wanted to have it both ways and demand open seas when it suited them and impose restrictions on foreign merchants when they found it to their economic advantage, in both the East Indies (Indonesia) and the West Indies.[3]

Historians generally label the commercial protection against foreign competitors by means of state intervention as mercantilism. Employing this interpretive framework is fraught with dangers, however, because of the different meanings of that theoretical model.[4] Some have even questioned the validity of mercantilism as an interpretive model. Without restating the various interpretations of mercantilism, I am using the term here to signify governmental efforts to prevent subjects of foreign

---

[1]C.R. Boxer, *The Dutch Seaborne Empire, 1600-1800* (New York, 1970), 90-92 and 102; and Jonathan I. Israel, *Dutch Primacy in World Trade, 1595-1740* (Oxford, 1989), 90 and 104-105.

[2]Immanuel Wallerstein, *The Modern World System. II: Mercantilism and the Consolidation of the European World-Economy, 1600-1750* (New York, 1980), 38.

[3]Boxer, *Dutch Seaborne Empire*, 92.

[4]See D.C. Coleman, "Mercantilism Revisited," *Historical Journal*, XXIII, No. 4 (1980), 773-791, for divergent interpretations of mercantilism.

countries to trade in regions under its jurisdiction for the purpose of limiting such rights to its own subjects and thus protect its national economy.

In their Atlantic commerce, the Dutch employed a mixture of mercantilistic protectionism and free trade access, depending on what suited them best. Initially, they had been instrumental in developing the Caribbean region, through capital investment and an efficient merchant marine, into a new system based on "advanced capitalist economics," in contrast to the exclusive markets of the Spanish and Portuguese American colonies.[5] As England and France began to apply mercantilistic policies during the seventeenth century and the Dutch found their commercial opportunities declining, their commerce became increasingly confined to their own overseas colonies.

Unlike several other European nations, the Dutch Republic was never able to induce much of its own population to emigrate to overseas settlements. This contributed to the failure of both their Brazil and New Nederland settlements.[6] In the Guiana region they were able to provide a supervisory staff to make tropical plantation economies thrive with slave labour brought in from Africa. For these areas the Dutch developed their own protective policies. Their Caribbean islands, particularly Curaçao and St. Eustatius, were not suitable for successful plantation development, and they were used primarily as commercial bases to penetrate the foreign markets in the region. Protective barriers were not an advantage here.

In addition to protectionism against merchants of other nations, the Dutch employed a system of exclusive markets through monopolies granted to particular Dutch companies. Thus, chartered joint-stock companies like the VOC (United East India Company) and the WIC (West India Company) were granted privileges within defined boundaries over their fellow nationals not affiliated with the company. By the end of the seventeenth century, however, the WIC's monopoly rights in the Atlantic

---

[5]P.C. Emmer, "The Dutch and the Making of the Second Atlantic System," in Barbara L. Solow (ed.), *Slavery and the Rise of the Atlantic System* (New York, 1991), 75-88.

[6]*Ibid.*, 84.

region had gradually been reduced to control over the Dutch Atlantic slave trade, and that was also reduced and finally terminated by 1740.[7]

This paper focuses on the economic policies and practices of the Dutch Republic with specific reference to its slave plantation colony of Surinam on the northern coast of South America. After 1682, Surinam was accessible to all Dutch merchants who paid the stipulated fees, with the importation of slaves the only remaining WIC monopoly. Foreign merchants were barred from the colony. The only exceptions were skippers from the British North American colonies. The reasons for this exception in mercantilistic exclusiveness and the resulting North American commerce with Surinam is the topic of this paper.

While researching Dutch Atlantic commerce, particularly the Dutch triangular Atlantic slave trade and the bilateral trade with Surinam, I was frequently struck by references to Americans ships in the harbour of Paramaribo, the capital and only port of Surinam. Since this phenomenon was unusual, rarely mentioned in the historical literature and never subjected to a systematic scholarly treatment, I decided that it deserves closer scrutiny.

An independent country since 1975, Surinam is not a place with great name recognition. It was originally settled by the English in 1651 as a slave plantation colony. In 1667 it was captured by a Dutch fleet not long after the British captured the Dutch colony of New Nederland, today's New York City and hinterland. In the subsequent peace settlement of the Second Anglo-Dutch War (1665-1667), Dutch negotiators apparently had no objection to surrendering New York in exchange for Surinam. The record is silent on motives, but having lost their colony in northern Brazil a decade earlier, the Dutch may have seen Surinam as a beneficial replacement.

Initially, the Surinam settlement was controlled by the Dutch province of Zeeland, but Zeeland authorities failed to revitalize the colony's economy to the level it had enjoyed under English administration. So in 1682, the States General (the Federal legislature of the Dutch Republic) finally took the initiative and approved a charter that provided a governing structure which placed the settlement under corporate ownership and management. The charter of 1682 was the foundation of

---

[7]Johannes Postma, *The Dutch in the Atlantic Slave Trade, 1600-1815* (New York, 1990), 201-204.

the Suriname Corporation (the so-called *Societeit van Suriname*) through which the city of Amsterdam, the West India Company, and the aristocratic Van Sommelsdijk family shared ownership and responsibility for the settlement.[8] These three charter members appointed a group of directors to formulate general policies and appoint a governor and other administrative officials to provide on-the-spot management of the colony.[9]

The primary purpose of the Surinam settlement was to produce tropical commodities for the benefit of its owners, and many plantations were established there for that purpose. In 1700 there were approximately one hundred sugar plantations. This number grew to 171 thirteen years later, and by the year 1800 there were about four hundred functioning plantations producing a variety of tropical produce, including sugar, coffee, cacao, and cotton.[10] But the population of Surinam remained relatively small. In 1700 there were approximately 1000 Europeans and 10,000 African slaves; by 1755 these figures had increased to about 1800 and 35,000 respectively, not counting escaped slaves or maroons and the indigenous population.[11]

The highest policy-making body of the Suriname Corporation was a group of directors representing the three shareholders, who met regularly (on average twice monthly) at the *West-Indisch Huys* in Amsterdam. Directors were drawn almost exclusively from Amsterdam merchant families, the patriciate; in most cases they were members or former members of the Amsterdam city council or mayors of the city, and those representing the WIC were invariably members of the governing board of its Amsterdam chamber. Most of them were also businessmen

---

[8]In 1770, after decades of conflict, the Sommelsdijk family was bought out by Amsterdam and the WIC.

[9]See G.W. van der Meiden, *Bestwist Bestuur: Een eeuw strijd om de macht in Suriname, 1651-1753* (Amsterdam, 1986), ch. 2.

[10]See R. Bijlsma, "Surinaamse Plantage-inventarissen uit het tijdperk 1713-1742," *West-Indishe Gids*, IV (1921-1922), 325-327; Van der Meiden, *Bestwist Bestuur*, 75; and Alex van *Stipriaan, Surinaams contrast: Roofbouw en overleven in een Caribische plantagekolonie 1750-1863* (Leiden, 1993), 33-34.

[11]Postma, *Dutch in the Atlantic Slave Trade*, 185. Because of the lack of any census, the demography of Surinam poses a difficult problem that has not yet been studied thoroughly.

with strong West Indian interests. Several were suppliers for the Surinam market and processors of Surinam commodities.[12]

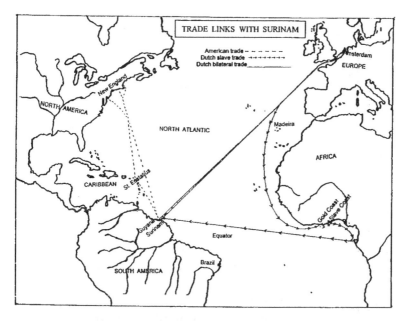

Figure 1: Map, "Surinam and Its Commercial Lifelines."

Although private shipping firms were allowed to do business in Surinam, after purchasing a permit from the Suriname Corporation, the corporate directors were also directly involved in outfitting ship consignments to Surinam. Furthermore, the directors appointed all government officials for Surinam, from the governor down to the teacher and the auctioneer. Stationed at Surinam, the appointed governors exercised supreme authority in the colony and were directly responsible to the directors in Amsterdam. Governors and their subordinates had to keep meticulous accounts of their transactions in Surinam, and they had to forward copies of their bookkeeping to Amsterdam. A flood of correspondence and papers passed in both directions across the Atlantic — commer-

[12]Algemeen Rijksarchief, the Hague (hereafter ARA), Societeit van Suriname Papers (hereafter SS), XXXII, 144. Several directors supplied meat for shipment to Surinam and were initially also involved in the outfitting of slave ships. Most of the minutes and resolutions of the meetings have been preserved; see ARA, SS, XVII-LXXXV.

cial and taxation records, legal and fiscal reports, as well as documents about the endemic squabbles between the governors and the planters.[13] Much of this paper work has been preserved, and it is because of that preservation that a rather accurate account of the commercial activities of Surinam can be studied, including the frequent comings and goings of North American ships.

The American shipping was by no means the most important contact between Surinam and the outside world. More significant was the triangular slave trade from Holland via Africa, which supplied the essential labour force for the plantations. Equally important was the extensive bilateral trade between the Dutch Republic and Surinam, which carried European immigrants and valuable supplies to Surinam and returned vast quantities of tropical commodities to Holland. The ship traffic between North America and Surinam was the third important life-line for the Surinam settlement, but it was significant nevertheless.

After years of research, I have been able to collect statistical information and generate data banks for each of these three commercial life-lines. The slave trade to Surinam encompasses approximately 600 shipping consignments for the years 1667-1795, the bilateral trade with Holland involves nearly 3600 shipping voyages during the 1683-1794 period, and the North Americans sent nearly 3900 ships to Surinam during the same period. One should keep in mind that the American ships tended to be much smaller than the Dutch ships – an average of sixty-two maritime tons compared to 140.[14] Dutch ships had far greater carrying capacity, and the value of their cargoes was therefore much higher. Publications on each of these commercial links are in preparation. Figure 2 provides a graphical comparison of these three branches of commerce. The information available in these data banks includes names of ships and captains, dates of arrival and departure, ports of origin and destination, the nature, quantity and value of the consignments, etc. Once all the data have been carefully edited and analyzed, a clear picture of the commerce converging on Surinam can be released.

---

[13]See Van der Meiden's *Bestwist Bestuur*, which can be translated as "government in conflict."

[14]The data on the Dutch slave trade have been published in Postma, *Dutch in the Atlantic Slave Trade*. The Holland-Surinam (bilateral trade) and the America-Surinam data banks are in the analysis and publication stage.

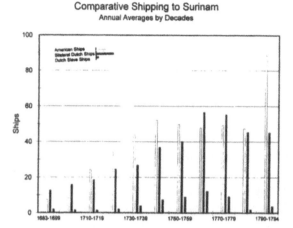

Figure 2: Graph, "Comparative Ship Traffic to and from Surinam."

The eighteenth-century Surinam settlement was an isolated community, far removed from the rest of the world, surrounded by the ocean on one side and impenetrable tropical rainforest on the other. The ocean side, and particularly where the Surinam river flows into the Atlantic, was Surinam's window to the world from which came mail, immigrants, new slaves, horses, food and supplies, but which also harbored dangers such as potential invasions (which actually occurred twice during the eighteenth century). The tropical rain forest, however, was perhaps more threatening and mysterious than the sea. It was controlled initially by the indigenous Indians, Caribs and Arawaks, with whom the settlement was at war during the end of the seventeenth century. Afterwards, the Maroons (runaway slaves) established their communities in the forests and they often attacked plantations. The plantations deep in the interior were most susceptible to such attacks and provided, therefore, the most precarious life. Paramaribo, the capital and only harbour of the colony, was the safest place for the settlers. Not only did it offer a modicum of urban existence, but with its constant flow of sailors, soldiers, merchants, and arriving and departing ships, it was the only place in the colony with some variety and excitement. From the perspective of the slaves, the great majority of the population, Surinam held all of the dangers described for Europeans, plus the agony of forced labour, constant harassment and exploitation by the masters, and little hope of manumission.[15]

It is clear that the Dutch intended at first to keep the Surinam colony inaccessible to foreign nationals. The 1682 charter stipulated unequivocally that no foreign ships should be allowed to enter the Surinam river and do business at the port of Paramaribo. With their own financial interest, the corporate directors in Amsterdam were also inclined to keep foreign merchants out of the colony. From the outset, however, these exclusion rules were occasionally violated. The records contain periodic references to American ships frequenting the Paramaribo harbour but rarely were any landings from other foreign ships recorded. We can only speculate on the reasons for these early American ships at Paramaribo. Perhaps they were old contacts dating back to the English period (1651-1667), or perhaps some skippers were New Yorkers who felt free to maintain an affiliation with their former Dutch compatriots in Surinam.[16]

The Surinam settlers and members of the colony's government invariably favoured admitting American ships, and they often allowed them to do business there in spite of the risk of being castigated by the authorities in Holland. Dutch ships were apparently unable to supply the Surinam population with adequate food and with horses to keep the sugar mills running. In 1685, Governor Van Sommelsdijck (1683-1688) pleaded with the corporate directors in Amsterdam:

> This colony is often destitute for all types of food...and especially for horses. During the past two years only one ship brought about 30 [European] horses, which were of poor quality and experienced a high death rate...more than half of them died. Planters are forced to use slaves to drive the mills. This colony could go to ruin unless horses are imported, as was done before. Scottish, New

---

[15]For a description of life in Surinam during the eighteenth century, see Gert van Stripriaan, *Roosenburg en Mon Bijou; Twee Surinaamse Plantages, 1720-1870* (Dordrecht, 1989); and Ruud Beeldsnijder, *Om werk van jullie te hebben; Plantageslaven in Suriname, 1730-1750* (Utrecht, 1994).

[16]The given names of New York skippers were usually recorded in Dutch: thus, Jan instead of John, and Hendrik instead of Henry.

England, and Norwegian horses are better for this climate
than Dutch horses. If only the foreign trade could be
opened for a while again, so we could export wood
products, molasses, and *Killdevil* [rum], this could bring
great relief to the inhabitants of Suriname.[17]

The "foreign trade" for which the governor pleaded must have been trade
with North American colonists.

The Suriname Corporation directors in Amsterdam appointed a
commission of three to study the problem of shortages. A few months
later the directors decided that the American importation of horses and
other draft animals might be tolerated, but the importation of food items
was explicitly declared unacceptable. The directors also decided to take
the issue to the States General, requesting a revision of the charter of
1682.[18] Such revisions did not materialize for another fifteen years,
however. Meanwhile, feeble efforts to bring in Irish and other European
horses were rarely successful and American horses were admitted
occasionally. A 1697 report listed the "important" news from Surinam as
follows:

...the great shortage of horses, which Dutch ships and
merchants cannot remedy because the voyages [across the
Atlantic] are too long. In addition, Dutch horses are too
big and cannot adjust here...Otherwise this colony would
be in good shape.[19]

In 1701, illicit foreign imports became a critical issue again. Few
American ships had been admitted to Paramaribo during 1696-1698 and
none in 1700, and Governor Paul van der Veen (1696-1707) complained
repeatedly about shortages of horses and food and the disaster that the
restrictions on foreign imports produced. Writing to Amsterdam in 1699,
he justified his recent breach of the foreign import ban: "Without

---

[17]ARA, SS, CCXII, 173.

[18]*Ibid.*, XVIII, 23 May 1685; XLVIII, 16 July 1685; and LXVIII, 27 September
1685.

[19]*Ibid.*, XIX, 7 April 1688; and XX, 14 September 1694.

admitting English ships...the militia might have revolted."[20] (North American colonial ships were regularly referred to as English.) After repeated pleas for foreign imports of food and horses, he finally presented to the Amsterdam directors a persuasive rationale: "Next to slaves, horses represent the second leg on which this colony walks." The directors in Amsterdam regularly discussed the issue of foreign imports to Surinam in their meetings throughout 1701. While insisting that the import ban on American food and merchandise remain intact, they concluded that the importation of American horses could be permitted, but only if there was a demonstrated shortage. However, if American horses were brought in, an import duty had to be levied on them, and the directors made clear that this relaxation of the rules was an exception to official regulations.[21]

After a few more years of haggling and negotiating, and with the approval of the Dutch States General, the directors of the Suriname Corporation adopted a special ordinance on 25 April 1704 that formally authorized North American ships to trade at the Paramaribo port with carefully defined restrictions. Accordingly, Americans were not only permitted, but required, to include horses in each of their consignments. Ships from North America were not allowed to bring European-grown grains and manufactured goods, nor manufactured commodities from Asia. (These were products that Dutch merchants, including some of the directors of the Suriname Corporation, could readily supply themselves.) The Americans were not allowed to export sugar from Surinam (later coffee beans, cocoa beans, and cotton were added to the list), but they were allowed to export molasses, rum, and wood products. But they were allowed to bring food items, building supplies, tobacco, alcoholic beverages, livestock, and supplies like candles and soap — all products that were grown or processed in the North American region and not in Europe.[22] The special ordinance of 1704 was a compromise that protected Dutch merchants from serious foreign competition, yet met the dire needs

---

[20]*Ibid.*, XXII, 22 September 1698; CCLXXXV, 28 February 1699; and CCXXVI, 15 October 1697.

[21]*Ibid.*, CCXXVIII, 28 January 1702; CCXXIX, 28 January 1702; XXI, 19 August 1701; and CCCL, December 1701.

[22]J.A. Schiltkamp and J.Th. De Smidt (eds.), *West Indisch plakaatboek; Plakaten, ordinantien en andere wetten, uitgevaardigd in Suriname, 1667-1761* (2 vols.; Amsterdam, 1973), I, 253-255.

of the Surinam settlers and allowed the colony to flourish and maximize its economic potential, to the benefit and interests of the Dutch owners and merchants.

Table 1
Horse Landings at Paramaribo
1683-1794

Years	Ships Arriving (documented)	No Record of Horses	Horses Total	Average per Vessel	Undocu- mented Estimate	Grand Total	Annual Average (per period)
1683- 1704	181	155	550	21.154	2325	2875	131
1705- 1709	77	1	1112	14.632	14.63158	1127	225
1710- 1719	243	5	2896	12.168	60.84034	2957	296
1720- 1729	343	3	6014	17.585	52.75439	6067	607
1730- 1739	437	1	5019	11.511	11.51147	5031	503
1740- 1749	522	74	5874	12.797	947.0065	6821	682
1750- 1759	498	56	3290	7.3274	410.3341	3700	370
1760- 1769	480	66	3860	9.1253	602.2695	4462	446
1770- 1779	494	289	563	2.7463	289	852	85
1780- 1789	465	364	831	7.8396	100	931	93
1790- 1794	463	446	111	5.0455	50	161	32
Totals	4203	1460	30120	121.93	4863	34983	312

Source: American-Surinam Databank.

North American merchants had to pay a hefty price for the privilege of trading in Surinam. They were subject to higher, as well as additional, fee payments than Dutch ships that anchored at Paramaribo.

American ship masters had to pay a tonnage fee of six guilders per *last* (one *last* or burden was equal to two maritime tons), plus five percent on all imported and exported goods, and three guilders for every horse landed at Paramaribo.[23] Careful accounts were kept of these duty payments, and the survival of many of them provides useful records for historians. Most of these papers have been preserved for the years 1705 through 1745, providing a very detailed account of the American trade. In 1742 the newly appointed and ambitious governor Jan Jacob Mauricius started keeping a daily administrative journal in which he also recorded arriving and departing ships and their cargoes.[24] The directors in Amsterdam liked this system so well that they had these journals bound and preserved, and subsequent governors maintained journals for the remainder of the century. Thus, while the taxation records were discarded, we have at our disposal much of the same data for the years after 1745, albeit less detailed. The three-year overlap (1742-1745) provides a convenient validity check on the two sets of documentation.

The records collected for this study of the North American trade add up to slightly more than 4200 shipping voyages, each with up to twenty-five variables in a record. An estimated three hundred of these consignments are assumed to have had British Caribbean islands as their operational base, but a home base is sometimes difficult to determine when the names of the ships and the captains are both in English, and stopovers at Caribbean ports were a common practice. It is safe to assume that about 3900 of these voyages had their operating base in North American mainland ports, primarily in the New England colonies.[25]

A desperate need for horses was one of the primary reasons for allowing American ships to enter the Paramaribo harbour, and the Surinam establishment was generally not disappointed with the American response. As shown in table 1, the Americans shipped at least 30,000

---

[23]These documents are distributed among other papers in ARA, SS, CCXXXIII-CCLXXVI. Dutch ships, by contrast needed to pay only 2.5 percent export duty and no import duties.

[24]For an account of the role of Mauricius in Surinam history see van der Meiden, *Bestwist Bestuur*, 91-127.

[25]Additional research in archives in the United States and Great Britain may eventually clarify the home ports of these ships. The statistics gathered by this author are in a computerized data bank under the title America-Surinam Databank.

horses to Surinam, primarily during the 1701-1770 period. An estimated 3000 horses may be added to account for missing documentation, either missing cargo statistics or undocumented arrivals of ships. The bulk of the horse trade to Surinam took place between 1705 and 1770, with annual averages reaching more than 600 horses during the 1720s and 1740s. The peak year was 1745, when more than 900 horses were landed at Paramaribo. The horses were used primarily as draft animals in the sugar mills, walking in circles to turn the heavy mill stones that crushed the sugar cane, and for farm chores and at lumber mills. Some riding horses were imported to Surinam as well. After 1750, horse imports began to decline as increasing numbers of sugar plantations relocated to the coastal lowlands, where running water was used to power the sugar mills.[26]

Table 2
Surinam Horse Imports by Port of Origin
1683-1794

Regions and Ports	Ships	Missing Data	Horses Documented	Estimate Undoc.	Grand Total	Average Load	Maximum Load
Middle Colonies	583	169	1882	338	2220	4.6	44
New York	323	91	1225	182	1407	5.3	44
Philadelphia	222	46	637	92	729	3.8	26
Unnamed Ports	38	23	20	46	66	1.3	6
New England	3203	950	28021	3800	31821	12.5	62
Massachusetts	1426	430	9368	1720	11088	9.4	57
Connecticut	183	42	3067	168	3235	21.8	58
New Hampshire	25	23	40	92	132	20	20
Rhode Island	1340	327	15278	1308	16586	15.1	62
Maine/Canada	41	30	96	120	216	8.7	32
Unnamed Ports	189	107	172	428	600	2.1	32
Southern Colonies	165	123	133	123	256	3.2	25
Unidentified Port D	252	179	84	358	442	1.2	32
Totals	4203	1421	30120	4610	34739	11	

Source: See table 1.

---

[26]Van Stripriaan, *Roosenburg en Mon Bijou*, 50-51. See also table 2, as well as the America-Surinam Databank for horse trade statistics.

New England traders, sometimes referred to as "the Dutch of England's Empire" because of their commercial entrepreneurial skills, brought the lion's share of the horses to Surinam (see table 2). Very few horses were shipped from the southern colonies, and the middle colonies also contributed only meagrely to this traffic. New York, the most active port in the middle colonies, shipped an average of five horses per consignment. By contrast, ships from Connecticut and Rhode Island carried an average of twenty-two and fifteen per vessel respectively. The Connecticut port of New London seems to have specialized in the horse trade, and the ships that carried its large horse consignments were often referred to as "horse jockeys." In terms of aggregate figures, however, Rhode Islanders were most active in the horse trade, carrying approximately fifty percent of the total number of horses landed at Paramaribo. Massachusetts was second to Rhode Island in total numbers, although it averaged fewer than ten horses per consignment.[27]

Average horse cargoes can be misleading, however, because there were so many ships that brought only a "token" horse to meet minimal requirements. Many ships were admitted without any horses, if they could prove through the ship's manifest that horses had been boarded but had died during the crossing. Nearly seventy percent of the horse-carrying ships landed fewer than three at Paramaribo (1886 out of 2738). Before 1770, American ships were regularly refused entry into the Paramaribo harbour if they did not bring horses. Occasionally, the absence of horses was used to force American captains to do transport services for Surinam authorities, who were particularly disagreeable when it became evident that horses had been sold at interim ports before arriving at Paramaribo.[28] After 1770, the demand for horses in Surinam dwindled and the absence of horses on arriving ships was no longer noted in the governors' journals, which suggests that the 1704 regulations requiring horse imports may no longer have been enforced.[29]

---

[27]John J. McCusker and Russell R. Menard, *The Economy of British America, 1607-1789* (Chapel Hill, 1991), 92; and Robert O. Decker, *The New London Merchants, 1645-1909: The Rise and Decline of a Connecticut Port* (New York, 1986), 32.

[28]Jeffrey D. Kratz, "The Colonial Balance of Trade: New England's Horse Trade with Dutch Suriname, 1750 to 1780" (Unpublished MA thesis, Mankato State University, 1995), 74; see also America-Surinam Databank.

[29]See America-Surinam Databank.

New England exported horses not only to Surinam, but also to other sugar colonies in the West Indies. Few historians have mentioned this trade, and until the traffic to other areas is scrutinized, the true extent of the overall horse trade will remain a matter of speculation. The horse trade to Surinam was certainly well known in its time, because the expression "Surinam horses" was familiar enough that when merchants like the Brown family of Providence placed advertisements for export horses in newspapers, they would use that term.[30]

A tragic element in this maritime horse trade was the extremely high mortality of animals. According to available statistics, approximately thirty-six percent of the horses boarded in North America did not make it to Surinam alive. This means that more than 56,000 horses must have been exported in order to land 36,000 (see table 1) at Paramaribo. Storms were the biggest killer of the horses, which were usually transported on the open decks of the small American ships or had temporary covers constructed for shelter. Horses were often washed overboard during storms or thrown overboard after sustaining injuries. Numerous references to such incidents are found in the Surinam and Rhode Island records.[31]

Voyages from the North American mainland to Surinam lasted an average of thirty-eight days, although this may have included stopovers at other ports. The port of origin seemed to make little difference in the average length of the crossing, except clearances from Philadelphia which took a few days longer than clearances from other American ports. The shortest registered voyage was ten days from Newbury Port (Massachusetts), but that seems to have been an exceptional case or an error in the documentation. Provisioning the horses, particularly a large consignment, required considerable space for fodder and water, as well as additional crew members. Forty to fifty horses per cargo was not uncommon; the

---

[30]See James Hedges, *The Browns of Providence Plantation: Colonial Years* (Cambridge, MA, 1952), 77, for a copy of such an advertisement in the Rhode Island *Gazette*. See also Kratz, "Colonial Balance of Trade," 73.

[31]ARA, SS, CCXLVIII, 625 (all thirty horses died as a result of a storm – 1721); CCLI, 272 (forty-five of fifty horses died at sea – 1724); CCLII, 4 (all twenty-five horses lost in a storm – 1725); and CCLIII, 226 (forty-seven of fifty horses died in a storm). See also John Carter Brown Library (JCBL), Brown Family Papers (BFP).

largest documented consignment was for sixty-two horses landed at Paramaribo.[32]

In addition to horses, North American skippers brought a variety of food items, building materials, and household supplies, as well as livestock like sheep, pigs, and geese. An excellent record of import and export duties paid in Surinam for the years 1705-1745 has been preserved; the records list all imported and exported items as well as their assessed values and the five percent duty payments.[33] Table 3 gives an overview of the value of these imports in five-year units. Statistics for later years are less detailed in the Surinam records. Supplementary data must be obtained from American archives. The Brown family papers in Providence, for example, provide a considerable amount of data on their trade with Surinam for the years after 1770.[34]

Table 4 lists the various items that were shipped to and from Surinam by fifty-one American ships during the year 1736. Prominent among the imports were large amounts of flour and fish. New York and Philadelphia shipped primarily grain and dairy products, while New England cargoes included large amounts of fish, tobacco, and lumber. Wine came primarily from the Madeira islands, which were also frequently listed as a destination for American ships.[35] The tobacco brought to Surinam was grown in Rhode Island and was generally considered of inferior quality, but the Surinamese had evidently taken a liking to this particular variety.[36] Many building projects in Surinam must have been constructed with American lumber, although Surinam also had its own lumber cutting yards and lumber was also a regular export item from Surinam.

---

[32]See America-Surinam Databank for voyage length, and tables 1 and 2 for maximum and average loads.

[33]Contained in ARA, SS, CCXXXIII-CCLXXVI. Table 3 has been extracted from these documents.

[34]JCBL, BFP. The analysis of these data have not been completed for inclusion in this paper.

[35]A Madeira wine measure, *pijp* contained ninety-two gallons.

[36]See Hedges, *Browns of Providence Plantation*, 30-35.

Table 3
Imports to Surinam by North American Ships*
705-1744

All Monetary values are in Dutch Guilders

Years	Ships		Value			Missing	Total Imports	Annual Average
	Documented	Data Missing	Documented Total	Cargo Average	Maximum Cargo	Data Estimate		
1705-09	77	2	123,980	1,610	11,224	3,220	127,200	25,440
1710-14	123	5	250,407	2,036	9,021	10,179	260,586	52,117
1715-19	120	1	236,854	1,974	7,020	1,974	238,828	47,766
1720-24	161	2	308,059	1,913	7,234	3,827	311,886	62,377
1725-29	182	2	329,810	1,812	6,360	3,624	333,434	66,687
1730-34	204	2	559,047	2,740	8,356	5,481	564,528	112,906
1735-39	233	0	396,597	1,702	7,515	0	396,597	79,319
1740-44	283	31	319,735	1,130	14,000	35,024	354,759	70,952
Aggregate	1,383	45	2,524,489	1,887	14,000	63,329	2,587,818	64,695

Note: *Horses not included

Source: See table 1.

Table 4
Surinam Imports and Exports
by North American Ships in 1736
Consignments of 51 ships

Imports

Categories	Sub-categories	Units	Measures	Value Dutch Guilders
Livestock	Sheep, Pigs, Geese	284		2634
Preserved Meats		653	Barrels	12868
Butter and Cheese		697	Barrels	9811
Fish	Codfish, Mackerel, Herring, Oysters, Eel	1001	Barrels	12569
Grain Products	Flour	1612	Barrels	21126
	Bread/Biscuits	108	Barrels	524
Alcoholic Beverages	Wine	8280	Gallons	24765
	Bier/Ale	65	Barrels/bottles	
Tobacco		30250	Pounds	5436
Building Supplies	Boards Shingles/Tar	154000	Square Feet	10783
Bricks		104000	?	1164
Produce	Onions, Peas	222	Barrels	2601
	Apples, etc.		?	
Household Supplies	Candles, Soap		Boxes	1724
Salt			Barrels	2901
Miscellaneous				300
Aggregate Imports (exc. horses)				**109206**
Horses		487	150 per Head	73050
Imports Grand Total				**182256**

Exports

		Units	Measures	Value
Molasses		?	Barrels	42906
Rum		45	Barrels	1515
Aggregate Exports		**2996**	**Barrels**	**44421**

Taxation at Parimaribo

	Unit/Value	Total
Horses (3 guilders per head)	487	1461
Tonnage Fee (6 guilders per last=2 ton)	1375	8250
5% Import Duty	109206	5460
5% Export Duty	44421	2221
Taxation Total		**17392**

Source: See table 1.

Table 5
Exports from Surinam to North America
1705-1744

Years	Ships		Values in Dutch Guilders				In Guilders	
	Documented	Data Missing	Export Total	Cargo Average	Maximum Cargo	Missing Data Estimate	Total Exports	Annual Average
1705-09	77	3	64,109	833	2,500	2,498	66,607	13,321
1710-14	123	5	125,671	1,022	3,095	5,109	130,780	26,156
1715-19	120	5	131,973	1,100	2,880	5,499	137,472	27,494
1720-24	161	4	226,639	1,408	3,281	5,631	232,270	46,454
1725-29	182	3	223,932	1,230	2,532	3,691	227,623	45,525
1730-34	204	4	243,489	1,194	2,814	4,774	248,263	49,653
1735-39	233	0	172,342	740	1,650	0	172,342	34,468
1740-44	283	30	218,667	773	1,974	23,180	241,847	48,369
Aggregate	1,383	54	1,406,822	1,017	3,281	50,382	1,457,204	291,441

Source: See table 1.

The aggregate value of the 1736 imports, not counting horses, was 109,206 guilders. The 487 horses imported were a relatively low annual figure for that decade. Estimated at 150 guilders a head, their total sales value would come to 73,050 guilders, bringing total imports for 1736 to 182,256 guilders. Duties paid in Surinam on these transactions totalled 17,392, which left a favourable balance of 165,064 guilders before other costs and profits were calculated.

Most important among the American exports from Surinam were molasses and rum, both sugar by-products that were not in demand in Holland. A rudimentary but potent type of rum, appropriately called "killdevil," was distilled in Surinam and exported by Americans. But the Americans seemed particularly interested in acquiring molasses because it was, as one historian called it, the "engine" of New England's commerce. Not only was molasses distilled into rum, but it was also regularly used in the barter trade that was still widely practised in colonial America.[37]

Table 5 shows the aggregate values of American exports from Surinam for the years 1705-1744, the period for which the most complete documentation is available. In five-year units it lists the number of consignments, the values of their cargoes, and annual averages. As well, it provides an estimate for unrecorded data or that which escaped the researcher's scrutiny.

As table 6 illustrates, the value of American imports into Surinam exceeded the value of exports on a ratio of nearly four to one. Horses represented almost half of the total import value for the years 1705-1744. The balance of trade, approaching four million guilders for this forty-year period, may seem rather insignificant in terms of international trade, and they are a reminder of the small size of the American ships at this time. One should also keep in mind, however, that imported goods were estimated for tax purposes and that the actual selling price may have been significantly higher. Furthermore, one guilder still had considerable buying power during the eighteenth century. For example, a horse would typically sell for approximately 150 guilders and eighteen sheep were taxed at 100 guilders at Paramaribo.[38]

---

[37]*Ibid.*, 30 and 38; chapter 2 is entitled: "Molasses, an Engine in the Hands of the Merchant."

[38]See America-Surinam Databank.

Table 6
Balance of North American Trade
1705-1745

	Horses	Unit Price	Totals All in Dutch Guilders	Taxes	
Horses Imported	18500	150	2775000	55500	f.3 per head
Goods Imported			3076962	153848	5 percent
Total Imports			**5596962**		
Exports			**1535393**	76769.7	5 percent
Tonnage Fees*				483600	f.6 per last
All Taxes at Surinam				769718	
Balance of Trade**			**3291851**		

Note: * - An estimated 1300 ships, averaging sixty-two last, at f.6 per last (one last is two tons).

** - Surinam imports minus exports and basic taxes and fees.

Source: Tables 1, 3, 5 and America-Surinam Database.

The commerce with Surinam was obviously very important to Americans because the products they had to sell were in demand in Surinam. The molasses they received in exchange for the products they exported stimulated their economy. But their favourable balance of trade with Surinam – which came primarily in the form of currency, Dutch bills of exchange, or Surinam exports – provided a powerful incentive. This enabled them to overcome the negative balance of trade that the American colonies had with Britain and enabled them to purchase the manufactured goods imported from England. The issue of the colonial balance of payment has been widely discussed by American historians but is far too complex an issue to address in this format. It is hoped that the data collected for this study will someday make a valuable contribution to that debate.[39]

From the British perspective, the American trade with Surinam was always under a cloud of illegality. The Navigation Laws introduced in 1651 put several commercial restrictions on foreign nationals as well as on American colonists, although the latter often ignored them. English planters in the Caribbean also wanted horses from North America and they wanted the North Americans to buy their molasses. They repeatedly protested against the North American trade with Surinam, but generally to no avail.[40] American merchants apparently found it more profitable to trade with foreign colonies such as Dutch Surinam.

Additional navigation laws became increasingly more stringent, however, making it more difficult for the North Americans to trade with foreign markets. The Molasses Act of 1733 and the Sugar Act of 1764 hampered the American trade with Surinam, but the Americans often found ways to circumvent the regulations by registering Madeira as their destination. Occasionally they also obtained falsified papers that camouflaged the Surinam origins of their cargoes in order to mislead the British colonial custom officials.[41]

Wars and international tension often disrupted shipping to and from Surinam, especially the trans-Atlantic traffic with Holland. This was particularly so during the turbulent war-filled years between 1690-1715, and again in the periods 1780-1784 and 1795-1815. A long period of Dutch neutrality from 1715-1780 made commerce relatively smooth and proficient. In time of war or threat of war, the Dutch often used the convoy system for their Atlantic crossings. American ships seem to have been less affected by these international crises. Even during the Revolutionary War with England, Americans kept arriving at Surinam when Dutch ships rarely managed to do so. The Fourth Anglo-Dutch War (1780-1784), which resulted from Dutch support to the American cause,

---

[39]This theme of the trade balance has been explored by several authors; see McCusker and Menard, *Economy of British America*, 71-88.

[40]Frank Wesley Pitman, *The Development of the British West Indies, 1700-1763* (New Haven, 1917), 197-202.

[41]Hedges, *Browns of Providence Plantation*, 5, 31, 43, 164 and 100-201. See America-Surinam Databank for destinations.

was devastating for Holland's merchant marine. The Dutch often had to rely on neutral foreign ships, including American, to transport their Surinam grown commodities to Amsterdam. Surinam was also affected by this war. Paramaribo became more of an international port, with increased shipping activity from a variety of countries, but particularly with the Caribbean islands.

In conclusion, Surinam depended on and was influenced by its various commercial life-lines. With Holland, Surinam had a symbiotic relationship that sustained its very existence. The approximately 185,000 slaves shipped by the Dutch from Africa to Surinam were crucial for the functioning of its plantation system.[42] The transportation system provided by the Dutch in the bilateral trade between Holland and Surinam was also indispensable. Not only did it bring essential personnel for the settlement, but also food, supplies, and all sorts of equipment. In return, the bilateral traffic shipped most of the tropical produce to Holland that generated the capital that sustained the Surinam settlement. But the American trade was also essential for the Surinam economy. Without the shipment of horses, food, and supplies from North America, the settlement might not have survived; it certainly would have been less productive.

The three primary commercial links with Surinam had a significant social impact on the Surinam settlement as well. The earlier mentioned isolation was diminished by these life-lines, for they provided communication with the outside world and brought merchants, sailors, and ship officers to the port of Paramaribo. Dutch ships spent an average of 130 days in Surinam, while American ships remained an average of eighty days, despite the fact that many American ships left shortly after their arrival.[43] The waiting time was not only needed for loading and unloading and for commercial transactions, but also for collecting outstanding debts.[44] This meant that there were always many Dutch and American sailors and officers at Paramaribo. Crew information is difficult to obtain, but if the larger Dutch ships had an average crew of twenty and American ships ten, then Paramaribo's population must have been increased by

---

[42]See Postma, *Dutch in the Atlantic Slave Trade*, chapters 8 and 9.

[43]See the Surinam-Holland and the America-Surinam Databanks.

[44]Hedges, *Browns of Providence Plantation*, 40. See the America-Surinam and Surinam-Holland Databanks for harbour days in Surinam.

several hundred temporary residents on a continuous basis.[45] Merchants often stayed longer than ship crews in order to sell their merchandise and collect debts. The port was clearly Paramaribo's biggest economic enterprise and its window to the world.

An interesting piece of artistic evidence of the American contact with Surinam is preserved in the St. Louis Art Museum. A large canvas produced by the New England artist John Greenwood and painted in Surinam during the 1750s portrays seventeen American ship masters engaged in a drunken orgy in a Paramaribo bar. The gentlemen pictured are believed to include captains Esek Hopkins and Nicholas Cooke; the latter became governor of Rhode Island during the American Revolution.[46]

The impact of Surinam on both the Dutch and the American economies of the eighteenth century is complex and difficult to assess. In general, Surinam was only a small piece in the economic puzzle, but specific communities like Amsterdam, Boston, Providence and New London undoubtedly felt the impact of the trade with Surinam. The aforementioned advertisement in the Providence, Rhode Island newspaper seeking "Surinam horses" (for shipment to Surinam) illustrates that fact. There is no doubt that the tropical produce shipped to Amsterdam was a significant contribution to the operation of the various refineries in Amsterdam.[47] Likewise, the profits made by New England merchants on the Surinam trade must have contributed to their ability to cope with their negative trade balance with England. The consequence of the trade with Surinam requires further research and analysis to determine its actual impact on other economies.

The American merchants persistently challenged the Dutch mercantile system at Surinam. Ultimately they succeeded in breaching that barrier because the settlers favoured their presence and the colony needed

---

[45]Reliable population figures for Paramaribo are not available for the eighteenth century. Estimates of the town's population range from fewer than 1000 at the beginning to approximately 4000 at the end of the century; See van Stripriaan, *Roosenburg en Mon Bijou*, 311; and G.A. de Bruijune, *Geographische Verkenningen 5: Paramaribo* (Bussum, 1976), 27.

[46]Hedges, *Browns of Providence Plantation*, 39-40; and America-Surinam Databank.

[47]J.J. Reese, *De Suikerhandel van Amsterdam van het begin der 17de eeuw tot 1813* (s-Gravenhage, 1908), 30-35.

the merchandise that they could supply. The Americans were also eager to purchase the sugar by-products that were not in demand in Holland. While the Dutch authorities initially resisted the American challenge, they ultimately yielded because of the symbiotic nature of this commercial relationship. Since both parties benefited in the long run, there were no compelling reasons to maintain the mercantilistic restrictions that were initially imposed on the trade with Surinam.

A Scottish Venture in the Newfoundland Fish Trade, 1726-1727

Olaf Uwe Janzen[1]

On the afternoon of 8 June, 1726, as it was making its way north through Pentland Firth between the Scottish mainland and the Orkney Islands, the merchant ship *Christian* of Leith was struck by a storm.[2] The ship's master, Alexander Hutton, was obliged to bear away and make for the shelter of Kirston Harbour, anchoring there at 5 pm. Not until 14 June did the winds shift sufficiently to allow the *Christian* to get underway once again. Finally, two days later and nearly two weeks after departing Leith, the ship's supercargo, Edward Burd Jr., was able to record in his journal with some satisfaction that the *Christian* had come abreast of the lonely rock of St. Kilda. Ahead lay the open Atlantic and their destination, Newfoundland.

[1]I am most grateful for the generous financial assistance that the research for this paper received through a Vice-President's Research Grant at Memorial University of Newfoundland (itself funded by the Social Sciences and Humanities Research Council of Canada) and a grant from the Institute of Social and Economic Research of the Memorial University of Newfoundland. I also thank the assistance provided to me by the staffs at the Scottish Record Office, the Scottish National Library, the Library of the University of Edinburgh, the Archives of the City of Edinburgh District Council, and The Merchant Company of Edinburgh. The hospitality and support extended to me during my visits to Edinburgh by the International Social Science Institute, Dr. Malcolm Anderson, Director, and especially the Centre of Canadian Studies, Dr. Ged Martin, Director, are much appreciated.

[2]This paper is based largely on a *Journal of a Voyage to Newfoundland, in 1726-1727* kept by Edward Burd, Jr., the *Christian*'s supercargo. The journal can be found in the Scottish Record Office (hereafter SRO) in Edinburgh, where it is catalogued as RH 9/14/102. Henceforth it will be cited as Burd, *Journal*. Additional documentation came from letters and accounts belonging to Edward Burd Jr. and catalogued separately by the Scottish Record Office as RH 15/54. The dates provided in the journal are all in the Julian or Old Style. Unless indicated to the contrary, all references to dates in this paper are also in the Old Style, except that the year is taken to begin on 1 January, not 25 March as was then customary.

The unscheduled stop in the Orkneys had almost certainly come as a relief to Burd, for he had been troubled by sea-sickness during the *Christian*'s first days at sea.[3] Yet the men who had chartered the ship would have viewed the delay at Kirston as an inauspicious beginning to a commercial venture which, by its novel nature, was filled with uncertainties. Stowed in the *Christian*'s hold were five tons of "Bisquett" in thirty-two casks, which the supercargo was to sell in Newfoundland; he was then to purchase a cargo of fish for delivery and sale in Spain, where the acquisition of yet another cargo, consisting of cork, wine, and fruit, was to be arranged for the final leg back to Scotland.[4] It was a dramatic departure from the kind of venture in which the investors had previously engaged, for not one of them had ever traded to Newfoundland — indeed, no Scottish merchant had ever participated regularly in the Newfoundland fish trade before the *Christian* began her voyage.[5] Yet the men who chartered the ship were not complete novices in maritime commerce. All were experienced both in domestic enterprise and in maritime trade with Europe. Moreover, they were linked by an informal but advantageous network of social, political and commercial contacts through which they could safely respond to new commercial opportunities like the Newfoundland trade. This paper will therefore consider the social, economic and political environment which drew them into the

---

[3]Reference to Burd's sea-sickness is made in a letter from his father, dated 23 July 1726, in SRO RH 15/54/4, A4. This was the first long-distance voyage for the 24-year-old Burd; National Library of Scotland, Edinburgh (hereafter NLS), MSS #5061, "Genealogical History of the Family of Burd of Ford and Whitehall" (1827), 106.

[4]Copy of instructions for Alexander Hutton, master of the *Christian*, and Edward Burd Jr., supercargo, 24 May 1726, in Burd, *Journal*, 10v-11.

[5]The earliest Scottish ship on record to venture to Newfoundland was the *Grace of God* of Dundee, which voyaged there and then to Lisbon in 1599/1600; W.A. McNeill (ed.), "Papers of a Dundee Shipping Dispute 1600-1604," in *Miscellany, Vol. X, of the Scottish History Society* (Edinburgh, 1963), 55-85, esp. 68, 73. However, the Scots never became a fixture in the trade, so that by the first half of the eighteenth century, any Scots found in Newfoundland were assumed by David Macmillan to be acting as "a 'cover' not only for the shipping out of colonial produce from the Southern plantation colonies and the West Indies to foreign European ports, but also as a 'blind' for importing large quantities of European goods...into all the British colonies...;" D.S. Macmillan, "The 'New Men' in Action: Scottish Mercantile and Shipping Operations in the North American Colonies, 1760-1825," in D.S. Macmillan (ed.), *Canadian Business History: Selected Studies, 1497-1971* (Toronto, 1972), 50-51.

Newfoundland trade at this time, as well as the circumstances of the voyage which seemingly convinced them not to repeat the experiment.

Scotland had only become part of the British North Atlantic commercial sphere with the Act of Union of 1707. For several decades before then, the Scottish economy had struggled within a European commercial environment that was increasingly mercantilistic and competitive. Scotland's leaders responded with a regime of mercantilistic regulations of their own in the hope of stimulating maritime commerce and economic growth while defending Scottish national sovereignty.[6] However, Scotland's small size made it extremely difficult to improve the country's balance of trade by encouraging exports while actively discouraging imports, with the result that the attempt would fail.[7] When the 1690s ushered in a series of economic crises, the stage was set for what Bruce Lenman has termed "a revolution of frustrated expectations" among Scotland's ruling classes.[8] Negotiations began that eventually led to economic and political union with England in 1707.[9] The immediate benefits of this measure to the Scottish economy included trade protection, access to North American colonial commodity trades and shipping, and

---

[6]Eric J. Graham, "In Defence of the Scottish Maritime Interest, 1681-1713," *The Scottish Historical Review* LXXI, 1,2; nos. 191/2 (April, October 1992), 88-109.

[7]Bruce Lenman, *An Economic History of Modern Scotland 1660-1976* (Hamden, CT, 1977), esp. Chapt. 3: "Crisis, Union and Reaction 1690-1727," 23-40. According to Lenman, Scotland's population stood at roughly 1.25 million in 1695.

[8]Lenman, *op. cit.*, 52. Famine, war, the protectionist policies of Scotland's mercantilist rivals, and the collapse of the Darien scheme had all exacted their toll; Lenman, *op. cit.*, 45-52; T.M. Devine, "The Union of 1707 and Scottish Development," in *Scottish Economic & Social History* V (1985), 23; Christopher A. Whatley, "Economic Causes and Consequences of the Union of 1707: A Survey," *Scottish Historical Review* LXVIII, 2, no. 186 (October 1989), 150-181.

[9]Scotland had proposed some form of economic union on at least three previous occasions; T.C. Smout, "The Anglo-Scottish Union of 1707. I: The Economic Background," *Economic History Review*, 2nd ser., XVI (1964), 457. But Union appealed to the English only when they became drawn to the political stability it would foster; Lenman, *op. cit.*, 52-53, Graham, *op. cit.*, 104-105. According to T.M. Devine, the English emphasis on the political advantages of Union rather than its economic ones meant that Scotland would be spared Ireland's fate of becoming an economic satellite; Devine, *op. cit.*, 29.

the revitalization of trade with Iberia and the Mediterranean.[10] Yet Union was not followed by the degree of trade expansion or prosperity that many Scots had expected. For one thing, trade now found itself encumbered by a more complex, energetic, and burdensome customs and excise establishment. For another, the weaknesses of Scottish manufacturing, such as the inferior quality of Scottish linen, were now exposed to the full force of competition.[11] In the words of T.M. Devine, the Scots soon learned that "Union provided a series of risks and an array of opportunities. Ultimately what mattered...was the Scottish response to these stimuli."[12] It was in this context that the voyage of the *Christian* to Newfoundland took place in 1726.

The ship had been chartered by eight merchants, most of whom were men of some stature in the Edinburgh commercial community. They included William Carmichael, James Newlands, Robert Dundas, William Hutton Sr., William Jamisone, Walter Scott, and Robert Smith Jr., all of Edinburgh or Leith, and Robert Robertson, a merchant of Glasgow. Two of the partners — Carmichael and Newlands — were both "baillies," or magistrates, a role which was not uncommon for prominent merchants to play in eighteenth-century Edinburgh. At least four of them — Hutton, Carmichael, Smith, and Scott — were also burgesses and guild brethren. Like his father before him, Hutton was a member of the Merchant Company of Edinburgh, holding several positions of trust within that organization before being elected its Master shortly after the *Christian*'s departure for Newfoundland.[13] Hutton, Carmichael, Newlands, and

---

[10]Graham, *op. cit.*, 107-108.

[11]Lenman, *op. cit.*, 60-62; Devine, *op. cit.*, 28, 31-32. For an analysis of the way in which the Union exposed defects in the linen industry and trade, see Alastair James Durie, "The Scottish Linen Industry 1707-1775 With Particular Reference to the Early History of the British Linen Company," (PhD thesis, University of Edinburgh, 1973), 3.

[12]Devine, *op. cit.*, 32.

[13]*Roll of Edinburgh Burgesses and Guild-Brethren 1701-1760* (Scottish Record Society, Vol. 62; Edinburgh, 1930), ed. Charles B. Boog Watson; Alexander Heron, *The Rise and Progress of the Company of Merchants of the City of Edinburgh 1681-1902* (Edinburgh, 1903), Appendix V, 390-392, "Masters of the Merchant Company;" The Merchant Company of Edinburgh (hereafter MCE), Minutes from 1681 to 1696 and Register of Entrants with the Company from 1681 to 1902; MCE, Minutes, vol. 2 (1702-1714).

Jamisone were also co-investors in several local enterprises, including a sugar refinery and distillery and a stage coach company in Leith. They were also partners in direct trade with Spain both before and after 1726, through which they would have developed commercial contacts in Iberia that would greatly simplify the challenge of engaging in the Newfoundland trade.[14] Devine maintains that such diversification in both overseas trade and the domestic economy, together with the effective use of a network of kin and close personal acquaintances, was typical of the greater Scottish merchants, who sought thereby to "minimize the insecurities of trade, and so...preserve their fortunes..."[15] William Hutton and his partners may not yet have been "great merchants" — Devine emphasizes that in the late seventeenth and early eighteenth centuries, the number of Scottish merchants with the necessary finance, experience and contacts to engage in overseas trade on a consistent basis would have been very small — but it is probable that they came close to qualifying, and it is almost a certainty that they aspired to become such. And the Newfoundland trade was a sensible one in which to realize such an ambition, for the entry requirements of the fish trade, at least in terms of capital, were fairly low.[16]

---

[14]SRO CC 8/8/106, Commissary Court Records, Edinburgh Testaments, March 26, 1742 to January 20, 1743, 118-118v, Testament of "the late William Hutton merchant in Edin. & Residenter in Leith;" SRO CC 8/8/98, Commissary Court Records, Edinburgh Testaments, 30 July 1736 to 23 April 1736, 241-244v, testament of the late Baillie James Newlands. In their letter to their agent in Barcelona, the partners referred to at least one previous commercial voyage to that port; William Hutton Sr. & partners to William French, 14 May 1726 in Burd, *Journal*, 17v. The *Christian* would journey to Spain for salt in 1734; SRO CC 8/8/106, Commissary Court Records, Edinburgh Testaments, March 26, 1742 to January 20, 1743, 118-118v, Testament of "the late William Hutton merchant in Edin. & Residenter in Leith."

[15]T.M. Devine, "The Social Composition of the Business Class in the Larger Scottish Towns, 1680-1740," in T.M. Devine and David Dickson (eds.), *Ireland and Scotland 1600-1850: Parallels and Contrasts in Economic and Social Development* (Edinburgh, 1983), 167; T.M. Devine, "The Merchant Class of the Larger Scottish Towns in the Later Seventeenth and Early Eighteenth Centuries," in George Gordon and Brian Dicks (eds.), *Scottish Urban History* (Aberdeen, 1983), 103-104.

[16]Gillian Cell commented on the degree to which "the Newfoundland fishery [was] run by men of limited capital;" G. Cell, *English Enterprise in Newfoundland 1577-1660* (Toronto, 1969), 6.

Of the several men who invested in the voyage of the *Christian* to Newfoundland, William Hutton appears to have been the key figure. He alone appears to have had some familiarity with the Scottish fishing industry and possibly in the European fish trade.[17] Scotland had long produced whitefish and herring for export to northern Europe. The control of the German, Dutch, and other Continental merchants over that trade was declining by the late seventeenth and early eighteenth century, and Scottish investors were anxious to take over their role. The conventional wisdom has been that lack of capital, combined with the continued dominance of German merchants in northern Europe, inhibited success, and that lack of experience discouraged significant development of a trade with southern Europe for several decades.[18] However, the Act of Union of 1707 was followed almost immediately by petitions to the Board of Trade for subsidies to support a trade in Scottish whitefish to the Mediterranean.[19] And six of the fifteen vessels that the *Christian* found at Barcelona in 1727 carried "dryed Cod fish, from Scotland." Indeed, according to Edward Burd Jr., Scottish fish was a preferred product in the Barcelona market, suggesting that Scotland's trade in fish with Iberia was better established by then than has hitherto been suspected.[20] While none

---

[17]Hutton owned a minority share in a fishing buss and fishing equipment at the time of his death; disposition, William Hutton to spouse Christian Thomson, 28 February 1737, SRO Register of Deeds (hereafter RD), Second ser., Durie's Office, 3/195.

[18]James J.A. Irvine and Ian A. Morrison, "Shetlanders and Fishing: historical and geographical aspects of an evolving relationship. Part I," *Northern Studies* XXIV (1987), 44-47; Hance Smith, *Shetland Life and Trade 1550-1914* (Edinburgh, 1984), 19, 22-23.

[19]J.D. Marwick (ed.), *Extracts from the Records of the Convention of the Royal Burghs of Scotland, Vol. IV, 1679-1711* (Edinburgh, 1880), 427-428, convention approved of several overtures for the encouragement of trade, 25 November 1707; *ibid., IV*, 511-516, "Memorial of several particulars concerning trade, and especially the fishing on the coast of Scotland," 9 April 1711.

[20]"Scots fish never fail to Sell here at about 1 p[8] p Quintall [112 lbs.] more than any fish that come to this place; The reason they give for it is this, that the Scots fish allwayes Stand the Summer better than any other: another advantage they have is, that they soke in double the quantity of Water that any other fish doe, Soe that with 1 lb of fish they sell another of Water." Burd *Journal*, 21. From this description, it seems likely that the Scots were selling stockfish, which used no salt in the curing process. Yet there is also the intriguing fact that during the closing years of the War of the Spanish Succession, several London merchants had employed William Taverner, a Newfoundland ship's captain and

of these points can be linked directly to the voyage of the *Christian*, we can assume that William Hutton and his partners had sufficient information at their disposal to encourage an attempt to broaden an existing bilateral commerce with Spain into a triangular pattern that included Newfoundland.

William Hutton not only brought some familiarity with the fishing industry and trade into the venture, he also brought the *Christian*, a ship which he co-owned with its sailing master and William's brother, Alexander Hutton.[21] This, however, may have been more a curse than a blessing. In its purpose, its cargo, and its route, the *Christian* was what was commonly called in the Newfoundland trade a "sack ship," one of at least fifty-five such ships reported in Newfoundland in 1726.[22] Sack ships were the freighters of the fish trade; they did not participate in the fishery itself, but instead brought provisions and gear to Newfoundland to be sold or exchanged for fish which they then delivered to the principal markets in southern Europe. There they took on cargoes of wine, cork, dried fruit and other Mediterranean products then in demand in northern Europe.[23]

---

trader, to develop a fishery on the northwest coast of Scotland. This might possibly have introduced the Newfoundland cure, using a combination of light salting and open-air drying, to Scotland; Public Record Office (hereafter PRO) Colonial Office papers, series 194 (hereafter CO 194), vol. 5, 109, copied in National Archives of Canada microfilm reel #B-208 (hereafter NAC Reel B-208), Petition of William Taverner to Lord Oxford, Lord High Treasurer, no date, enclosed with William Taverner to the Lords Commissioners for Trade & Plantations, 31 March, 1714. Equally intriguing is the fact that the Letter of Credit with which the partners backed the bills of exchange drawn by their supercargo in Newfoundland was secured by London merchant Claud Johnson and witnessed by a servant of J. Taverner, quite possibly one of William's relatives. Johnson might eventually prove to be the critical link between the investors in the *Christian* and Newfoundland.

[21]"Disposition, William Hutton to spouse Christian Thomson," 28 February 1737, SRO Register of Deeds (hereafter cited as RD), 2[d] ser., "Durie's Office," 1 December 1736 - 30 April 1737. The ship was almost certainly named after William's wife.

[22]From the annual "State of the Fishery at Newfoundland (1726)," PRO CO 194/8, 42 (NAC Reel B-210).

[23]According to Peter Pope, "sack" derives from *vino de sacca* or "wine set aside for export." P. Pope, "Adventures in the Sack Trade: London Merchants in the Canada and Newfoundland Trades, 1627-1648," *The Northern Mariner/Le Marin du nord* VI: 1 (January 1996), 1. See also Cell, *English Enterprise*, 6; Davis, *Rise of the English Shipping Industry*, 235-238; Ian K. Steele, *The English Atlantic 1675-1740: An Exploration of*

At seventy tons burthen, the *Christian* was fairly typical of Scottish ships of that era, but it was small for a sack ship.[24] It also proved to be a slow sailer; quite apart from the locational disadvantages of setting out from Leith and the unfortunate weather encountered during the first week of the voyage, the *Christian* needed more than six weeks to arrive at St. John's from St. Kilda, or almost twice the time taken by West Country ships in crossing the Atlantic.[25] Burd blamed the slow passage on fickle winds and the necessity of heaving to at night once they encountered icebergs, though he subsequently conceded that the ship had also been "leaky in the Passage."[26] Yet the journey later from Newfoundland to Spain would be just as slow. It would seem, therefore, that the *Christian* was not well suited to a trade governed by a tight annual schedule.[27]

Communication and Community (New York, 1986), 81.

[24]Sue Mowat, *The Port of Leith: Its History and Its People* (Edinburgh, 1994), 288; T.C. Smout, *Scottish Trade on the Eve of Union 1660-1707* (Edinburgh & London, 1963), 47-52. Peter Pope challenges the "conventional historical wisdom," that English sack ships were usually larger than the fishing ships they served; Pope, "Adventures," 15, fn. 16. However, the fifty-five sack ships at Newfoundland in 1726 averaged just over a hundred tons each, while the ninety-four fishing ships recorded that year averaged just under fifty-six tons each; "State of the Fishery for 1726," PRO CO 194/8, 42 (NAC Reel B-210).

[25]The *Christian* arrived at St. John's over eight weeks after her departure from Leith; the average voyage between the West Country and Newfoundland took about five weeks, and could take as little as three weeks; Steele, *The English Atlantic*, 82. Ironically, the distance from Leith to Newfoundland (about 640 leagues according to Edward Burd Jr.'s calculations, or about 1920 nautical miles) was not much greater than the distance between the Lizard and St. John's, Newfoundland (1804 nautical miles, according to Steele, *op. cit.*, 342, fn. 10).

[26]Edward Burd Jr. to William Hutton Sr., 17 September 1726, in Burd, *Journal*, 9-9v. Though hardly the ship's fault, "the Wind being right out of the Harbour," nevertheless it seemed somehow a fitting conclusion to the trans-Atlantic voyage that the *Christian* had to be towed through the Narrows into St. John's harbour by a boat from the warship *Argyle*.

[27]The full duration of a sack ship's triangular voyage — from home port to Newfoundland to Southern Europe and back to home port — normally took just about a full year. This brought the sack ship to its home port just in time to be refitted for the next year's voyage. A delay at any stage of the voyage could have serious repercussions not only for the profits earned on that stage but could also ruin any hope of profit for the

Apart from these limitations, which clearly went unrecognized as they prepared the ship for its voyage, the partners made careful and sensible preparations for the new venture. Captain Hutton and Edward Burd Jr. were instructed to make for "St Johns, Ferryland, or the Bay of Bulls, or any Harbour thereabouts." There they were to sell the biscuit stored in the hold "to the best advantage, rather to Masters of Ships, than to the ffishermen upon the Island." They were then to acquire "where you best can" a cargo of "good Merchantable fish, well dryed & fair to the eye," without "Spots or blemishes," for subsequent delivery to Barcelona, Spain. There the investors' agent would arrange for the sale of the fish and the acquisition of a partial cargo of cork before the *Christian* began the homeward journey. The ship would stop only at San Lúcar, north of Cadiz, to complete its cargo with sherry and fruit.[28]

The instructions suggest that the partners had secured sound advice before venturing into the Newfoundland trade. For instance, they had taken the essential step of arranging a letter of credit from Claud Johnston, a merchant in London with good connections in the fishery, to support the bills of exchange that Burd would have to write when purchasing fish in Newfoundland.[29] Secondly, Burd's instruction to purchase fish from "Masters of Ships" rather than from "the ffishermen upon the Island" suggests that the partners sensed that it would be easier to collect bad debts from migratory fishermen who returned seasonally to England than from those who lived permanently in Newfoundland. Yet the unfamiliarity of the partners in that trade is also apparent. Burd learned later that the partners would have been wiser to secure their letter of credit through an Exeter merchant, because most of the fishing ships at

voyage in the following year. See Jean-François Brière, "Le commerce triangulaire entre les ports terre-neuviers français, les pêcheries d'Amérique du nord et Marseille au 18e siècle: nouvelles perspectives," *Revue d'histoire de l'amérique française* XL: 2 (automne 1986), 193-214.

[28]Copy of instructions for Alexander Hutton, master of the *Christian*, and Edward Burd Jr., supercargo, 24 May 1726, in Burd, *Journal*, 10v-11.

[29]Letter of Credit from Claud Johnston, April 28, 1726, SRO RH 15/54/4, A2. The worth of Johnson's credit was attested by Solomon Merrett, John Spackman, John Lloyd and David Milne. The supercargo later described the first three as "verry well known in Newfoundland but especially Merrett & Hoyte [*sic*; the original clearly identifies him as Lloyd] are best known in fferryland." See Burd *Journal*, 10v.

Ferryland, where the *Christian* eventually bought its fish, were based in that West Country town.[30] Of greater concern was the decision to appoint Edward Burd Jr. as supercargo. As the representative of the chartering party on board the *Christian*, it was his responsibility to attend to the accounts of the cargo and any other commercial affairs of the ship. Though no longer as common in commercial ventures as in the previous centuries, supercargoes were still found in newer trades "where firm business connections had not yet been established."[31] Yet Burd's appointment appears to have been governed less by business logic than as an apprenticeship for young Edward and a favour to his father, with whom William Hutton had served as Merchant Councillor of Edinburgh years before.[32] Burd therefore lacked the necessary judgement within the Newfoundland trade that came with experience.

The young supercargo's limited skills were quickly put to the test. As soon as the ship had moored in St. John's harbour, Burd accompanied Captain Hutton ashore to pay their respects to Captain Robert Bouler, the naval commodore at Newfoundland.[33] Within hours of their arrival — perhaps even as they were being received "verry Kindly" by Captain

---

[30]As Burd explained, "any body that have a mind to purchass a Cargoe here, would doe well to get their Credit upon Exeter, because this saves trouble to those they buy their fish from, in having their money remitted in them, from London or Bristoll; They will allwayes sell their fish a Ryall a Quintall cheaper for Exeter Bills, than for Bills upon either of the other two places." Burd, *Journal*, 12v-13.

[31]Ralph Davis, *The Rise of the English Shipping Industry in the Seventeenth and Eighteenth Centuries* (Newton Abbot: David & Charles, 1962), 170-171.

[32]Helen Armet (ed.), *Extracts from the Records of the Burgh of Edinburgh, 1701 to 1718* (Edinburgh, 1967), 27, entry for 23 September 1702. T. McAloon views Burd's presence on the *Christian* as "a finishing school for his commercial training." McAloon, "A Minor Scottish Merchant in General Trade: the case of Edward Burd 1728-39," in John Butt and J.T. Ward (eds.), *Scottish Themes: Essays in Honour of Professor S.G.E. Lythe* (Scottish Academic Press, 1976), 17.

[33]The British government stationed two warships at Newfoundland to patrol and protect the fishery; see Gerald Graham, "Britain's Defence of Newfoundland," *Canadian Historical Review* XXIII: 3(September 1942), 260-279; on Robert Bouler, see entry by Michael Godfrey in David Hayne (gen. ed.), *Dictionary of Canadian Biography, Volume II: 1701 to 1740* (Toronto, 1969), 89-90. Bouler's ship, *Argyle*, a fifty-gun fourth-rate warship, remained at St. John's throughout the season; *Ludlow Castle*, Captain St. Lo, was stationed at Placentia.

Bouler — Captain Weroy of the *Crown* galley of London broke the price of fish at sixteen shillings or thirty-two ryalls per quintal. This was a full shilling higher and two weeks sooner than Burd had been led to expect, for which reason, the supercargo confided in his journal, Captain Weroy "was heartily cursed by allmost every body."[34] Yet Weroy's impatience was understandable during that summer of 1726. For many years the British fishery at Newfoundland had been severely disrupted, first by war, and then by a mysterious refusal of the cod to come inshore as they normally did each spring.[35] The fishery was just beginning to recover, so that landings in 1726 were the best in decades.[36] Nevertheless, the fish did not come inshore as early in the season as they once had in former, better times, so that the season was well advanced and the weather no longer as favourable for a good cure by the time large volumes of fish were being processed.[37] Moreover, as the fishery began to recover, so did the demand among buyers — hence Captain Weroy's attempt to snatch an advantage by offering an unexpectedly high price. How Burd must have envied

---

[34]According to Burd, "even the Boat keepers themselves told that they did not expect above 30 Ryalls," Burd, *Journal*, 30 July 1726. "Breaking the price" refers to the practice by which buyers met in St. John's to settle on a price agreeable to all; the practice still prevailed in 1806 when it was described by Governor Erasmus Gower; see Shannon Ryan, *The Ice Hunters: A History of Newfoundland Sealing to 1914* (St. John's, 1994), 40. Captain Weroy must have violated the custom in order to assemble a cargo as quickly as possible, knowing that the higher cost of purchasing the fish would be off-set by getting to market early enough to command an even better selling price. Weroy expected to set out from Newfoundland on 7 September, or two full weeks before the *Christian* began her voyage to Spain; Alexander Wylly to Edward Burd Jr., 5 September 1726, SRO RH 15/54/4, A10; Burd, *Journal*, 22 September 1726.

[35]Keith Matthews, *A History of the West of England - Newfoundland Fisheries* (PhD thesis, Oxford University, 1968) 307; see also Steele, *English Atlantic*, 81. The French inshore fishery also experienced poor yields during this period; see Laurier Turgeon, "Le temps des pêches lointaines: permanences et transformations (vers 1500-vers 1850)" in Michel Mollat (directeur), *Histoire des Pêches Maritimes en France* (Toulouse, 1989), esp. 149-152, and Jean-François Brière, "Le reflux des terre-neuviers malouins sur les côtes du Canada dans la première moitié du XVIIIe siècle: réponse à un changement du climat?," *Histoire sociale/Social History* XII: 23(May 1979), 166-169.

[36]Shannon Ryan, "Abstract of returns for the Newfoundland fishery 1698-1833; compiled from CO 194 papers" (St. John's, 1969).

[37]R. Bouler, "Answers to Heads of Inquiry," PRO CO 194/7, 37 (NAC Reel B-210).

Captain Rannie, the Scottish master of a London sack ship, who had arranged to purchase a cargo of bank fish at twenty-seven ryalls per quintal before he left England![38] For the young supercargo, it was an abrupt and unpleasant initiation into the unpredictability of the Newfoundland fish trade.

In his quest for a cargo of fish for the voyage to southern Europe, Burd sought out the advice and services of Captain Richard Newman, the fishing admiral of St. John's that year.[39] Over a glass, Newman advised Burd to seek his fish in Torbay, a rather exposed harbour just to the north of St. John's, assuring him that the price there would be three or four ryalls cheaper. In company with Captain Hutton and Captain Newman, Burd therefore paid a visit to Torbay, only to discover that the boat-keepers there would only sell their fish at half a ryall below the St. John's price. In place of optimistic predictions of bargain prices, Captain Newman now advised that nothing better could be expected. Subsequent haggling failed to bring about an acceptable compromise.[40]

Burd could not disguise his annoyance with "His L^dShip [Captain Newman, who] did not doe such fair things as he promised."[41] Leaving Hutton and the crew in St. John's to attend to repairs to the ship's hull, he therefore made his way to the outports south of St. John's in search of his elusive cargo. His first stop was Bay Bulls, where he was assured by Mr. Henley, a local merchant, that with the help of two boat-masters there and a third from Toad's Cove, a cargo could be scraped together. This, too, however, failed to work out. The man from Toad's Cove never showed

---

[38]Burd *Journal*, 5 August 1726. Later, as *Christian* sailed by the Azores, she spoke a pink of London, bound for Alicante with a cargo of saltcod from St. Pierre (which was then a British possession), for which purchase had been arranged before she set out for the fishery at a price of 25 ryalls per quintal; *ibid.*, 24 October 1726.

[39]Captain Newman's status as "fishing admiral" was a custom of the fishery; "the first Ship in the Harbour is Lord or Admirall of that Harbour, & the Captain sits Supream Judge of all differences that happen in the place, from whose sentence there is no appeal but to the Commodore." Burd, *Journal*, 13. The fishing admiral also took his choice of fishing room or berth, making this "a worthwhile prize of local control for the first ship there each year." Steele, *English Atlantic*, 83; see also Matthews, *op. cit.*, 21.

[40]"30 Ryalls if the ship went to Torbay [to pick up the fish] or 31 if they brought the fish about to St Johns; I offered them 29 & 30." Burd, *Journal*, 6 August 1726.

[41]Burd, *Journal*, 4 August 1726.

up, and then one of the Bay Bulls boat-masters backed out of any deal.[42] It must have been with a mounting sense of frustration that Burd proceeded to his next destination, Ferryland, one of eighteenth-century Newfoundland's more substantial settlements. Founded in the previous century as a proprietary colony, Ferryland by 1726 had nearly as many permanent inhabitants and more private dwellings as St. John's.[43] It attracted more fishing ships and more sack ships than St. John's, because it produced more fish — more, in fact, than any other community on the island.[44] Much of Ferryland's prosperity by then rested on both a thriving inshore fishery and the banks fishery — Burd claimed that "This place is the most frequented by the Bankers of any in the Land."[45] Indeed, it was precisely for this reason that Burd had been drawn to Ferryland in the first place, for he had been advised that "a cargoe of Bank fish...wou'd doe fully as well as the Shoar for a Spanish Mercate."[46] Moreover, bank fish cost less. Burd therefore approached Captain Thomas Holdsworth, who had been recommended to him as "one of the best men in the place," and the two quickly worked out an arrangement whereby Burd would purchase 1,500 quintals of "dry merchantable Bank & Shoar fish" at fourteen shillings six pence per quintal from Holdsworth and several other boat

---

[42]Burd, *Journal*, 8, 9, and 10 August 1726. Toad's Cove is known today as Tors Cove.

[43]"State of the Fishery for 1726," PRO CO 194/7, 42 (NAC Reel B-210).

[44]Compare the numbers in "State of the Fishery for 1726" in PRO CO 194/7, 42 (NAC Reel B-210); according to Burd, "There commonly fishes here between 30 & 40 sail of Ships from 50 to 150 Tons, the greatest part of them belong to a small town in the River of Exeter called Limpston...;" Burd, *Journal*, 22 September 1726.

[45]Burd, *Journal*, 22 September 1726. The preference of southern European markets for lightly salted dry cod or "poorjack" had committed British fishermen to the inshore fishery since its origins in the sixteenth century. The offshore banks were ignored until the failure of the inshore fishery after 1713 left them with few alternatives; Matthews, *op. cit.*, 311-312; C. Grant Head, *Eighteenth Century Newfoundland: A Geographer's Perspective* (Toronto, 1976), 72-74. The British shift to the banks was pioneered by New England in the 1680s; Daniel Vickers, *Farmers & Fishermen: Two Centuries of Work in Essex County, Massachusetts, 1630-1850* (Chapel Hill, NC, 1994), 149-150.

[46]Burd, *Journal*, 5 August 1726.

keepers, while Holdsworth accepted 6,000 pounds of his biscuit at fourteen shillings per hundredweight.[47]

Was it a good deal? Burd insisted that "This was the best bargain I could make" if his ship were to make an early departure for Spain. It was also with some relish that he would later report that the price of fish had soared by mid-September to sixteen and even seventeen shillings per quintal, and that many of the buyers would go away with only half their lading; "they would now give any thing for fish, but they are not to be had."[48] Yet there is an understandably defensive tone to Burd's remarks. For one thing, shortly after arriving in St. John's he had declined an offer to sell all of the biscuit at fifteen shillings per quintal "till I saw whither or not wee Stayed in the Place." Had the *Christian* arrived even sooner, his biscuit would have sold at an even better price. Instead, there were now so many sack ships in Newfoundland that he had to sell his biscuit in lots, at fourteen shillings per hundredweight or less.[49] Burd also knew that his biscuit would have sold at a better price earlier in the season. Unless a sack ship timed its arrival earlier than the others — and there was little doubt that the *Christian* was unlucky in this regard — it could not hope to sell its cargo at the highest possible price.[50]

Nor could a sack ship hope to purchase fish at the most advantageous price if it arrived too late in the season. This may explain Burd's curious confidence that bank fish would do as well as shore fish in the Spanish market. Ordinarily, bank fish rarely matched shore fish in quality,

---

[47]Burd, *Journal*, 11, 12, and 13 August 1726; "Contract Betwixt Tho: Holsworth & Edward Burd junior 1726," SRO RH 15/54/4, A14. 800 quintals of the purchase consisted of bank fish, the rest was shore fish.

[48]Burd at Ferryland to William Hutton Sr., 17 September 1726, in Burd, *Journal*, 9-9v.

[49]Burd, *Journal*, 13 August 1726. "I expected allwayes that the price of bread would have risen, but Such great numbers of Ships coming & all of them Bringing some, Still kept the price Low." Burd, *Journal*, 11 September 1726. Burd would later claim that "Bread was sold in the Spring at 20 s^h p % [hundredweight]." Burd, *Journal*, 15.

[50]Timing was immensely critical to a sack ship, both for the sale of its cargo and the purchase of fish. In response to Burd's request for advice on "what things was wanting in this place" Burd was told that "unless you Could be a Erly Shipe one Dare not venture To advise,..." Alexander Wylly (St. John's, Newfoundland) to Edward Burd Jr., 13 December 1726, SRO RH 15/54/4, A22.

because bank fish was heavily salted and stored for several weeks in the hold of the banking vessel before being brought to shore.[51] All this salt had to be rinsed away before the final transformation into the familiar saltcod could be completed. According to Captain Bouler, the difference in quality between the two meant that shore fish usually fetched two ryalls per quintal more than bank fish "and this year in most places it was five Ryalls a Quintall dearer than the Bank fish."[52] This suggests either that the collapse of the inshore fishery during the decade after 1713 had compelled even the discerning Spanish market to accept bank fish, or that the *Christian*'s late arrival in Newfoundland, together with the large number of sack ships at Newfoundland that summer, had led Burd into a questionable decision.

By 18 August, the *Christian* was in Ferryland, anchored "as near to Cap' Holdsworth's Stage as possible..." The bread was unloaded and Holdsworth was delivered his share. The hold was then readied to receive the saltcod. Burd was still hopeful that the *Christian* could complete its lading and depart for Spain before the end of the month. This, however, was not to be. The business of transferring fish into the hold was one that required good, dry conditions. Instead, "bad Weather" set in, forcing Burd to wait for clearer skies. When, after nearly ten days, the weather failed to improve, Burd was unable to stand the delay any longer; "bad Weather" or no, the process of loading the fish on board was allowed to begin.[53]

It was a time-consuming process, taking three weeks to complete. In part, the slow pace was necessary because of the care with which the fish had to be stowed in the hold. Then there was the blustery weather,

---

[51]Burd recorded detailed observations on the British fishery at Newfoundland in his *Journal*, 12v-15. Head claims that "Complaints of declining quality of product became frequent in the first decades of the [bank] fishery." Head, *op. cit.*, 74.

[52]Capt. R. Bouler, "Answers to the Heads of Inquiries," 13 October 1726, PRO CO 194/7, 32 (NAC Reel B-210). A British merchant would insist later in that century that the southern European markets "will never take bank fish if they can get shore;" evidence of Mr. Jefferey to the British Parliamentary inquiry, 1792, cited in Matthews, *op. cit.*, 312.

[53]Burd, *Journal*, 27 August 1726. The unfavourable weather conditions were widespread; on 5 September, Alexander Wylly would write Burd from St. John's that "the Badness of the Weather for this Three Weeks past, has very much Hindred the Ships here." See SRO RH 15/54/4, A10.

which continued to interfere with the loading process and occasionally even interrupted it.[54] The principal factor slowing the process down, however, was that the fish was delivered, not in a few large lots but rather as numerous consignments, one as small as two quintals, more typically in lots of fifty or sixty or ninety quintals. Most came from Holdsworth himself or from people who were paying off their debts to him by delivering fish for his account.[55] Several smaller lots were supplied by other byeboat men and planters.[56] Finally, on 16 September, the last ten quintals were taken on board; the last of the bread had been sold scant days before.[57] Shortly before noon on 22 September, after another delay occasioned by contrary winds, the *Christian* made sail, much to the obvious delight of Edward Burd Jr., who bid "adieue to fferryland & all the Rogues in it."[58]

---

[54]See Burd, *Journal*, various entries between 27 August and 16 September 1726.

[55]It was common for eighteenth-century merchants to advance supplies on credit to boat-keepers against repayment in fish at the end of the season; similarly, boat-keepers advanced supplies on credit to their servants against wages. The truck system, long vilified for its seemingly exploitive character, has recently been subjected to considerable scrutiny, leading to more complex and balanced conclusions about its nature. See for instance Matthews, *op. cit.*, 177-178; W. Gordon Handcock, *Soe longe as there comes noe women: Origins of English Settlement in Newfoundland* (St. John's, 1989), 137, 232-234; and Sean Cadigan, *Hope and Deception in Conception Bay: Merchant-Settler Relations in Newfoundland, 1785-1855* (Toronto, 1995), 105, 116-117.

[56]Both planters and "byeboat men" were inshore fishermen using small boats and employing seasonal workers or "servants" to fish and to cure the catch. The nominal difference between the two was that the byeboat men were migratory fishermen resident in England. However, both Matthews and Handcock emphasize that there was little difference between the two groups, since planters often spent only a few years in Newfoundland before returning permanently to England while byeboat keepers frequently over-wintered in Newfoundland; Matthews, *op. cit.*, 170; Handcock, *op. cit.*, 26.

[57]Burd still had 25 hundredweight of biscuit left. To the end, he had hoped that the price of bread would rise, "but Such great numbers of Ships coming & all of them Bringing some, Still kept the price Low." He therefore managed to secure no better price than twelve shillings per hundredweight for the remaining biscuit; Burd, *Journal*, 11 September 1726.

[58]Burd, *Journal*, 22 September 1726. While conceding "of the best of them...that they are not such great Rogues as some of their Neighbours," Burd warned that "the verry honestest of them will cheat you if he can hansomely & therefor its impossible for one that

Burd's relief was understandable. The voyage from Scotland to Newfoundland had been tedious and slow. Precious time had been spent securing the best price possible. Yet more time had been lost to bad weather and the laborious process of bringing the fish on board and stowing it in the hold. Some self-congratulation was perhaps justified merely for having secured a cargo at a reasonable price — at least one sack ship went away empty, despite offering three ryalls per quintal more than Burd had paid.[59] Nevertheless, this would have brought the super-cargo little comfort. His success in buying a lading of fish was offset by his failure to sell his biscuit at the price he wanted.[60] Yet any relief Burd may have felt at leaving Ferryland was premature. Little did he know, as the Newfoundland coast disappeared over the stern, that before him lay yet more frustrations and tribulations. The *Christian* was still making its way to the Strait of Gibraltar when it began to be overtaken by vessels which had departed Newfoundland as much as three weeks behind it — further proof, if any were needed, that the *Christian* lacked the speed desired for the trade.[61] Upon arriving at Gibraltar on 15 November, Burd expressed optimisim that they would soon reach Barcelona where "ffish...gives a great price...a' 7½ Dollars [per hundredweight]." Honesty, however, forced him to concede that the *Christian*'s slow passage from Newfoundland almost certainly would bring them to Barcelona behind the rest of the trade, "tho' wee were the first Ship from Newfoundland bound to our Port."[62] Adding to his unease were rumours that war between England and Spain was imminent. A more immediate concern were the fickle winds that hindered *Christian*'s departure from Gibraltar and

---

deals with them to be too much upon his Guard," adding that "this may Serve for a Character of the greatest part of the people that fish in the Country, as well as of those in this place."

[59]"A boat came here this day from a Ship of 300 Tons that lay at Bay of Bulls, & offered 32 Ryalls p quintall but could not have his Cargoe." Burd, *Journal*, 5 September 1726.

[60]Burd to his father, September 1726, SRO RH 15/54/6, B5.

[61]Burd, *Journal*, 10 November 1726.

[62]Burd's letters of 15 November 1726 to Claud Johnson, William Hutton Sr., and Mark Pringle, all in Burd, *Journal*, 16-16v.

dragged the journey to Barcelona out to more than two weeks. There, more bad news awaited them. The local demand for fish — never very elastic — had largely been satisfied by ships that had arrived earlier. By the time Burd and Captain Hutton made their way ashore, prices had tumbled and customers were "verry cool in buying."[63] An even worse catastrophe was the discovery that much of the fish in the *Christian*'s hold had spoiled during the voyage, greatly diminishing its value.[64] George French, the investors' agent in Barcelona, drew attention to "the Moistness of the fish" which, during a long trans-Atlantic passage, would have caused the cargo to become heated in the cramped hold.[65] Several possible factors, all arising from the inexperience of the investors and the supercargo, may explain how this could have happened. Possibly the bank fish taken on board had not been completely cured, leaving too high a moisture content.[66] Alternatively the fish may have been contaminated by rain during loading. Then, of course, there was that great constant, the unfortunate *Christian*, slow "and Not extrard^y tight."[67] Bad judgement or a slow, leaky ship, it made little difference; the venture to that point was anything but a success.

Having unloaded and disposed of the fish in Barcelona, Burd and Captain Hutton now encountered difficulty in putting together a return

---

[63]In contrast to the 7½ dollars a quintal Burd had optimistically predicted in Gibraltar, the best price obtained upon arrival in Barcelona was six dollars; Burd, *Journal*, 7 December 1726. Burd estimated Barcelona's annual demand for saltcod at about 30,000 quintals.

[64]Of the 1500 quintals of fish received in Ferryland, only 217 quintals were judged first quality; over a thousand quintals were second grade, and more than 200 quintals were third grade; see "Accompt Sale of 1500 Quintals Poorjack from Newfoundland," Burd, *Journal*, 18v.

[65]George French to William Hutton Sr. & Co., 12 January 1727, SRO RH 15/54/4: A3. It undoubtedly came as small comfort knowing that "the Same fate Attended all the Ships with fish that arrived this Season att this port." *Ibid.*

[66]In his "Answers to the Heads of Inquiry" in October 1726, Commodore Bowler had indicated that the late appearance of the cod that year, combined with a wet summer, had made it difficult to cure the fish properly; PRO CO 194/8, 38v (NAC Reel B-210).

[67]Burd in Barcelona to his father, no date, SRO RH 15/54/6, B1; Gregory French to William Hutton Sr. & Co., 12 January 1727, SRO RH 15/54/4, A3.

cargo. An unusually bad season meant that cork was not only scarce and expensive but also poor in quality. Mr. French therefore advised the *Christian* to take on several small cargoes — some wine for Cadiz, some empty wine pipes for Mataró, and more wine for delivery to Gibraltar.[68] French claimed that freighting these small cargoes would be more rewarding for the owners than continuing to wait for cork to appear, a prospect he regarded as "good for Nothing."[69] Yet each cargo meant an additional delay, so that, by the time they departed their last port of call at Villasa, the season for a quick passage to the Straits was over.[70] More than a month was spent sailing to Gibraltar, fighting gales all the way, only to learn that a long-anticipated conflict between England and Spain had at last begun. Gibraltar was besieged, and all trade was immobilized.[71] There the *Christian* remained until the middle of March, when a convoy was finally arranged. The war with Spain also meant that the original plan to pick up wine at San Lúcar had to be abandoned. Instead, the *Christian* had been obliged to sail in ballast as far as Bordeaux. There, Edward Burd Jr. made his departure in order to sample the delights of France, while Captain Hutton proceeded to the island of St. Martin-de-Ré, off La Rochelle, to load salt with the hope of salvaging something out of the voyage for the investors.[72]

It seems highly unlikely, however, that the venture could have earned a profit by the time the *Christian* returned to Leith. We know nothing about the cost of the biscuit that had been shipped to Newfoundland so that we are unable to determine whether a profit was made on that leg of the voyage. However, the poor quality and low price of the fish

---

[68]Charter party between Richard Neiland (Barcelona) and Alexander Hutton, 8 January 1727, SRO RH 15/54/6: B54.

[69]SRO RH 15/54/4: A3, Gregory French to William Hutton Sr. & Co., 12 January 1727. Burd surely was not amused to learn subsequently that a week after the *Christian* sailed from Villasa for Gibraltar, French had "more Cork than Youl be able to take in." Gregory French to Edward Burd Jr., 23 January 1727, SRO RH 15/54/6: B53.

[70]Villasa would probably have been Vilasar de Mar, a tiny port north of Barcelona and just south of Mataró.

[71]Burd, *Journal*, entries for 14 January to 14 February 1727.

[72]Edward Burd Jr. to his father, 6 June 1727, SRO RH 15/54/6, B7.

when the ship reached Barcelona almost certainly meant that any profit on the second leg of the voyage was insignificant.[73] The small freights carried between Barcelona and Gibraltar would hardly have covered the expenses of sitting idle for a month in Gibraltar or travelling from there to Bordeaux in ballast. The final leg, with salt from Bordeaux to Leith, probably earned very little. Against all that, there would have been the chartering costs, insurance, wages for the crew, port costs, the costs of outfitting and maintaining the ship, and so on, which, while not indicated by the available records, would almost certainly have exceeded the revenues generated by the voyage.

If, therefore, the 1720s seemed a propitious moment for Scottish investors to venture into the Newfoundland trade, the voyage of the *Christian* seemed also to demonstrate that success would not come easily. The partners in the *Christian* had included knowledgeable businessmen familiar with the Spanish trade and who appear to have made reasonable decisions, tempered with commendable caution. They lacked only three things which, in the end, proved fatal to the experimental venture. First, they lacked familiarity with the Newfoundland fish trade. Much therefore depended on their supercargo, Edward Burd Jr., whose responsibilities it had been to sell one cargo and acquire another. These he carried out with energy and initiative, and sensibly followed all the normal procedures typical of any trade of that day. In the end, however, general competence was not enough. A supercargo had to know the peculiarities of the particular trade as well, and it was here that Burd showed his weakness. The ultimate responsibility for the quality of the fish purchased in Ferryland rested upon his shoulders. That it failed to meet the standards of the market when delivered to Barcelona must be partly laid at Burd's door. The sound judgement that comes with experience and a healthy measure of good fortune were essential ingredients he had yet to acquire. Second, the investors lacked a suitable ship. The *Christian* proved itself to be too slow and too leaky for a trade in which the commodity was perishable and where delays threatened the profits of each leg of a voyage that was governed by a tight annual schedule. Finally, the investors lacked that most essential ingredient of any commercial venture, but especially the Newfoundland fish trade — luck. From the start, the voyage of the

---

[73]Ignoring for a moment various sundry charges, commissions, etc., the fish cost slightly under £1100 in Ferryland, and sold for about £1142 in Barcelona (5832 ryalls, two sols at an exchange rate of forty-seven pence per ryall); Burd, *Journal*, 26 February 1727.

Christian was dogged by misfortune — bad weather, lousy timing, a poor year for fish, a poor year for cork, even a war between England and Spain. It is therefore little wonder that William Hutton and his partners did not persist in their commercial experiment. Instead, they appear to have concluded that the time had not yet come for Scots merchants to engage in the Newfoundland trade, for they vanished from the trade as abruptly as they had ventured into it.

The Consolidation of Bilbao as a Trade Centre in the Second Half of the Seventeenth Century

Aingeru Zabala Uriarte

The Consulado of Bilbao, an offshoot of the Consulado of Burgos, was conceived in principle as a common space for merchants and shipmasters, traders and carriers, in which each group had a more or less important role to play.[1] The Consulado's first ordinances, which included working regulations and which may therefore be considered its deed of foundation, were drafted in the sixteenth century and remained in effect until the mid-eighteenth century, although not without a number of modifications. These modifications were basically dictated by experience and referred almost exclusively to trade.[2] Indeed, the fact that such modifications affected mercantile issues and not transport suggests the extent to which the interests of shipmasters and carriers lost ground to those of merchants and traders. Throughout the sixteenth century, and particularly in the first half of the seventeenth century, the maritime importance of Bilbao diminished as it gained prominence as a commercial centre.[3]

The increasing influence of the group of merchants in the Consulado, a result of Bilbao's burgeoning economy and, to some extent perhaps, the decline of Burgos, enabled the city on the Nervión river to consolidate its position as a trading centre, and brought with it the typical consequences of such a development. The Consulado found itself dealing increasingly with litigation and disputes between merchants while at the

---

[1]R.S. Smith, *Historia de los Consulados de Mar (1250-1700)* (Barcelona, 1978), a translation of *The Spanish Merchant Guild: A History of the Consulado (1250-1700)* (Durham, NC, 1940).

[2]T. Guiard, *Las Ordenanzas del Consulado de Bilbao (tres conferencias leídas por...)* (Bilbao, 1931).

[3]T. Guiard, *Historia del Consulado, Casa de Contratación de Bilbao y del Comercio de la Villa de Bilbao* (2 vols., Bilbao, 1914).

same time having to develop new areas of mercantile activity and to adjust its ordinances to the new situation thus created.

Throughout the seventeenth century, all kinds of measures were introduced to endow Bilbao with the qualities necessary to compete, within its limits, on the same level as the major European trading centres. This meant, essentially, upgrading its commercial tribunal, to deal with the growing number of disputes; developing and regulating the credit market, consisting mostly of bills of exchange and promissory notes; keeping a close watch on the way the merchants as a whole worked, and even inspecting their books; providing the city with resources to tackle insurance and contraband-related problems; and, finally, strengthening its competitiveness on the international market by offering a tax situation as good as, if not better than, other places and consolidating its export offer, as a guarantee for the growing import activity.

Clearly, this could not all be achieved at once. It is true that, almost from the start, Bilbao made major efforts to keep up on the international scene, developing preferential trading relations with other centres such as Nantes and Bruges, where it enjoyed certain reciprocal tax privileges.[4] Yet these links had fallen into disuse by the mid-seventeenth century because the agreements on which they were based had become outdated by then, either because it was no longer possible to comply with them or because trade habits in general had moved on. Instead, Bilbao's commerce was compelled to adapt to the new times and to modernise its operational structures if it expected to retain its international status.

Even so, while the process of turning Bilbao into an advanced mercantile zone was not actually delayed, it did have to develop in a rather tense atmosphere. Tension was caused by the lack of harmony between the groups of merchants involved. At the beginning of the seventeenth century, the community of foreign traders working in Bilbao was quite large – as it remained some 150 years later – and the local people from Bilbao and the province of Vizcaya in general used every means in their power to achieve a certain level of control over their trading centre. This they eventually managed, though not without confrontations between opposing communities, by hindering the foreigners' activities, delaying or even refusing them permission to reside in Bilbao,

---

[4] J. Ybarra y Bergé, "Vizcaínos en Brujas," *Boletín de la Real Sociedad Vascongada de Amigos del País San Sebastian*, VIII (1952), 345-356.

subjecting them to more or less discriminatory treatment, with no possibility of appealing to their consuls, who were also denied residential permission, and even persecuting them whenever international conflicts gave them the opportunity. Foreigners were also vulnerable to attacks on their trading activity, where the locals could take full advantage of comparative advantages and, in some cases, create them artificially.

So it was in this context that, largely in the second half of the seventeenth century, Bilbao created for itself a set of instruments, additional to the ones it had used for the previous hundred years, which enabled the city to take its position as one more commercial centre involved in international trans-Atlantic trade.

Developments at the Port: A Framework of Reference

Shifts deriving from international conflicts apart, a global analysis of the seventeenth century would show us that activity at the port of Bilbao as a whole, measured in river traffic, did not grow. Every year, 180 vessels sailed up the river Nervión to the anchoring ground at Olabeaga or the river wharves and then back out to sea again. Nevertheless, while river traffic in the sort of situation we shall be looking at remained relatively stable, the same cannot be said of trade, at least if average duties are used as a measure of commerce, as they clearly increased.[5]

Although this picture needs to be modified slightly, the sensation of increasing commercial activity throughout the seventeenth century remains. First, the port was highly sensitive to the activities of the corsairs, who plagued the seas throughout that century.[6] Second, the performance of economic variables was subject to currency fluctuations. Clearly, any global idea of the century should be treated with a certain amount of caution.

The adverse situation lasting from 1623 to 1630 affected traffic, which stagnated over a long period without actually going into recession. Signs of recovery did not become evident until 1655. From this year until 1669, substantial increases were registered in activity, with an average of

---

[5] Archivo Foral de Bizkaia (Provincial Archives of Bizkaia; AFB), various, box 28, ref. 7 (old system).

[6] E. Otero Lana, *Los corsarios españoles durante la decadencia de los austrias. El corso español del Atlántico peninsular en el siglo XVII (1621-1697)* (Madrid, 1992).

250 vessels a year mooring at the port. However, from 1672 on, traffic went into serious decline which in global terms left the situation much as it was at the beginning of the century, although conditions were never quite as bad as they were in the 1620s, when less than a hundred ships were registered in some years. And yet, in contrast to the fluctuations in traffic, the value of business done rose systematically throughout the century, when measured against the value of the goods entering Bilbao and to exports of iron and wool (admittedly, this is different in itself from the evolution of business). Trade increased, but commercial value rose most sharply between 1650 and 1672. A short but difficult cycle began after 1681 and lasted until 1693, when trading recovered to reach previously-attained levels. Such seemingly different performances are not difficult to understand, basically because every year the average value of goods imported by each vessel increased almost systematically. By the end of the century, the 300 *maravedis* each ship paid in average duties (proportional to the value of the shipment), had become 1100 or 1200 in most years, with the average value multiplied by a factor of four.[7]

Although using such information to draw conclusions about the evolution of commercial activity has its risks, testimonies from the merchants themselves do enable us to get a clearer picture of this development beyond purely quantitative variables. In 1649, for example, in an attempt to lay the foundations for improved organisation of trade, the Consulado agreed with the existing Bilbao postal service on an express system for communicating business news from San Sebastián and, from there, with the rest of Europe. At first, and with the likelihood that a service that "takes and brings letters from the businessmen of this Borough" would be loss-making, the possibility of subsidising the service was discussed. However, in 1664, we read that "now that the increase in commerce has been recognised...and that business has gone well and is now going well, so that the ordinary post...is well developed," the need for subsidies had disappeared. Indeed, in 1666, it was acknowledged that

---

[7]See P. Erkiaga Lasa, "Bilboko merkatalgoa XVII mendean" (Unpublished PhD thesis, University of Deusto, 1977). This is a magnificent, highly detailed study of average duties which, sadly, remains unpublished, though it is available at the University for consultation.

the mail service to and from San Sebastián sold more than the same service for Castile. It was very much a sign of the times.[8]

This policy left its mark on the Consulado's General Accounts as a number of loans outstanding from previous years were amortised and new investments were undertaken, including everything from new head-quarters to a new vessel for service and special duties, all clearly reflecting the buoyant situation of business. However, during the recession of the 1680s, in 1683 to be precise, when the "calamity of the times had diminished commerce," the San Sebastián postal service was subsidised once again and the Contractation House returned to a policy of loans and debts, directly as a result of war and also partly because the war led to a general decline in commerce in Bilbao. In short, the evolution in the number of vessels would seem to be the best indication of the merchants' frame of mind, and in this interpretation it can be said that, while the century was fairly homogeneous, expansion was more evident during the years between 1655 and 1670. It was therefore in this period that the Consulado, from a position of strength, tried to modernise and improve the competitiveness of Bilbao's trade.

The Activity of the Consular Tribunal

Leaving aside a range of possible minor qualifications, the activity of the Consular Tribunal is a reasonable indicator of two phenomena, one relating to the evolution of trade and commerce and the other to the process of institutionalisation of the Mercantile Tribunal as arbitrator in business disputes. While exogenous factors likely had less influence on this evolution than on traffic or commerce, they do exist. In times of international conflict, special bills were occasionally granted to trade with countries at war and were registered in the Tribunal's Legal Documentation. One example is illustrative: in 1695, of the forty-one documents registered with the Consular Tribunal, more than half were sea letters, which had no bearing on the institutionalising process mentioned. More subtle is the inclusion of ship's protests amongst this documentation, because although they are due to an external factor, in this case the state

---

[8]AFB, Various, Consulado, "Libro de Decretos de la Casa de contratación de esta Noble Villa de Bilbao," begun in 1662. These books, registered as Books of Minutes, numbered under the old archiving system as box 35, in reg. 2, correspond to the years 1594-1662. Reg. 3 stretches from 1662 to 1692 and reg. 4 covers 1692-1704.

of the sea, they are a further sign of the modernisation and development at Bilbao, as such documents are fundamental in claiming for damages from maritime insurance companies. Even so, they should not be given too much importance, as there are insurance policies that insist on declarations being made to the Notary of the first port reached, independently of its status.

The data speak for themselves. Only ten lawsuits survive from the sixteenth century and, up to 1628, there are but sixteen in total. The period from 1629 to 1631 is conflictive, but from then until 1647 the tribunal was not exactly overworked, as only one or two lawsuits survive for each year.[9] It is quite likely that many documents have disappeared, presumably lost rather than systematically destroyed. Even so, it is reasonable to assume that the evolution of the surviving lawsuits will reflect the general evolution of real cases, whether records remain or not. In any case, the surviving lawsuits are of interest as a testimony to the development and consolidation of the tribunal of the Consulado, as one of a number of activities designed to bring the institution into line with the techniques of its time.

From 1647 to 1662, the pace remained slow at the Tribunal, with some three or four lawsuits a year. However, between 1662 and 1676 the Tribunal matured. This was facilitated in part by the pace of growth in commerce, at least to the end of the 1660s, and partly by the sharp economic crisis which aggravated conflicts and forced more people to seek redress from courts and tribunals in general. The tribunals' work load became much less onerous when trade languished to a remarkable degree in the 1680s, only to increase heavily again in the following decade, when the Consular Tribunal's activities became a recognised part of the economic scene.

Obviously, the consolidation of the Consular Tribunal took a long time and met with some opposition, not least from other legal bodies such as Crown representatives, foreign communities, who preferred to be tried by their own Consuls, or by individuals who occasionally found it more in their interests to have recourse to ordinary justice rather than accept the special characteristics of a commercial court. The Consulado's vigorous defence of its jurisdiction led to substantial consolidation, so that between

---

[9]AFB, Judicial. A section of this collection is devoted to the Consular Tribunal, for which documentation was kept by the *Corregidor* (the chief magistrate) rather than by the Consulado.

1650 and 1700, in the face of much hair-splitting and frequent disputes, the Tribunal gained valuable experience and became more expert, and its prestige and acceptance grew. Indeed, the expertise and importance of the Consulado of Bilbao was acknowledged throughout the Spanish monarchy until the second half of the eighteenth century. In this respect, the main difficulty always came from the community of foreign traders, who applied to be given, and be judged by, their own Consuls, thus escaping the Contractation House's jurisdiction.

The increase in commerce led the English to name, or rather to attempt to name, a consul in Bilbao in 1660 who would charge a fee on English activities at the port. But opposition was so great that by 1662 the person appointed to the post had still not managed to take possession. At around the same time, the French also tried to establish a consul in Bilbao, but immediate opposition was encountered from the Consulado, the city and the government of the *Señorío* of Vizcaya.[10] However, in most cases, the foreign communities declared that they were happy with the Consulados, and did not officially ask for their own consuls. This was left to their respective Governments, or to the people who actually aspired to the job. The only one to be accepted in the Consulado's jurisdiction was the consul "of Holland, who agreed neither to receive taxes nor use exemptions or fees, accepting the title only and agreeing to assist his fellow countrymen in their dealings, as a mere solicitor or procurator of the Dutch."[11]

Notwithstanding this opposition to the designs of their respective parliaments, foreign communities remained firmly settled in Bilbao and continued to play an active role during the first half of the eighteenth century.[12] Nevertheless, and despite their economic importance in the second half of the seventeenth century, it was firmly established that commercial agents in Bilbao had to submit, without exception, to the Tribunal of the Consulado, except for degrees of appeals.

---

[10]F. Sagarminaga, *El Gobierno Foral del Señorío de Vizcaya* (10 vols., Bilbao, 1892; reprint, Bilbao, 1988), II, 197-198.

[11]Guiard, *Historia del Consulado*, II, 308-309.

[12]J.J. Laborda, "Comercio y Mercaderes en Bizkaia 1700-1730. Aproximación al estudio de la Sociedad del Señorío de Vizcaya y de la Machinada de 1718" (typescript, Bilbao, 1973).

Negotiation of Bills[13]

The first Ordinances of the Consulado do not include regulations governing the drawing and negotiation of bills in Bilbao, whether commercial drafts or promissory notes. In fact, an exhaustive study of notary protocols, where protests of bills should in principle be registered, shows that until 1660, for various reasons, bills were either not drawn on Bilbao or, if they were, the dealings were rarely registered.[14]

Even so, some references make it clear that in Bilbao, as in other ports, there were times when the Spanish regulation of international maritime trade made drawing difficult. On 7 February 1626 a royal decree stipulated that "the *maravedis* in which the merchants sell their goods shall be taken away in other goods of the kingdom and not in gold, silver or coin." This was cancelled by another decree in 1629 by which it was permitted "to negotiate with foreign kingdoms by means of bills of exchange without the obligation to register the merchandise or give guarantees of taking the value out in other goods." It was however, some time before such bills were drawn on Bilbao, or at least there are no records of such activity.[15]

Then, between 1660 and 1669, the number of bills of this kind negotiated accelerated, causing so many problems that the Consulado was obliged to intervene. It acknowledged in 1669 that, "as there is no settled style governing the terms in which protests of letters in this city should be made," a substantial number of lawsuits had arisen. It therefore established that such protests would have to be made to a notary within a

---

[13]In 1979-1980, Carlos Municio carried out detailed research in the Provincial Historical Archive of Bizkaia (AHPV), searching all Notary Protocols from the seventeenth century to locate protested bills. Municio never actually wrote about the results of the research, and I am therefore most grateful that on this occasion he has kindly passed the information on to me.

[14]Between 1630 and 1659, only eight protests appeared, and none before that date; AHPV, Protocol 3747, Simón de Severicha, 2 December 1630; 4634, Martínez de Larrabeitia, 27 March 1634; 5385, Juan Bautista Larrazabal, 10 May 1647; 2561, Domingo Arexmendi, 8 July and 12 September 1652; 2563, Domingo Arexmendi, 4 February 1653; and 5194, Antonio de la Llana, 28 March 1659.

[15]Guiard, *Historia del Consulado*, I, 274.

period of twenty days from the maturity date.[16] For example, in 1662, Juan de Arechavala protested a bill valued at 20,000 *reales* and in respect of which Nicholas Wescomb, the payer, said that, not yet having received order to pay it, but expecting to receive such order, "shall pay said bill in due course," and "asks and requires as many times as is necessary that said Juan de Arechavala retain in his power said bill in the sixty days contained therein, without sending it."[17] This was by no means exceptional. A year later, Wescomb had to deal with a similar problem and "said that until now he had not order nor notice...to accept said bill, and it might be that said order would arrive when the sixty days contained in said bill were to expire."[18] Such difficulties, arising out of the desire to proceed with a bill free of time limits (something that the Consulado's regulations tried to prevent), were frequent throughout the 1660s.

To give official status to this consideration, they had recourse to the King. In 1671, a Royal Provision was received approving the agreement, although it was suspended for a time because other centres, such as Seville, Malaga and Cadiz, might have felt discriminated by the move. Once they all agreed, it was put into practice. But by 1675, "though by means of the content of said ordinances many debates and differences experienced before their introduction had ceased," the use of bills in commerce had generated much additional equivocation which also required regulation. At the meeting of 9 September, a six-point article was agreed to deal with this issue. Besides confirming the need to protest a bill before a notary, maturity dates were affirmed and defined according to where the draft was made: forty days for Madrid and environs and sixty for Andalucía, Portugal and so on. But above all, point six established that a partial protest could be made, i.e., when a percentage of the bill was paid, the document had validity for the remainder, and on that basis it could be dealt with through the ordinary channels.

---

[16]AFB, Various, Consulado Libro de Decretos, 1692. A further clarification was made at the same meeting in 1669: "Many lawsuits and disagreements have occurred because the persons on whom fall the bills, to be paid in silver, pay them in *doblones* at 32 *reales* of silver each *doblón* worth 2 *escudos*."

[17]AHPV, Protocol 5199, Antonio de Llana, 26 April 1662.

[18]*Ibid.*, Protocol 5201, Antonio de Llana, 12 March 1663.

We should not, however, suppose, that the measure was well received or at least applied everywhere, as might be deduced from some of the lawsuits on record, because it would seem that it entailed certain changes to traditional customs, to which some appealed for protection. In 1672, with the response from Seville just received, it was declared that, once the term defined within a bill of exchange had been fulfilled, it was "the custom in Spain between men of business...to wait a fortnight."[19] But what in 1672 might be interpreted as a certain lack of enthusiasm for new measures can only be described, by 1681, as resistance to more or less acceptable changes. A bill at the beginning of the year argues that "22 November, in the English style, is counted and calculated 2 November in the Spanish style, so that the use matures this 2nd day of the month (February) [i.e., sixty days later]; the fourteen days of grace the payers of such bills usually and should enjoy expire on the 16th of this month and on that same day the payment would be made."[20]

Others attempted to outmanoeuvre or simply ignore the regulation, by negotiating bills on their free decision, which meant that the drawbacks they aimed to put to an end remained active. In 1673 one man protested a bill maturing on 4 May by making the demand for payment in the presence of a notary on 27 April of the same year, a disconcerting move to say the least.[21] Similar irregularities can be discovered in succeeding years, although they are more the exception than the rule. Such practices eventually disappeared.[22]

However beneficial the process might have been considered, it was not always peaceful. On 13 December 1681, a considerable disturbance ensued when a notary tried to send a claim on a bill before the maximum period established had finished, as the notary, "considering himself a party, and with much anger and impassioned display," tried to persuade the judges at the Consulado to deal with his demand, even "unsheathing his sword and dagger, desirous of killing them." The resulting furore reaffirmed the Consulado's conviction of the need for

---

[19]*Ibid.*, Protocol 5412, Sebastián de Goicoechea, 5 November 1672.

[20]*Ibid.*, Protocol 2657, Juan Bautista Asturiazaga, 6 February 1681.

[21]*Ibid.*, Protocol 2647, Juan Bautista Asturiazaga, 27 April 1673.

[22]*Ibid.*, Protocol 5293, Domingo de Gaminde, 9 December 1676.

regulation, and the institution ordered the ordinances to be reprinted, because by then they had run out of copies, and used the opportunity to add a new regulation on the drafting of bills in an appendix.[23]

Even so, in the majority of cases the process of regulation was increasingly accepted, although some explicit acknowledgements of the following sort were made in protests in 1680: "if it comes into his hands before the term of sixty days has expired, for said bill, he shall pay it."[24] More explicitly, in an exceptional case in 1681, we find precise references to the new regulation in a protest that states: "to be free to make said payment in virtue of the decrees and ordinances of the Contractation-House of this Borough confirmed by H.M. for having passed the terms in which said bill should have been made known."[25] As a result, and in general, from the dates that mark the legalisation of the Consular agreement, business conducted with this kind of document was fully regulated and almost all protests were henceforth properly grounded, and not on more or less unstable or unpredictable terms or for other dubious motives, as it was stated that such dealings were made for "reasons that shall be written to the giver of the bills" or because resources were lacking, and so on.

In addition to its work on this important question, the Consulado also intervened in other aspects of the negotiation of bills, specifically on issues having to do with changes in payments, changes not so much in the value of different national currencies but more regarding the appraisal which, as a result of the peculiar Spanish financial situation, had to be made of the amounts in which payments of such bills for Bilbao or other Spanish trading centres were specified. In 1678, the Consulado agreed that "the contracts made to this day be in effect, according to the manner in which they were struck and agreed by sellers and purchasers. But, from now on, said contracts being in silver, must therefore be paid in such, and not in any other coin, and being in gold, must therefore be paid in pieces of four for each one doubloon, without no reduction...and avoiding by

[23]AFB, Various, Consulado, Libro de Actas (1680-1699), box 28, reg. 7.

[24]AHPV, Protocol 5218, Antonio de Llana, 3 June 1680.

[25]*Ibid.*, Protocol 4602, Antonio de Hostendi, 30 April 1681.

this means the great inconveniences that have been experienced in said reductions to the great prejudice of commerce."[26]

The majority of bills were, however, agreed in fixed currency without causing major difficulties. In an almost overwhelming majority, bills were agreed in *reales* of eight. Specifications were actually introduced in some protests: "400 ducats at 375 *maravedis* of silver each ducat, excluding the *reales* of Peru and any other coin current before the Royal Provision of 1642." The *peso* had always to be in line with the Consulado's stipulation of eight *reales* of silver for each one. All this did not, however, prevent discrepancies from occurring.

In this context, it was not enough to fix criteria on bills of exchange. In 1687, it was acknowledged that the regulation had virtually brought disputes in the business of bills to an end. But it had not wiped out the problem completely. As we have already seen, five lawsuits were recorded in the 1660s, and twelve in the 1670s, with a maximum for the second half of the seventeenth century of three in 1679 alone. Once the regulation had been consolidated, the number of cases fell to two in the 1680s and three in the 1690s, and that at a time when commerce was in a trough.

In general terms, however, the regulation was so successful that in 1685, having confirmed the usefulness of regulating maturity periods, and, with a view to avoiding other drawbacks deriving from other "species of bills" such as promissory notes, bearer warrants and collections, they decided to regulate them in the same way.[27] The several characters of the promissory notes were regulated in such a way as to permit the creditor to demand payment from any of the signatories, always provided that the claim was made in a given period, since after such a period, the debtor could only make partial claims to each party, the term being established as the thirty days after maturity. As with bills, the regulations permitted partial issues and, consequently, partial demands. Commerce with such notes, not so much as in themselves but in the claims deriving from non-payment, was regulated, time being given for claims to be made even from endorsers to whom, by this means, the notes could be returned for settlement.

---

[26]AFB, Various, Consulado, Libro de Actas, 1663-1680, box 28, reg. 8.

[27]*Ibid.*, Judicial, 2125/015 (1676).

By incorporating these ordinances, the Consulado regulated a sector that had been passed over in the initial drafts, not so much from ignorance but rather because, in the case of bills of exchange at least, practice had shown regulation to be unnecessary. However, from 1660 onwards, the practice of drawing on Bilbao began, and increased rapidly, forcing the Consulado's magistrates to take steps to avoid the disputes that arose largely from the lack of definition of the mercantile documents themselves. This they did by regulating their use and treatment. In the process, they also laid the foundations for more effective internationalisation of Bilbao's commerce and trade.

Here then is the key: protested bills occurring sporadically before 1660, and became a much more regular phenomenon from that year on in what was a growth process. That process was rooted fundamentally in the commercial situation but also reflecting developments in the use of a mercantile tool. In these conditions, the number of protested bills varied in normal years between five and twelve per year (twenty times during the thirty-nine-year period between 1660 and 1700), exceeding the higher figure fifteen times. In such cases, like the years between 1679 and 1683, or 1691 or even 1696 and 1697, the figures were relatively high, more than thirty-five protests being registered each year.

It is true that we do not know how many bills were drawn on Bilbao in the seventeenth century. All we have are the records of the protests and this clearly has more to do with the economic situation than any other factor. Even so, the substantial developments surrounding this kind of document in the protocols of local notaries provides proof of the success of the implementation of a commercial traffic in bills in the local market after 1660.

The incorporation of additional regulations was by no means intended as a reform of the ordinances. In this respect, things did not reach the state of the French commercial ordinance (1673) although, together with the Marína ordinance (1681), it was to form a substantial part of the doctrinal body used in the eighteenth century (1737) for the global reform of the Ordinances of Bilbao.[28] Moreover, aspects that were fundamental to the development of trade, such as the regulation of mercantile companies and freightment, would not be tackled by the

---

[28]E. Gactó Fernández, *Historia de la jurisdicción mercantil en España* (Seville, 1971).

Consulado of Bilbao until the eighteenth century.[29] During the second half of the seventeenth century, then, both issues went largely unrecognised and remained disorganised, as well as being unregulated, which almost certainly caused problems that the new ordinances would attempt to solve. Even so, such problems, whatever they were, could not have been very noticeable since, even though action was taken on bills of exchange, merchants in Bilbao at the time apparently saw no reason to regulate further and nothing was said about them in the edition of the ordinances the Consulado published at the end of the seventeenth century.

Coin and Currency Control

Money was of course another factor in achieving the necessary confidence. Spain's delicate monetary situation caused a number of major scares and also made some of its coins easy meat for fraud. In these conditions, the Consulado informed the civil authorities of the *Señorío* of Vizcaya of its concern. Luckily, both the local authorities and Crown representatives involved moved rapidly. Between 1669 and 1670, at the slightest sign of irregularities in the sector, the public authorities reacted with unusual severity, forestalling almost any subsequent attempt at fraud and bringing a remarkable degree of security to Bilbao as a trade centre.

The procurators of Bilbao were the first to bring the question to the attention of the *Juntas Generales* (General Assembly) of Vizcaya, accusing the foreigners – who else? – of withdrawing genuine coins, reducing their weight and then returning them to circulation.[30] The measures taken to avoid fraud of this kind were simple enough, but did not eliminate it completely, as they only adjusted the price of the coin to its real value. It was proposed, via a series of "necessary comparisons, with weights adjusted to all kinds of doubloons and *escudos*, *reales* and *medios*" and by ensuring that the worth of coins in circulation depended on their weight in silver or gold, to "avoid all the dishonesty of trafficking with lack of weight." Another measure consisted of prohibiting in Vizcaya the use of a coin known in both legal and the thriving fraudulent

---

[29]C. Petit, *La Compañía Mercantil bajo el régimen de las ordenanzas del Consulado de Bilbao, 1737-1839* (Seville, 1980); and R. Fernández Guerra, "El fletamento en el litoral cantábrico durante el siglo XVIII" (unpublished manuscript, Gijón, 1992).

[30]Sagarminaga, *El Gobierno Foral...*, II, 259-260, resolution for 1669.

circulation as the *molino*. Circulating the coin was made an offence in the *Señorío* and anywhere within a distance of twelve leagues. Finally, it was proposed that counterfeiters should be efficaciously persecuted.[31]

Even so, at first plenty of people were ready to defraud by this means. The Señorío even authorised counterfeiters to be killed freely if they used weapons to defend themselves. According to the *Actas* of 1670, "Lucas de Urisa and another man called Marcos the countryman resisted with firearms and escaped and are now at large in the Señorío." That same year two counterfeiters were garrotted. This was quite an unusual step, as records of this kind of death penalty being used in the Señorío are rare.

Despite such drastic measures, counterfeiting was not completely stamped out. In 1674, a mule was bought with counterfeit coin.[32] More significantly, an extended counterfeit coin production and distribution ring was dismantled in 1675. More than twenty people were accused in Axpe and Arrazola; some died in prison.[33] In 1677, the Chief Magistrate opened an inquiry after counterfeit coins were found in the river at Bilbao.[34] Proceedings were brought against three locals for counterfeiting a coin known as the *molinillo* in 1680, basically because the Señorío had prohibited its circulation, even legally, in its jurisdiction. In this case, though, as well as being counterfeit, the coin was obviously too light-weight and flimsy.[35]

After 1680, there were no more cases of counterfeiting until well into the eighteenth century, so it is fair to say that the severity with which the authorities acted in the most important cases effectively ruined the counterfeit business. From the initial generalised accusation directed

---

[31]*Ibid.*, 264, resolution for 1670.

[32]AFB, Judicial 197/008 (1674), Criminal prosecution brought by the Chief Magistrate of Durango against the manufacture of counterfeit coin used to pay the 103 ducats for the sale of a mule.

[33]Varied documentation on the case exists in AFB, Judicial. The first document refers to resistance to the authorities and subsequent injuries and wounds and is in 1288/015 (1674); for the moment, the rest are in 196/37; 197/1-7 and 25-26; 198/8, 9 and 10; 2213/1 to 10 and 2214/1 to 5. Further documents may well come to light in the future.

[34]*Ibid.*, 2212/007, 2 October 1677.

[35]*Ibid.*, 2046/029, 16 January 1680.

against the foreigners of reducing the weight of silver coin, the authorities moved against the actual counterfeiting, usually of poor quality, and distribution done by local people. No foreigner was ever in fact accused of such activities.

The objective of maintaining confidence in trade was duly achieved. Indeed, in the tumultuous years after the civil war, and the disturbances of 1718, such confidence took no more knocks, despite the fact that, in the seventeenth century, the behaviour of coin and currency and, in the following period, "prizes" of silver, meant that counterfeiting continued to be an interesting proposition.[36]

Improvements in Competitiveness

As local trade was based on a long-standing, and very specific, equilibrium, the locals looked to change such conditions by working on the variables closest to hand.

The original set-up was simple. Wool and iron were loaded at Bilbao, while incoming boats brought varied cargoes, and not just to make the voyage to Bilbao worthwhile. Loading wool and iron was complementary; while there were alternatives to Basque iron, even in Spanish markets, wool had virtually no competition and international demand was solid.[37]

Controlling wool was a major, perhaps decisive, factor for Bilbao's trade, but there are indications around 1673 that the product was effectively controlled by foreigners, who not only advanced money to the sheep-owners but also subjected them to extortion, as they "managed to pay in commodities, introducing them against the law and giving them the value they wanted." The wool owners could do nothing about this as the foreigners were their only buyers, and they were even forced to pay for the transport costs of the wool to the North and the risks of the insurance,

---

[36]*Ibid.*, 1755/001, 1694. A counterfeit piece-of-eight appeared in Mondragón in the same year.

[37]Sagarminaga, *El gobierno floral...*, II, 237: "although the iron worked with the minerals of the Señoría in its district and in the surrounding provinces is of a quality unmatched anywhere in the world, and Philip IV ordered that anchors for his ships should be made with this iron alone, iron of greatly inferior quality is brought from Liège and Germany to Seville and other parts of Anadalucía, because it is cheaper."

and made to use the foreigners' own carriers, usually Dutch or English.[38] With this state of affairs, the foreigners were considered to own the wool trade, to the point where "if any local shipped them on his own account, the wool of the sale from the north arrived, with such impost and the wool sold at such low price that they obliged him not to repeat the experience."[39]

Bilbao trade was bound to be fragile while this situation continued. So, despite the difficulties such a move entailed, "from the second half of the seventeenth century, men from Bilbao figure among the exporters of wool from Segovia. People with Basque names also began to appear as owners of migrating flocks."[40] To be more precise, around 1680 a group of traders from Bilbao decided to become directly involved in the wool trade, trying to dislodge the foreigners.[41] Although the process has barely been studied, we have enough information to be able to say that by around 1687 the same people, and in particular the Mesta, who fifteen years before had complained about the situation described above, now felt that things had changed and that the foreigners were losing control of the wool trade.

Of course, a frontal assault of this kind on the wool trade required heavy investment; capital was needed to continue advancing to the sheep owners the kind of sums that the English and Dutch had previously paid. One estimate puts these advances (which, given the nature of the trade, were programmed for more than a year ahead) at 400,000 *reales*, the same amount that in 1673 the Community of Merchants of Burgos, in an

---

[38]E. Larruga, *Memorias políticas y económicas* (45 vols., Madrid 1787-1800), XXVII, 290 ff. and XXVIII, 28 ff. My thanks to Luis María Bilbao for these references.

[39]AFB, Judicial 2081/007, 1672. This is an interesting lawsuit in which are found half a dozen letters referring to the wool trade, including such features as quality, interest and payments. Among other things, the Dutch insisted on paying in kind. This is one of the cases in which the locals tried to negotiate directly with the North. (126 ff.)

[40]A. García Sanz, *Desarrollo y crisis del Antiguo Régimen en Castilla la Vieja* (Toledo, 1977), 241, n. 62.

[41]According to Guiard, "nine important Bilbao merchants took the initiative of going to Castile to contract wool directly" around that time; *Historia del Consulado*, I, 387. The nine were Martín de Aranguren, Diego de Allende, Francisco de Gallartu, Antonio de Zumelzu, Antonio de Zarrabeitia, Antonio de Landazuri, Martín de Guendika and Pedro de Gacitua.

attempt to centralise the wool trade in their city to the detriment of Bilbao, said it had available, but which by 1687 it could no longer afford. Yet they would not have managed to get very far even if they had been able to pay, as traders from Bilbao had pre-empted them.

Even so, control over wool was always precarious. In the last years of the seventeenth century, with the competition from Burgos comprehensively seen off, other attempts were always likely to be made, the majority regularly coming, in the eighteenth century particularly, from the central Spanish administration, which fully understood that control of a product in such demand was an essential extortion factor for Bilbao commerce and trade.

Nevertheless, despite everything, local merchants were fully aware at what was a key moment in the seventeenth century that if Bilbao was to be firmly established as a trade centre, their relations with the suppliers of the main export product had to be regularised. This did not necessarily mean control over production, but certainly entailed edging foreign competition out of the way.

There is no doubt that the move was highly successful, although perhaps success did not come quite as quickly as some interested witnesses would seem to suggest. At the beginning of the eighteenth century, for instance, problems were still being recorded. However, the initiative enabled Bilbao traders to go on the offensive and use the stable export trade in wool and the customs fees deriving therefrom to their advantage against the attacks from the Crown, which was always looking for ways to curb "freedoms" and increase its control over local activity.

In short, local merchants took advantage of the years when trade prospered, between 1655 and 1670, to prepare a profound change, largely with regard to international commerce, in the status of Bilbao as a trade centre. In a single, relatively short period, they established the fame, prestige and expertise of the Consular Tribunal (1662-1676), opened Bilbao up to the international business of bills and promissory notes from 1660 onwards, regulating the business in 1669, and also restructured the way money moved (1670-1675). Once these measures had taken effect, the way was clear for the assault on the wool trade in 1680.

Obviously, the period saw many other major events and conflicts, as Guiard's invaluable work, regularly quoted here, makes clear. But other phenomena, particularly the traffic in bills, which Guiard virtually ignores, were in fact the most profound and important stimuli of change.

In the following years, until the reform of the Ordinances in 1734, the Bilbao mercantile community continued to detect further anomalies and deficiencies in the system they had to work with, and commissioned some of its members to write a set of new Regulations. However, despite being much more mature, wide-ranging and precise than the preceding ones, these were nowhere near as important as those discussed in this article as far as opening up new areas of trade, creating new opportunities and changing perspectives was concerned.

So it can be said that the second half of the seventeenth century was a key period in the consolidation of Bilbao as an efficient trade centre on Europe's Atlantic seaboard. Indeed, judging by the decline of other well-established centres within the Spanish monarchy, Bilbao was to prove one of the few capable of carrying on substantial international activity in the eighteenth century.

Cutting Out The Middleman?
American Trade In Northern Europe, 1783-1815

Daniel A. Rabuzzi [1]

John Greene Proud[2], supercargo for several ships owned by the large New York firm Minturn and Champlin[3], wrote from French-occupied Hamburg to his principals in June 1810: "The resources of this market in Capital and a Spirit of Speculation so far exceed that of any other in this quarter that is open to us."[4] A week later, however, writing to London bankers, Proud sounded a note of caution: "Our mutual N.Y. friends have had some pretty considerable and on the whole advantageous business in this quarter under my direction — but the Prospect is now exceedingly cloudy and if we are enabled to wind up present Affairs in safety and without Loss it is as much as can be expected."[5] By October he characterizes the Hamburg, and by implication North Sea/Baltic, market as "nearly as bad

[1]For their assistance, I thank Silvia Marzagalli, Edward Tebbenhoff, Ernst Pijning, and the staffs at the Maryland Historical Society and the Library of Congress/Manuscripts Division.

[2]J.G. Proud (1776-1865), born New Bedford, Massachusetts; married and became merchant in Baltimore; failed c. 1808; became supercargo for New York merchants Minturn and Champlin, Port Grinnell Minturn and Fish, John P. Mumford, and Elias Kane.

[3]Minturn and Champlin were one of the largest US merchant-shipowners around 1800 (failed during War of 1812). Part of leading constellation including Grinnells, Fish, and Mumford, all originally from New Bedford (hence Proud's connection) and Newport. See Robert Albion, *The Rise of New York Port 1815-1860* (New York, 1939), 44 and 244-248; Joseph Scoville, *The Old Merchants of New York City* (New York, 1872, 3 vols.), III, part 1, 105, 151, 242, and 318; III, part 2, 190-194; Reinhard Spindler, *New York und der amerikanische Indienhandel (1784-1812)* (Stuttgart, 1994), 238, 377, 435 and 505.

[4]Maryland Historical Society (MHS), Ms. 1530, Redwood Collection (RC), box 6, Proud Letterbook no. 1, Proud to Minturn and Champlin, 9 June 1810.

[5]*Ibid.*, Proud to John Lewis, Brown and Co., 15 June 1810.

as it can be,"[6] in November, his opinion drops lower still: "With respect to commerce I hope it is not entirely annhilated but you may consider it as dead for the present."[7]

Having been detained by Danish privateers, nearly shipwrecked off Rostock, and frustrated at every turn by French *douanieres* and duplicitous German merchants, supercargo Leonard Matthews[8] of the schooner *Nonsuch* was even more scathing about American trade prospects in northern Europe at that same time. From Hamburg, he informed his principal, merchant and later mayor of Baltimore George Stiles[9], in February 1811 that: "The shape given to commerce in this country, and which involves your interest so deeply, is to me a source of infinite regret, but no human foresight could guard against it."[10] He was long since disenchanted with north European markets: "I am heartily sick of Europe, and wish very much to go home, but when that happy period will arrive is very uncertain."[11] Writing to a fellow American supercargo, Matthews expressed his disgust, asserting that the German merchants would "fleece you like the devil, for it is, unfortunately for us, the

---

[6]*Ibid.*, Proud Letterbook no. 2, Proud to Minturn and Champlin, 26 October 1810.

[7]*Ibid.*, Proud to Minturn and Champlin, 7 November 1810.

[8]Dates unknown. MHS, Dielman-Hayward biographical file, lists a "Leonard Matthews" marrying in 1817, and Samuel Jackson's *Baltimore Directory* for 1819 lists him as a merchant.

[9]Stiles (1760-1819) began as a sea captain for the very important Baltimore firm S. Smith and Buchanan and became one of Baltimore's leading merchants. His wholly-owned schooner *Nonsuch* was one of the most famous privateering ships during the War of 1812. See MHS, filing case A, s.v. "Stiles" (esp. *Baltimore Sun*, 9 November 1949); and Jerome Garitee, *The Republic's Private Navy* (Middletown, CT, 1977), 30, 42, 87, 162, 201-202, 236 and 264.

[10]MHS, Ms. 2508, Letterbook of schooner *Nonsuch* (*Nonsuch* Letterbook), Matthews to Stiles, 5 February 1811.

[11]*Ibid.*, Matthews to A.W. Preuss, 14 December 1810. Matthews was forced to stay in Europe for over a year. The penultimate entry in the letterbook, dated 5 April 1811 to W. Peterkin in Copenhagen, reads: "I cannot depart for America before my affairs are closed and when that will be no mortal can say."

prevailing opinion of the merchants in this country, that the United States will have no more trade to these parts of the world..."[12]

Although perhaps more severe as a result of the Napoleonic conflict, the experiences of Proud and Matthews were by no means uncommon for maritime merchants from the fledgeling US. Lack of trust, lack of knowledge, missed timing and miscues: such experiences were bound to be common as Americans launched themselves into markets previously excluded to them under Great Britain's Navigation Acts. And launch they must, for conversely they lost many privileges once enjoyed as colonials under those self-same Acts. For the Americans, the rules of the commercial game had changed dramatically; they had, however, no choice but to continue playing, given the vital role of maritime trade within the American economy.

Scholars have long recognized the paramount importance of overseas commerce to the US during the first decades after independence.[13] Much has been written in general terms about the insatiable commercial spirit of post-revolutionary Americans, and in aggregate terms about the growth of the early American economy and the creation of new trade routes by Yankee merchants.[14] We are less often told, however,

---

[12]*Ibid.*, Matthews to R.W. Goodrich, Memel, 19 March 1811.

[13]Stanley Elkins and Eric McKitrick, *The Age of Federalism: The Early American Republic, 1788-1800* (New York, 1993), esp. 65-73, 92-113 and 375-449; John Belohlavek, "Economic Interest Groups and the Formation of Foreign Policy in the Early Republic," *Journal of the Early Republic*, XIV, No. 4 (Winter 1994); David Fitzsimons, "Tom Paine's New World Order: Idealistic Internationalism in the Ideology of Early American Foreign Relations," *Diplomatic History*, XIX, No. 4 (Fall 1995); and Merrill Peterson, "Thomas Jefferson and Commercial Policy, 1783-1793," *William and Mary Quarterly*, 3rd ser., XXII, No. 4 (October 1965).

[14]Gordon Wood, *The Radicalism of the American Revolution* (New York, 1991), chaps. 14, 17 and 18; Elkins and McKitrick, *Age of Federalism*, 381-386, 413-414 and 441 ff.; John McCusker and Russell Menard, *The Economy of British America 1607-1789* (Chapel Hill, 1985), 370-376; Curtis Nettels, *The Emergence of a National Economy 1775-1815* (New York, 1962), 65-69, chaps. 10-11; Merrill Jensen, *The New Nation: A History of the United States during the Confederation 1781-1789* (New York, 1965), 175-184 and chap. 9; Donald Adams, "American Neutrality and Prosperity, 1793-1808: A Reconsideration," *Journal of Economic History*, XL, No. 4 (December 1980); Claudia Goldin and Frank Lewis, "The Role of Exports in American Economic Growth during the Napoleonic Wars, 1793 to 1807," *Explorations in Economic History*, XVII, No. 1 (1980); and James Shepherd and Gary Walton, "Economic Change after the American Revolution: Pre- and

exactly how this spirit operated on a daily basis and what techniques individual merchants used to create new markets or to plug into existing ones where they had no prior presence. We need more micro-analyses to test and/or complement our macro-level theses.[15] Looking at the risk-taking decisions and tactics of merchants in one specific overseas market — as opposed to the national strategies of politicians and universal schemes of political economists — will help us better understand the early American economy and the shaping of an American commercial consciousness.

The specific market — or, more accurately, set of overlapping markets — is that of northern Europe, defined as eighteenth-century people defined it: the continent north of Cape Finisterre, plus Scandinavia, with a particular emphasis on the Baltic. Few scholars have studied the trade of America with the Baltic,[16] whereas vast attention has been paid to the dramatic opening of Yankee commerce with China, Indonesia, India, Turkey, and Latin America.[17] Tea, cloves, and opium continue to

---

Post-War Comparisons of Maritime Shipping and Trade," *Explorations in Economic History*, XIII, no. 4 (1976).

[15]Cf. Stuart Bruchey, *Robert Oliver, Merchant of Baltimore 1783-1819* (Baltimore, 1956); John McMaster, *The Life and Times of Stephen Girard: Mariner-Merchant* (Philadelphia, 1918); and John Reinoehl, "Post-Embargo Trade and Merchant Prosperity: Experiences of the Crowninshield Family, 1809-1812," *Mississippi Valley Historical Review*, XLII, No. 2 (September 1955). All three include details on merchant activity in northern Europe.

[16]A comprehensive survey includes Robert Greenhalgh Albion, *Forests and Sea Power* (Cambridge, MA, 1926), chaps. 4 and 8; J. William Fredrickson, "American Shipping in the Trade with Northern Europe 1783-1860," *Scandinavian Economic History Review*, IV, No. 2 (1956); Aage Raasch, *Niels Ryberg, 1725-1804* (Aarhus, 1964), 141-154; Raasch, "American Trade in the Baltic, 1783-1807," *Scandinavian Economic History Review*, XIII, no. 1 (1965); Alfred W. Crosby, *America, Russia, Hemp, and Napoleon: American Trade with Russia and the Baltic, 1783-1812* (Columbus, OH, 1965); David McFadden, "John Quincy Adams, American Commercial Diplomacy, and Russia, 1809-1825," *New England Quarterly*, LXVI, No. 4 (December 1993); and Stephen Patrick, "Marylanders in the Nascent Russo-American Trade, 1776-1783," *Maryland Historical Magazine*, XC, No. 1 (Spring 1995).

[17]James D. Phillips, *Salem and the Indies* (Boston, 1947); William Fowler, Jr., "'Trye All Ports': The Port of Boston 1783-1793," in Conrad E. Wright (ed.), *Massachusetts and the New Nation* (Boston, 1992); G. Bhagat, "Americans and American Trade in India, 1784-1814," *American Neptune*, XLVI, No. 1 (Winter 1986); Spindler,

capture the imagination in a way that flax, tar, and iron do not, but the glamor of the oriental or other distant trades should not blind us to the importance of the north European markets. Or, rather, we should keep the tropical goods in view but expand our field of vision: Americans greatly valued the north European ports — even when it meant running the many risks that so plagued the supercargoes Proud and Matthews, for example — because these provided key markets for precisely the commodities Americans were keen to re-export from Batavia, Bengal, or Bahia.

Looking at the north European markets will also shed light on the much-discussed issue of whether Americans wished to cut out the British middleman they had been forced to use (and had grown so accustomed to using) before 1783, and the degree to which they actually did so.[18] For the young US, reliance upon or independence from the former metropole, especially in trade matters, was an issue of central importance not only for purely economic reasons but at least as much for political and psychological reasons. The acrimonious national controversy over the Jay Treaty in 1794-1796 is but one example of the issue's importance.[19] For American traders venturing into northern Europe after 1783, there would be no lack of British middleman available: both the English and the Scots had been

---

New York; Rhys Richards, "United States Trade with China 1784-1814," *American Neptune*, LIV, supplement (1994); Jonathan Goldstein, *Philadelphia and the China Trade, 1682-1846* (University Park, PA, 1978); James Field, *America and the Mediterranean World, 1776-1882* (Princeton, 1969), chap. 2; and Peggy Liss, *Atlantic Empires: The Network of Trade and Revolution, 1713-1826* (Baltimore, 1983), chap. 5.

[18]Gordon Bjork, "The Weaning of the American Economy: Independence, Market Changes and Economic Development," *Journal of Economic History*, XXIV, No. 4 (December 1964); Norman Graebner, "New England and the World, 1783-1791," in Wright (ed.), *Massachusetts and the New Nation;* Alison Gilbert Olson, *Making the Empire Work: London and American Interest Groups, 1690-1790* (Cambridge, MA, 1992), chap. 12; and David M. Williams, "The Rise of United States Merchant Shipping on the North Atlantic, 1800-1850: The British Perception and Response," in Clark Reynolds (ed.), *Global Crossroads and the American Seas* (Missoula, MT, 1988).

[19]"The outpouring of popular feeling over the Jay Treaty...was more directly responsible than anything else for the full emergence of political parties in America..."(Elkins and McKitrick, *Age of Federalism*, 415.)

active in the "East Country" trade since the Late Middle Ages.[20] Did the Americans use the British to gain access to the new markets, and, if so, in exactly what ways?

Forbidden by the Navigation Acts to trade directly with Europe north of Finisterre, Americans knew little of that region before the Revolution (much less so than they did about southern Europe). Americans had some contacts with the Dutch, gained via the West Indian trade, and probably through the rice trade as well, which the English freed for northern Europe in the 1750s; the Dutch emerged during the war and its immediate aftermath as the United States' banker and one of its most important trading partners.[21] For similar reasons, Americans knew something of northwestern Germany. At least as early as the 1740s, some Chesapeake tobacco planters had very close ties to Bremen and Hamburg merchants resident in London.[22] In 1755, with the liberalization of the rice trade, the first ships arrived in Bremen from South Carolina; a modest three rice ships arrived yearly on the Weser through 1776.[23] Pre-revolutionary contacts with the Baltic were even more fleeting and were, moreover, illicit. The Danish Sound Toll registers record just fifteen ships with home ports in British North America entering the Baltic between 1741 (the first ever recorded) and 1776.[24]

Given the previous lack of significant direct contact, American merchants and shipmasters in the 1780s and 1790s had a great deal to

---

[20]Ph. Dollinger, *Die Hanse* (4th ed., Stuttgart, 1989), 252-253; T.C. Smout, "Scottish Commercial Factors in the Baltic at the End of the 17th Century," *Scottish Historical Review*, XXXIX (October 1960); Gordon Jackson, *Hull in the Eighteenth Century* (Oxford, 1971); and Herbert Kaplan, *Russian Overseas Commerce with Great Britain during the Reign of Catherine II* (Philadelphia, 1995).

[21]P.J. van Winter, *Het aandel van den Amsterdamschen handel aan den opbouw van het Amerikaansche Gemeenebest* ('s-Gravenhage, 1927); and Peter Hoekstra, *Thirty-Seven Years of Holland-American Relations, 1803 to 1840* (Grand Rapids, MI, 1916).

[22]Planters' daughters sometimes married German merchants. See Jacob Price, "One Family's Empire: The Russell-Lee-Clerk Connection in Maryland, Britain, and India, 1707-1857," *Maryland Historical Magazine*, LXXII, No. 2 (1977), 179.

[23]Franz Josef Pitsch, *Die wirtschaftlichen Beziehungen Bremens zu den Vereinigten Staaten von Amerika bis zur Mitte des 19. Jahrhunderts* (Bremen, 1974), 10.

[24]Fredrickson, "American Shipping in the Trade with Northern Europe," 109.

learn about northern Europe. In this, they were no worse off than their political leaders: the new American government itself faced a daunting task of self-education on every front. Adams, Madison, and Jefferson, for instance, were thirsty for knowledge of all kinds, and worked with verve to obtain timely and accurate data. Even so, much of what any American had to work with was outdated or erroneous: the Founders relied, for example, on histories published in the 1650s and 1670s for their under-standing of the Dutch Netherlands.[25] Recent travel accounts, despite their idiosyncratic nature and often dubious observations, had to fill the gap; especially popular portrayers of northern Europe were Wraxall (1774; 4th ed. 1807; abridged 1796), Coxe (1784; 5th ed. 1802; abridged 1809), and Carr (1805; abridged 1806).[26] Fortunately, detailed geographical works on northern Europe were available by the time of independence: the German A.E. Buesching's hugely popular *Erdbeschreibung* was translated into English in 1762 and 1778.[27]

Buesching's geography was, however, a six-volume work and therefore probably beyond the means of many merchants. More affordable were the commercial handbooks, newspapers, and gazetteers that appeared with increasing frequency in the late eighteenth century.[28] For example, a substantially revised and expanded edition of Samuel Ricard's

---

[25]Jan Willem Schulte Nordholt, *The Dutch Republic and American Independence* (Chapel Hill, 1982), 109. For an overview of the books on commerce and navigation that were available to leading Americans, see James Madison's 1783 "Report on Books for Congress," in W. Hutchinson and W. Rachal (eds.), *The Papers of James Madison* (Chicago, 1969), 62-115.

[26]Nathaniel Wraxall, *A Tour through Some of the Northern Parts of Europe* (London, 1774); William Coxe, *Travels into Poland, Russia, Sweden and Denmark* (London, 1784); and John Carr, *A Northern Summer; or, Travels round the Baltic* (London, 1805).

[27]A.E. Buesching, *A New System of Geography* (London, 1762); and Buesching, *An Introduction to the Study of Geography, or, A General Survey of Europe* (London, 1778). Madison ordered the former for the Library of Congress.

[28]Daniel A. Rabuzzi, "Eighteenth-Century Commercial Mentalities as Reflected and Projected in Business Handbooks," *Eighteenth-Century Studies*, XXIX, No. 2 (1995-1996); and Jochen Hoock, "Kommunikationsstrukturen und raeumliche Erfahrung in der geschaeftlichen Welt des 18. Jahrhunderts," in M. Espagne and M. Werner (eds.), *Transferts: Les relations interculturelles dans l'espace Franco-allemand (XVIIIe et XIXe siècle)* (Paris, 1988).

classic *Traité Général du Commerce* was published in 1781, which contained detailed information about virtually every port-city in northern Europe.[29] In 1805, Joshua J. Oddy published his encyclopedic *European Commerce*, which included masses of data on the Baltic.[30] By the 1820s, even secondary ports in the Baltic, such as Stralsund in northern Germany, were well enough known to Americans to warrant separate entries in standard (*non*-commercial) reference works.[31]

Books and newspapers only sufficed as background sources of information on northern Europe; merchants depended more heavily on personal experience and private intelligence as they broached new markets there and elsewhere. In any event, those merchants who saw potential in the North hardly waited for others to write home about it first: more-or-less steady contact with that region began already in 1776. As early as June of that year, a Baltimorean ship loaded iron, deals, and hemp in St. Petersburg.[32] The New Englanders were the predominant pioneers, however; beginning no later than 1780, they corresponded with merchants in and then sent ships to St. Petersburg and Riga, Gothenburg, Copenhagen, and Hamburg.[33] For example, Minturn and Champlin, the firm for whom our Mr. Proud was supercargo, was very active in the

---

[29]Samuel Ricard (revised and expanded by Thomas Antoine de Marien), *Traité Général du Commerce* (Amsterdam, 1781). Ricard's first edition came out in 1686 and had been revised throughout the century. A 1799 edition published in Paris included the subtitle "revue et l'état actuel de commerce de l'Amérique."

[30]J.J. Oddy, *European Commerce* (London, 1805). The first American edition (1807) omitted the port statistics.

[31]See, for example, "Stralsund," s.v. in Abraham Rees, *The Cyclopedia, or Universal Dictionary of Arts, Sciences, and Literature* (Philadelphia, 1805-1825).

[32]Patrick, "Marylanders in the Nascent Russo-American Trade," 36.

[33]Crosby, *America, Russia, Hemp, and Napoleon*, 42-44; Phillips, *Salem and the Indies*, chap. 4; Fowler, "'Trye all Ports,'" 43 and 51; Raasch, "American Trade in the Baltic," 38; Benjamin Labaree, *Patriots and Partisans: The Merchants of Newburyport 1764-1815* (Cambridge, MA, 1962), 97; and James Hedges, *The Browns of Providence Plantation: The Colonial Years* (Cambridge, MA, 1952), 288 and 303.

early German and Danish trades.[34] (Both Minturn and Champlin were originally from Newport, before moving to New York; Champlin began his Baltic endeavors while still resident in Rhode Island.) Scandinavian and German merchants were just as eager to trade with the Americans: the first ships from Copenhagen, Bremen, and Hamburg arrived in the new US already in 1783.[35] Trade with Sweden and the Dutch Netherlands also got underway during the war. By 1801, with the restoration of direct trade between Antwerp and the US, Americans had established commercial ties to all the major ports of northern Europe.[36]

To enter a new market on anything more than a sporadic basis, the American merchant needed first to know merchants abroad: the key challenge was to make personal contacts and to build trusting relationships. Merchants, then as now, could pursue two general strategies. They could use a broad gauge approach, indiscriminately seeking contact with a large number of potential clients in hopes of obtaining at least a few positive responses. Or, they could narrow their focus and cultivate a handful of carefully selected opportunities, usually via third-party introductions and recommendations. Most merchants marketed both ways, at least at some point in their careers.

The former strategy was tedious and probably yielded only a low percentage of positive replies relative to the volume of inquiries. (To use a French example: in 1764, a Bordeaux merchant sent circulars to over 230 German and Central European houses, of which some thirty, or thirteen percent, became customers.)[37] It was, on the other hand, well-suited to a beginning merchant with few contacts, because he could glean names of possible customers at no or low cost from a wide variety of sources. It was, in other words, the eighteenth-century version of today's mass mailings, and just about as well received. A German merchant

---

[34]Lynne Withey, *Urban Growth in Colonial Rhode Island: Newport and Providence in the Eighteenth Century* (Albany, NY, 1984), 94-95.

[35]Raasch, "American Trade in the Baltic," 57; Pitsch, *Beziehungen Bremens*, 13-14; Guenter Moltmann, "Hamburgs Oeffnung nach Uebersee im spaeten 18. und im 19. Jahrhundert," in A. Herzig (ed.), *Das Alte Hamburg (1500-1848/49)* (Berlin, 1989), 52.

[36]Karel Veraghtert, "The Port of Antwerp and America, 1790-1900," in Reynolds (ed.), *Global Crossroads*, 53.

[37]Hoock, "Kommunikationsstrukturen u. raeumliche Erfahrung," 53.

resident in Nantes and trading to America during the first decade of the 1800s recounted that "the houses to whom they [i.e., circulars] were sent...had every reason to be sick of them;" one day his principal received a large packet from the US, only to discover inside, not the hoped-for consignment orders, but "some thirty of our circulars...which the recipients had amused themselves by re-enclosing to our address."[38]

Perforce by virtue of their being newcomers to North European commerce, however, American merchants after the war of independence used circulars widely despite the low yield. A typical example is the circular ("A New Scene of Commerce has opened with this Country") sent by the Baltimore firm Samuel and John Smith in early 1784 to thirty-eight firms in eighteen European port-cities.[39] (Indicative of colonial North America's trade patterns, all but six firms addressed were in England or southern Europe, with one firm each in Dunkirk, Ostende, Rotterdam, Amsterdam, Altona, and Hamburg.) In most cases, they merely drum for business in their accompanying letter, but in a few cases — such as with Henry van der Smissen and Sons in Altona — they actually start trading:

> We now do ourselves the Honor to commence a Corre-
> spondence with your very respectable House The most
> favorable Commendations of which we have from our
> mutual Friend, Wynkoop & Seiman [sic] whose Letter of
> Introduction we now inclose together with our Invoice
> and Bills Lading for twenty Hhd Tobo which you'll
> please sell immdly for our Account...We have shipp'd
> this small parcel of Tobacco merely to make trial of your
> Commerce If on trial it appears flattering, we shall be
> glad to join you in extending it...Unless the Merchts of

---

[38]Vincent Nolte, *Fifty Years in Both Hemispheres, or, Reminiscences of the Life of a Former Merchant* (New York, 1854), 47-48.

[39]MHS, Samuel Smith Papers (SP), Ms. 1152, Letterbook I, 15 April 1784. On this leading Baltimore firm, see Frank Cassell, *Merchant Congressman in the Young Republic: Samuel Smith of Maryland, 1752-1839* (Madison, WI, 1971); and Garitee, *Republic's Private Navy*, 21-23, 29 and 203.

your country fall on a mode of giving Credit no very extensive Commerce can exist with your Country.[40]

Note that the Smiths combine the mass circular with letters of reference where they can. Differing little from current custom, introductions from "a mutual Friend" can be crucial in gaining a hearing. As is known to anyone who spends time with eighteenth- and nineteenth-century merchant correspondence (or today's for that matter), such letters are legion in the archives. What we wish to know is whether American merchants were typically introduced to their north European counterparts by the British playing middleman once again, or whether the Yankee newcomers eschewed the British in favor of making their own contacts. The short answer is, a little of both; but what impresses most is how swiftly the Americans forged their own connections. Americans could not cut out the British middleman in finance and insurance, even if they had wished to, but then no merchant on the Continent could afford to do so either: by 1800 the "bill on London" and, to a lesser extent, the Lloyd's policy had become indispensable to global trade. Increasingly after 1783, however, the Americans took control of their own commodity transactions and built up the direct correspondence with north European merchants.

The selective cultivation of leading north European merchants took many forms, some quite elaborate and initially peripheral. I suggest that the West Indies, that cockpit of international trade in the eighteenth century, provided American merchants with many initial contacts among Dutch, Danish, and German traders, long before 1783. The prime importance of the Caribbean trades to the North American colonies and the cosmopolitan nature of commerce at entrepots such as St. Thomas and St. Eustatius are very well documented.[41] (Caribbean commerce would

---

[40]MHS, SP, Letterbook, I, Smith to van der Smissen and Sons, 12 May 1784. For information on this important Altona firm, see Karl Schwebel, *Bremer Kaufleute in den Freihaefen der Karibik* (Bremen, 1995), 181. Wynkoop and Siemen were merchants in Philadelphia with connections to Baltimore merchants. See, for example, MHS, Hall Papers (HP), Ms. 1300, account of wine sale by Wynkoop and Siemen for account of J. Spear, Baltimore merchant, 16 January 1787. The Philadelphia Siemen may have been from Hamburg.

[41]John Coatsworth, "American Trade with European Colonies in the Caribbean and South America, 1790-1812," *William and Mary Quarterly*, 3rd ser., XXIV, No. 2 (April 1967); J.L. Willis, "The Trade between North America and the Danish West Indies,

loom large even at the top level of American government: for example, the US's first Secretary of the Treasury, Alexander Hamilton, began his career as a clerk, then merchant, for a prominent St. Croix firm with strong ties to New York.)[42] It is likely, therefore, that many American merchants first became acquainted with their north European equivalents through the West Indian back door and that they parlayed this acquaintance into direct trade relations after 1783.

Extensive, systematic archival work is necessary to demonstrate this hypothesis conclusively, of course, but a few examples may suffice as suggestive illustrations. The Baltimore house of Samuel and John Smith, noted above in connection with the sending of circulars, began operations in 1784 upon the return of John from the West Indies. One of their West Indies correspondents in the 1790s (by which time they were known as S. Smith and Buchanan, and had become one of the US's leading firms), was Edward Hall Jr. at Aux Cayes on St. Domingue (today, Les Cayes in Haiti).[43] Hall in turn corresponded with St. Thomas firms such as Roetgers and Gaedicke, and Stricker and Peneke, all of whose principals had come from northwestern Germany and had strong ties to Bremen.[44] The Heinrich Ludwig Stricker in the firm above may well have been related to the John Stricker listed as a merchant in every Baltimore directory between 1799 and 1819 (Germans routinely anglicized their first names in Baltimore); the Baltimore Stricker, in any event, imported coffee from Aux Cayes in 1801.[45]

1756-1807" (Unpublished PhD thesis, Columbia University, 1963); Barbara Tuchman, *The First Salute* (New York, 1988), chaps. 1-2 and 7; Cornelis Ch. Goslinga, *The Dutch in the Caribbean and in the Guianas 1680-1791* (Assen, 1985); Willem Klooster, "Illicit Riches: The Dutch Trade in the Caribbean, 1648-1795" (Unpublished PhD thesis, University of Leiden ,1995); Theodor Link, *Flensburgs Ueberseehandel von 1755 bis 1807* (Neumuenster, 1959); and Schwebel, *Bremer Kaufleute*.

[42]Elkins and McKitrick, *Age of Federalism*, 94-95.

[43]MHS, HP, Letterbook (1798-1800), Hall to S. Smith and Buchanan, 6 April 1799. Here Hall seeks commissions from S. Smith and Buchanan's "friends" in Hamburg, Bremen and Copenhagen.

[44]Schwebel, *Bremer Kaufleute*, 246-254.

[45]MHS, Customs Records, Ms. 1209, "Entry for Import Only," 2 May 1801, for Stricker aboard *Intrepid*.

Hall also corresponded with James Grant Forbes, merchant at Port-au-Prince, who was almost certainly brother of John Murray Forbes, US consul in Copenhagen, Hamburg, and Stettin from 1801 to 1819.[46] Hall had other potential channels into northern Europe, should he have chosen to exploit these. For example, Hall apparently shipped coffee and sugar to Tilmann Rucker in Bremen.[47] Thirteen years earlier, in 1788, Hall had stayed with Matthew Rucker while on a trip to Bordeaux.[48] The Ruckers were almost certainly related to the important Hamburg firm Rucker and Wortman, which traded extensively with both the West Indies and with Bordeaux.[49] Hall also had close relations with "Charles" B. Kuhlmann, merchant first in Haiti and later in Bordeaux; Kuhlmann had a brother in Curacao and, I believe, either a brother or a cousin among the German wine-merchants resident in Bordeaux.[50]

Batavia may have been another source of indirect contacts for American merchants. Our supercargo Matthews' principal, the later mayor of Baltimore George Stiles, began his career as a captain for S. Smith and Buchanan (making numerous voyages, by the way, to St. Croix and St. Eustatius).[51] In 1799 and again in 1802, Stiles captained the *Samuel Smith* to Batavia on charter to the Dutch East Indian Committee

---

[46]MHS, HP, Letterbook (1802-1804), Hall to Forbes, 3 and 28 August, and 27 October 1802; and 2 January, 24 April and 15 May 1803. See Frederick Allis (ed.), *Guide to the Microfilm Edition of the Forbes Papers* (Boston, 1969); and Library of Congress, Manuscripts Division, Forbes Papers, part VI, reel XLII, 1, folders 10 and 14.

[47]MHS, HP, "Bill of Lading," 3 October 1801, for *Neutralitet*, Capt. Kleine.

[48]*Ibid.*, Hall to Pallard, Lullin, Charton and Co. (Marseilles), 9 October 1788.

[49]Schwebel, *Bremer Kaufleute*, 163-165; Wolfgang Henninger, *Johann Jakob v. Bethmann, 1717-1792; Kaufmann, Reeder und kaiserliche Konsul in Bordeaux* (Bochum, 1993), 57; and Pierre Jeannin, "La clientèle étrangère de la maison Schroeder et Schyler, de la Guerre de Sept ans à la Guerre d'Indépendance," *Bulletin du Centre d'histoire des espaces Atlantiques*, New ser., III (1987), 43 and 76.

[50]Henninger, *Von Bethmann*, 56 and 183.

[51]MHS, SP, Letterbook, II (1786-1794), master's orders, 1 January, 15 April and 22 December 1789.

(the post-French occupation successor to the VOC).[52] Other Baltimore and Salem merchants also chartered vessels to the Committee at that time. What relationships might American shipmasters and supercargoes have struck up among the north European commercial sorts who visited Batavia or, for that matter, Calcutta, the Ile-de-France, and Canton?

American merchants were not, however, forced to rely solely on such indirect sources of potential north European contacts. In particular, Baltimore quickly forged deep direct ties with Bremen and Hamburg, based at first on the tobacco which the "Hanseatics" had eagerly imported via Great Britain during colonial times, and then on a wide array of Caribbean goods for which Baltimore acted as entrepot. German linens formed the return cargoes. These ties arose as much from outreach by Bremen and Hamburg firms as from marketing by the Baltimoreans. Leading Bremen merchants such as C.D.A. Delius and F.J. Wichelhausen quickly found Baltimore correspondents, and then sent relatives over the Atlantic to help conduct their growing North American trade.[53] By 1800 numerous Bremeners and other Germans had established themselves in Baltimore (and, to a lesser extent, in Charleston, Philadelphia, and New York); many of them traded regularly with relatives and others back in the Old Country.[54] Firms original to Baltimore — S. Smith and Buchanan, for example — entertained visiting Bremen merchants who soon became fast correspondents.[55]

Bremeners were not the only north Europeans courting the new Americans. Two of the houses most instrumental in the early trade between the US and northern Europe — Niels Ryberg and Co. in

---

[52]E.S. van Eyck van Heslinga, *Van compagnie naar koopvardij; De scheepvaartverbinding van de Bataafse Republiek met de kolonien in Azie 1795-1806* (Amsterdam, 1988), 60 and 141.

[53]Pitsch, *Beziehungen Bremens*, 13, 15, 18 and 20; and William Fry, *Fry's Baltimore Directory* (Baltimore, 1812), for H.D. Wichelhausen, merchant.

[54]Examples include von Kapff and Brune/Brune and Dannemann: MHS, Clarke-von Kapff and Brune Papers, Ms. 1754; Garitee, *Republic's Private Navy*, 40; and Karl Schwebel, *Aus dem Tagebuch des Bremer Kaufmanns Franz Boeving (1773-1849)* (Bremen, 1974), 116. Friese: MHS, Friese Shipping Accts., Ms. 933. Karthaus: MHS, Keidel Papers, Ms. 2073. Also present: Goverts, Seekamp, Anspach, Graf, Kalkmann, Hurxthal, Hammer, and Hoppe.

[55]Schwebel, *Tagebuch Boeving*, 28.

Copenhagen, and John Parish and Co. in Hamburg — were exceedingly swift in exploring American opportunities.[56] Ryberg contacted Americans in Europe as early as 1782; he became, for example, a very important correspondent for Minturn and Champlin beginning in 1786, and introduced the Newport/New York firm to the St. Petersburg trade.[57] Parish began his American operations already during the War of Independence. (Parish had emigrated from England, but his firm was thoroughly German by the late 1700s.) He approached S. and J. Smith of Baltimore in 1783, for instance.[58] Our two supercargoes made wide use of Parish and Co. during their tumultuous time trying to get American goods past the restrictions of the Continental System. Mr. Proud, representing Minturn and Champlin, was so close to Parish that he frequently dined at Parish's home.[59] Mr. Matthews, supercargo for George Stiles' *Nonsuch*, could not claim the same degree of intimacy, but did make Parish his very first contact upon his arrival in Europe.[60]

The Germans, Dutch, and Danes could not, of course, supplant the British, nor did Americans want them to do so. American merchants saw the northern continentals as supplemental sources of business; the newcomers wanted the widest possible set of contacts to work with, and seem to have cooperated happily with all parties so long as they gained entree into the north European markets. In any case, British merchants worked closely with merchants throughout northern Europe. During the war years, and especially during the first years of the Orders in Council embargoes and the Continental System, places such as Cowes on the Isle

---

[56]Rasch, "American Trade in the Baltic," 57; Crosby, *America, Russia, Hemp, and Napoleon,* 55; and Richard Ehrenberg, *Das Haus Parish in Hamburg* (Jena, 1925), 23-24.

[57]Withey, *Urban Growth,* 95.

[58]MHS, SP, Letterbook, I, Smith to Parish and Thompson, Hamburg, 17 August 1784.

[59]MHS, RC, box 5, Proud to wife Eliza, 18 December 1809.

[60]MHS, *Nonsuch* Letterbook, Matthews to Parish, 18 June 1810. Matthews regretted that, due to detention by Danish privateers, he was unable to present "those testimonials, previous to a correspondence, which I should otherwise have considered indispensable."

of Wight and British-occupied Heligoland became crucial listening posts and warehouses for American merchants shipping to northern Europe. As it was typically formulated, a ship sailed from, say, Boston bound for "Cowes and a Market, which Market will probably be to Rotterdam, Amsterdam, Hamburgh, or Bremen."[61]

Certainly, in emphasizing the creation of direct American trade links with northern Europe, we do not want to ignore or underestimate the continuing role of the British merchants. As one commentator wrote in 1784: "England may be considered as a great Inn, on the road from America to the Northern parts of Europe, where the Americans may repose themselves, till they procure knowledge of the best market to send their goods."[62] London and Liverpool firms appear prominently in the correspondence of American merchants doing business in northern Europe, with Baring Bros. and Co. probably most frequently consulted.[63] Also important were Jas. McKenzie and Alex. Glennie (London), and Cropper Benson/Rathbone Benson (Liverpool).[64] In 1801, the American consul in Hamburg went so far as to assert that "almost every ship is

---

[61]Library of Congress, Manuscript Division, Bourne Papers, IX, Isaac Mansfield, Marblehead, to Bourne, 4 February 1801; T. Auldjo, US consul at Cowes, to Bourne, 28 February 1801; *ibid.*, X, Jan H.C. Heneken, Philadelphia, to Bourne, 10 May 1801, stating that most US ships bound for Holland stopped at Cowes.

[62]Richard Champion, *Considerations on the Present Situation of Great Britain and the United States of America* (2nd ed., London, 1784), 106, quoted in Kenneth Morgan, "The Organization of the Colonial American Rice Trade," *William and Mary Quarterly*, 3rd ser., LII, No. 3 (July 1995), 450.

[63]MHS, RC, box 6, Proud Letterbook, I, Proud to Baring, 22 June 1810; McMaster, *Stephen Girard*, II, 79 and 82-85; and Philip Ziegler, *The Sixth Great Power: Barings 1762-1929* (London, 1988), 61-66.

[64]MHS, McBlair Papers, Ms. 1355, box 6, folder marked "Michael McBlair, Correspondence from 1800-1826," letters to MacKenzie and Glennie, 3 October and 20 November 1800; MHS, SP, Letterbook 3, Smith and Buchanan to Rathbone and Benson, Liverpool, 1 September 1794 and 19 January 1795; MHS, RC, box 6, Proud Letterbook, II,, Proud to Cropper Benson, Liverpool, 3 August 1810. For Cropper, Benson, Rathbone, see Stanley Chapman, *Merchant Entreprise in Britain* (Cambridge, 1992), 73, 82-89, 94 and 104.

under direction of London correspondents."[65] Nor should we overlook the frequent interaction of American merchants and supercargoes with British or British-origin firms throughout northern Europe itself, for example, with Belfour, Ellah, Rainals and Co. at Elsinore (the crucial chokepoint at the Danish Straits, rivalled only by Gibraltar and the Texel as a center of maritime intelligence), with Low and Smith in Gothenburg, or with Cramer and Smith in St. Petersburg.[66]

Yet, if Great Britain was "a great Inn," the Americans quickly set up hostels of their own on the continent. Already in 1783, leading American merchants came to the Netherlands to open offices.[67] And they began to network among themselves and with other Americans, sometimes at the highest levels of government. For example, Robert Gilmor of Baltimore co-founded in 1783 a short-lived American company in Amsterdam, before returning to the Chesapeake to establish one of the most important firms in the young US. His introduction to the powerful Amsterdam merchants Wilh. and Jan Willink came from none other than future-president John Adams, with whom Gilmor breakfasted in Paris (the Willinks were in the very first syndicate issuing credit to the new-born US, and had become very well known to Adams in that connection).[68]

Perhaps no American merchant was better at networking than Sylvanus Bourne, consul in Amsterdam in the early 1800s. A native of Massachusetts, Bourne had married a Baltimorean. He quickly made contact with Bremen merchants such as Wichelhausen and Delius, who

---

[65]J. Pitcairn to S. Bourne, 22 January 1801, quoted in Winter, *Amsterdamschen handel*, I, 131.

[66]MHS, RC, box 5, Proud to Eliza Proud, 9 November and 18 December 1809; box 6, Proud to Balfour Ellah Rainal [sic], 20 March 1810; Proud to Cramer Brothers, St. Petersburg, 18 and 29 May, 26 June, 1 July and 24 August 1810; Proud to Low and Smith 26 June, 21 August and 17 October 1810. For Cramer and Smith, see Marten Buist, *At spes non Fracta: Hope and Co. 1770-1815* (The Hague, 1974), 211, 220 and 511. For Low and Smith, see Bertil Andersson, *Goeteborgs Handlande Borgerskap...1806-1825* (Gothenburg, 1977), 56.

[67]Winter, *Amsterdamschen handel*, I, 92.

[68]MHS, Robert Gilmor, Jr. Papers, Ms. 387, reel 2, Family Memorandum Book; and Winter, *Amsterdamschen handel*, I, 135.

would have been known from their Baltimore connections (see above).[69] Likewise, he communicated with leading Hamburg houses such as Matthiessen and Sillem, and Luis and Jencquel, and with the largely American-oriented firm Homberg Homberg Freres in Le Havre.[70] Most importantly, however, Bourne worked closely with fellow Americans to compete head-to-head against both the British and the Dutch in obtaining American-sourced consignments. In this he was ably assisted by two of his wife's uncles: Baltimore merchant William Taylor, and former merchant, then president of the Bank of Baltimore, George Salmon.

Taylor consigned large quantities of tobacco and other products to Bourne, and both Taylor and Salmon marketed hard on Bourne's behalf in efforts to channel consignments to their in-law and away from other merchants in Amsterdam.[71] For instance, Salmon introduced to Bourne in 1801 Humphrey Pierce, "a very respectable Merchant in this place [i.e., Baltimore] and a shipper of coffee to your address on board the Vessel that carries this letter: it may be much to the advantage of your House by cultivating this friendship of Mr. Pierce, in attending closely to his interests, and commands, respecting this his first consignment to you — it will give me much pleasure to learn from him hereafter, that you have conducted this business to his satisfaction."[72] A month later, describing his efforts to get leading Baltimore merchants John McKim and Jeremiah Yellot to consign to Bourne, Salmon wrote: "I shall not miss an opportunity my Dear Friend to promote the interest of your House, Two or Three old Houses in your City interferes too often, I don't know what Kunckle has done in other places [e.g., Philadelphia, New York, Boston], but I am

---

[69]Library of Congress, Manuscript Division, Bourne Papers, VII, F.J. Wichelhausen to Bourne, 11 December 1799; and F. Delius to Bourne, 18 December 1799.

[70]*Ibid.*, IX, Homberg to Bourne, 18 April 1801; Matthiessen to Bourne, 24 April, 1801; and X, Luis to Bourne, 22 May 1801.

[71]*Ibid.*, VII, Salmon to Bourne, 20 February 1800; Salmon to Rebecca Bourne, 30 June 1800; VIII, Bourne to unknown, 28 November 1800; Salmon to Bourne, 16 December 1800; XIII, Taylor to Bourne, 12 October 1803; Taylor to Bourne, 13 February 1804; and Salmon to Bourne, 28 February 1804.

[72]*Ibid.*, IX, Salmon to Lange and Bourne, 15 April 1801.

sure he has prevailed but little here."[73] "Kunckle" and the other "old Houses" (probably Willink, and Crommelin) were the venerable Amsterdammers themselves, forced to compete hard against an upstart Yankee in their very midst for choice American business.

Relatively few Americans took the step taken by Bourne and established themselves in Europe for any long period of time; until sometime after 1815, there was no permanent network of American factors and merchants abroad, such as the Scots and the English had developed outside Great Britain (or the Germans outside Germany).[74] Perhaps the start-up and overhead costs were too great for many Americans. Perhaps American merchants were wary of specific long-term commitments — a commercial equivalent of the US foreign policy to avoid entanglement? — and preferred instead opportunistic flexibility. Of course, with greater flexibility came not only greater possible spot-market returns, but also the risk that European correspondents would take advantage of Americans whom they saw as mercenary or only semi-serious short-termers. One catches a whiff of this risk in Smith and Buchanan's complaint to a new consignment agent in 1795 that they had been "extremely ill-treated" in Hamburg previously and had considered declining further business in that port, but that they had "been induced to ship to your address a very small parcel of coffee" as a cautious, almost begrudging, re-entry into the Hamburg market.[75]

What American merchants seeking markets in northern Europe created was thus neither a great inn nor more than a handful of hostels but an ever-shifting series of bivouacs which sprang up wherever profit beckoned. Manueuvering adroitly to circumvent both the Orders in Council and the Continental System, for example, Americans congregated for a season on Heligoland and Sylt, in Toenning and Varel and Emden,

---

[73]*Ibid.*, X, Salmon to Bourne, 30 May 1801.

[74]Cf. Chapman, *Merchant Enterprise*, 131: "Until at least the middle of the nineteenth century, US firms preferred the 'adventure' kind of enterprise, with the ship's captain fulfilling the main entrepreneurial role."

[75]MHS, SP, Letterbook, III Smith to Lorent Am Endre and Co., Hamburg, , 24 June 1795.

in Hamburg, Copenhagen, and Gothenburg.[76] The Minturn and Champlin supercargo Proud described Heligoland in 1809 as: "this curious spot of *Rock*...barren as the Place is by nature it is at present a Place of much consequence and crowded with merchants."[77] Doing business in Toenningen and Hamburg, Proud depicts a bustling community of merchants from Baltimore, Philadelphia, New York and other American places.[78] Partly owing to their monolingualism, however, and partly it seems from choice, the Americans tended to stick together. Lodging over the winter in Hamburg with a fellow Baltimorean, Proud admitted that he had little "intercourse with the Inhabitants."[79] He observed that:

> ...if we Americans are but seldom to be found in those
> domestic Parties [i.e., Hamburg balls and 'masks'] I must
> do the Hamburgers justice to suppose it more owing to a
> Backwardness on our part than in a want of Hospitality
> on theirs — for being ignorant of their language and
> differing somewhat in manners, we are naturally disposed
> to decline rather than look for their Civilities...[80]

What the Americans did look for were profits. Towards that end, Proud was febrile in his efforts to find and exploit new mercantile contacts. Forced to visit Copenhagen when one of Minturn and Champlin's ships was seized by Danish privateers, Proud initiated a relationship, praising: "the house of Dunsfelt & Co...to whom I hope you will both take an opportunity of making suitable mention. That house is one of the most solid and respectable at that place [Copenhagen]...I must

---

[76]The first five places were not normally sites of trade but became so, as loopholes in the Continental System. Oddy, *European Commerce*, 345, noted in 1805: "Tonningen was scarcely known to the world, till the blockade of the rivers Elbe and Weser, by which circumstance it has got into great notoriety."

[77]MHS, RC, box 5, Proud to Eliza Proud, 16 July 1809.

[78]*Ibid.*, 21 July, 28 August and 18 October 1809.

[79]*Ibid.*, 18 December 1809.

[80]*Ibid.*, 16 February 1810.

request that you will on any occasion remember them."[81] The *Nonsuch* supercargo Matthews had a similar experience: while likewise defending his vessel from privateers' claims in the Danish Admiralty Court, Matthews was introduced to Duntzfelt, and was pleased with their service.[82]

Both Proud and Matthews were introduced to Duntzfelt by the Hamburg firm of Parish (see above). Increasingly, however, the Americans were able to dispense with even a north European middleman. For example, Matthews started his correspondence with the important Koenigsberg firm J.C. Jacobi, by noting that his principal Stiles was a "particular friend" of Smith and Buchanan "with whose respectable House you are acquainted and who furnished me with a letter to you."[83] Stiles had started as a captain for Smith and Buchanan; Baltimoreans were helping each other crack the Baltic markets. And they started to do so very early, not just as a result of the hothouse atmosphere during the French Revolutionary-Napoleonic era. Smith and Buchanan themselves, for instance, were introduced to the leading Hamburg firm Vogt and Sieveking in 1789 by another one of Baltimore's largest shipowners.[84]

By the early years of the nineteenth century, commercial networks created by and for Americans were so strong that even Amsterdammers began to tap into them. In other words, in some cases Americans were not only able to eschew European marketing expertise but could even offer some of their own to the Europeans. For instance, Amsterdam merchant T.H. Backer wrote to Baltimore merchant Ambrose Clarke in 1804: "I am very thankfull and under great obligations to my friends Messrs. Levering

---

[81]*Ibid.*, Box 6, letterbook #2, Proud to Minturn and Champlin, 21 July 1810. For Dunzfelt & Co., see Ole Feldbaek, *India Trade under the Danish Flag, 1772-1808* (Copenhagen, 1969), 169 ff.

[82]MHS, *Nonsuch* Letterbook, Matthews to Stiles, 24 June 1810; Matthews to Parish, 7 July 1810; and Matthews to Duntzfelt, 24 August and 18 September 1810.

[83]*Ibid.*, Matthews to Jacobi 23 June 1810. On Jacobi, see F. Gause, *Die Gesch. d. Stadt Koenigsberg* (2 vols., Cologne, 1968), II, 183 and 189.

[84]MHS, SP, Letterbook, II, Smith to "Voght and Seiveking," 11 November 1789. The "mutual friend" was Charles Ghequiere, on whom see Geoffrey Gilbert, "Maritime Enterprise in the New Republic: Investment in Baltimore Shipping, 1789-1793," *Business History Review*, LVIII, No. 1 (Spring 1984), 20.

and Mayer and Brantz for the favor of recommending you to my house, and I hope to convince you by my attentions for your interest that you will have no reason to complain of their introduction."[85] Levering and Brantz were both Baltimore merchants; Brantz was born in Stuttgart, and had probably been a merchant in Amsterdam before moving on to Baltimore.[86]

In summary: American merchants in the period 1783-1815 did not, in northern Europe at least, so much cut out the British middleman, as reduce him to one of several vectors for entry into new markets. American merchants were restlessly proactive in their attempts to insinuate themselves into the centuries-old markets of northern Europe, and should be credited with a considerable amount of ingenuity and grit in those attempts. I am not, however, proposing that we consider American mercantile prowess at that time as what has been called a "romanticized...legend."[87] On the other hand, it is unfair to denigrate the success of American merchants as being nothing more than dumb luck resulting from their neutral status during the French Revolutionary-Napoleonic wars.[88] It is worth noting that Yankee tactics for entering north European markets differed significantly from those used in trading with other areas. In Latin America, for example, American merchants cultivated relations with high-ranking officials rather than with local merchants, and relied upon relatives living as merchants on the foreign

---

[85]MHS, Clarke-von Kapff and Brune Papers, Ms. 1754, box 4, folder 18, Backer to Clarke, 20 November 1804, referring to a first-time consignment by the latter of clayed sugars.

[86]MHS, Dielman-Hayward Biographical file, s.v. "Lewis Brantz;" note the existence of the Amsterdam firm Couderc Brantz Changuigon. Several Leverings (Peter, Nathan), merchants in Baltimore, c. 1800-1815. Note that our *Nonsuch* supercargo Matthews married a Levering. Mayer unidentified.

[87]Goldin and Lewis, "Exports in American Economic Growth," 22. The authors are persuasive in downplaying the overall impact on the US economy of merchant activity overseas between 1793 and 1807.

[88]Cf. John Forbes, "European Wars and Boston Trade, 1783-1815," *New England Quarterly*, XI (1938), 719: "This extraordinary burst of prosperity was artificial and entirely the result of fortuitous circumstances. It took no superabundance of business acumen for the Yankee trader to seize the opportunity to profit by the embarrassment of the really first-class maritime powers and absorb their trade."

scene; they did not do these things in the north Atlantic and Baltic trades.[89]

Luck, foresight, daring, tenacity, and charm all played a role in this story.[90] Supercargo Matthews, who for all his lamentations appears to have turned a tidy profit for his principal Stiles, captured something of the mixture: "I have met so many adverse circumstances during this voyage that at present they go over me like a gentle breeze, and all the gales of misfortune can not produce a heavy swell in my spirits."[91] Supercargo Proud, who likewise seems to have executed well for Minturn and Champlin, writes from Hamburg of his "busy Cares and Perplexities," but then pulls up his braces: "I must conclude, to go and talk about Coffee, Tobacco, etc. on the Exchange..."[92] And there, I think, we too should conclude.

---

[89]Linda Salvucci, "Anglo-American Merchants and Stratagems for Success in Spanish Imperial Markets, 1783-1807," in J. Barbier and A. Kuethe (eds.), *The North American Role in the Spanish Imperial Economy 1760-1819* (Manchester, 1984).

[90]Cf. Stuart Bruchey, "Success and Failure Factors: American Merchants in Foreign Trade in the Eighteenth and Early Nineteenth Centuries," *Business History Review*, XXXII, No. 3 (Autumn 1958).

[91]MHS, *Nonsuch* Letterbook, Matthews to Peterkin, Copenhgan, 5 April 1811.

[92]MHS, RC, box 5, Proud to Eliza Proud, 19 and 22 June 1810.

A Vital Link in Wartime:
The Organization of a Trade and Shipping Network Between the United States and Bordeaux, 1793-1815

Silvia Marzagalli[1]

The outbreak of war in Europe in 1793 provided a notoriously unique opportunity to the shipping and trade of the United States, which benefited greatly from American neutrality. Exports increased from $17 million dollars in 1791 to $93 million in 1801 and $108 million in 1807.[2] Scholars have been interested primarily in the short and long-term impact of this growth on the economy of the United States. Historians have also paid attention to the impressive development of shipping activities in major port cities and the ventures of captains and seamen across the world oceans. However, little interest has been paid to the rapid establishment and consolidation of new trade networks. This paper will analyze the extension and the organization of American shipping and trade to Bordeaux which, on the eve of the French Revolution, was the major French port.

Franco-American relations in these years have been studied essentially within the framework of diplomatic history.[3] Insofar as trade between the two countries is concerned, only certain specific aspects, such

[1]I would like to thank the Institut für Europäische Geschichte, Mainz (Germany); the Peabody Essex Museum, Salem, Massachusetts; and the John Carter Brown Library, Providence, Rhode Island, which have greatly facilitated this research project through their grants, and Gayle Brunelle who helped correct this manuscript.

[2]*American State Papers, Commerce and Navigation* (reprint, Wilmington, 1973), I, 153; II, 85; and III, 28.

[3]Alexander De Conde, *The Quasi-War: The Politics and Diplomacy of the Undeclared War with France, 1797-1801* (New York, 1966); Henry Blumenthal, *France and the United States: Their Diplomatic Relations, 1789-1914* (Chapel Hill, 1970); Albert Hall Bowman, *The Struggle for Neutrality: Franco-American Diplomacy During the Federalist Era* (Knoxville, 1974); and Clifford L. Egan, *Neither Peace Nor War: Franco-American Relations, 1803-1812* (Baton Rouge, 1983).

as the license trade or privateering, have received comprehensive study.[4] Scholars who analyzed the growth of American trade were understandably not particularly interested in commerce to France, since it played only a limited role in the expansion of the foreign trade of the United States.[5] One could expect that French scholars would show more interest in these matters. However, even if Paul Butel and Jeanne Chase have underlined the American presence in the trade of Bordeaux, we still lack a detailed analysis of the role played by the Americans during the French Wars.[6] In particular, while French and American merchants did establish some commercial relations before 1793, the rapidity with which the trade and shipping network between the United States and Bordeaux was organized after the outbreak of the war is intriguing, and calls for explanation.

It is relatively easy to understand *why* this trade grew: the opportunities for profit in war time were appealing enough to motivate merchants, and the increasing difficulties of European neutral carriers gave North American merchants a strong comparative advantage. It is of course possible to delineate the evolution of trade during this period and even to identify the irregularities in its patterns, thus analyzing *when* and *how much* this trade grew. Yet Franco-American commercial relations in this period cannot be reduced to a purely quantitative analysis of shipping and trade. At best, the data can only provide us with the necessary framework by which to understand *how* merchants, both in France and in the United States, organized their trade networks in order to face the difficulties of war and maintain international exchanges. What strategies

---

[4]Frank Edgar Melvin, *Napoleon's Navigation System: A Study of Trade Control During the Continental Blockade* (1919; reprint, New York, 1970); and Ulane Bonnel, *La France, les États-Unis et la guerre de course, 1797-1815* (Paris, 1961).

[5]The most comprehensive study of American foreign trade is still Anne Clauder, *American Commerce as Affected by the Wars of the French Revolution and Napoleon, 1793-1812* (1932; reprint, Philadelphia, 1972). See also the relevant chapters of E. Johnson, *et al.*, *History of the Domestic and Foreign Commerce of the United States* (2 vols., 1915; reprint, New York, 1964), I.

[6]Paul Butel, "Guerre et commerce sous la Révolution et l'Empire: les négociants français et le 'refuge' américain," *Revue d'histoire économique et sociale*, LV (1977), 433-451; and Jeanne Chase, "War on Trade and Trade in War: Stephen Jumel and New York Maritime Commerce (1793-1815)," *Bulletin du Centre d'histoire des Espaces Atlantiques*, IV (1988), 111-161.

did they use in order to set up this trade network? And who took the initiative?

Shipping and Trade between the United States and Bordeaux

Before any attempt is made to answer these questions, it is necessary to understand that any study of Franco-American trade relations and of American shipping to France in this period is complicated by the poor state of quantitative sources, both on the American and on the French side. Port and custom house records are often incomplete, and even when they exist, they do not provide an exhaustive picture. American custom records were organized on a uniform national basis only in 1789 and have not always been preserved. Those of Boston, for instance, are lost, and while contemporary commercial newspapers offer very succinct information on clearances and entrances, they cannot provide a very reliable substitute.[7]

Even when the records of clearances and entrances for a specific American port are provided, they offer, by definition, evidence only on the *direct* trade between the two countries. As far as the role of American shipping for Bordeaux or for any specific area is concerned, these records are inadequate, since they do not give any indication of the ports the ship might have visited after it sailed from the United States and before it returned. The ship *Charlotte*, Samuel Morgan master, for instance, cleared from Providence to Bilbao at the beginning of October 1801, but her cargo was in fact sold in Bordeaux, where she arrived on 8 February 1802. She left France two months later, selling the return cargo in St. Thomas and Port-au-Prince.[8] The ship was therefore recorded by the Providence Custom House neither as clearing to France nor as coming from there.[9] Official US sources are therefore unable to provide a

---

[7]Newspapers underestimate port activities in Boston by about twenty percent according to John D. Forbes, "The Port of Boston, 1783-1815" (Unpublished PhD thesis, Harvard University, 1937).

[8]John Carter Brown Library (JCBL), Brown Family Papers (BFP), Box 52, Ship *Charlotte*, V__C52.

[9]National Archives (NA), Records of the United States, Record Group (RG) 36, Port of Providence, Entries and Clearances, Custom House, III (microfilm copy at the Rhode Island Historical Society).

complete picture of American trade to France. Of course, family papers can often provide vital complementary information, as was the case with the *Charlotte*. Yet this kind of record exists only in a few instances, despite the richness of American merchants' papers.

Nevertheless, and despite the incomplete nature of the sources, it is possible to reconstruct the main features of American shipping and trade to Bordeaux from 1783 to 1815 and to discover that the role of American shipping to France was in fact much more important than simply ensuring direct trade between the United States and France. American vessels did much of the carrying trade within Europe as well as between Europe and the Indian Ocean, and these voyages were not necessarily recorded by American customs. In order to evaluate the importance of American shipping and trade for Bordeaux, one must complete the information provided by American statistics and records with French sources. As French administration was disrupted by the numerous political changes which took place between 1789 and Napoleon's *coup d'état* in 1799, the Paris National Archives do not provide complete sets of data. Moreover, fire destroyed the Bordeaux port records in 1919, so that evidence of clearances and entrances for the Revolutionary and Napoleonic period are extremely scarce.

We do, however, have the records of the American consul in Bordeaux which have not yet been used by historians.[10] From May 1797 to 1816, he recorded every American ship entering Bordeaux.[11] The *Charlotte*, for instance, appears as entering Bordeaux from Bilbao and she cleared on 26 March 1802 for New Orleans. Unfortunately the consular records for 1805 and almost entirely those of 1806, which probably composed an entire volume, are missing. Each record states, among other things, the name of the ship, the date of her arrival in Bordeaux, the names of the shipowners and their residence, the port of clearance and the detailed nature of the inward cargo. This declaration is signed by the

---

[10]Charles A. Keene, "American Shipping and Trade, 1798-1820: The Evidence from Leghorn," *Journal of Economic History,* XXXVIII, No. 3 (1978), 681-700, evaluated similar records for Livorno, Italy.

[11]The volume containing the records from May 1797 to December 1804 is in private hands. I would like to express my gratitude to Mr. L. Marcus, who provided me with precious information from this volume. The volume for November 1806 to 1816 is at NA, RG 84, C20, vol. 215.

captain. When the ship left Bordeaux, the consul noted the date of departure, the destination and the outward cargo. These records represent therefore an extremely valuable, uniform source, which provide information on the main features of the American shipping to Bordeaux, even if it is necessary to complete the missing years with other sources.

The Evolution of American Shipping and Trade to Bordeaux

As the aim of this paper is to delineate trade networks, any quantitative analysis of shipping will be limited to a general framework which will allow us to understand the context and the irregular patterns of this trade.

The commercial relationship between France and the United States officially began on 6 February 1778, when the two countries signed a treaty of alliance and commerce. During the War of American Independence, France supplied the thirteen colonies mainly with arms and munitions. From 1778 to 1783, the United States exported to France two and a half times fewer goods than they imported from France.[12]

Despite great expectations in France for the future development of Franco-American commercial relations — both from the merchants and from the government — trade between the United States and France remained insignificant in the first decade after peace was restored in 1783. The French quickly discovered that they could not possibly compete with British merchants in the American market. French cargoes were often inadequate to meet local demand in the United States. Moreover, French merchants also lacked capital to sell on long-term credit, as the British did. Once they understood that Americans were not disposed to buy, at exorbitant prices, old-fashioned manufactured goods which they could no longer sell in Europe, the French merchants gave priority to traditional trade within the French colonial empire, a trade they knew well and which was profitable.

---

[12]Edmond Buron, "Statistics on Franco-American Trade, 1778-1806," *Journal of Economic and Business History*, IV (1932), 571-579; and J.F. Stover, "French-American Trade during the Confederation," *North Carolina Historical Review*, XXXV (1958), 399-414. On this early phase of trade relations between Bordeaux and the United States, see Mac Carvin Lowes, "Les premières relations commerciales entre Bordeaux et les Etats-Unis d'Amérique (1775-1789)," *Revue historique de Bordeaux*, XX (1927), 214-226; and XXI (1928), 31-39, 75-90 and 128-140.

Ironically, in this context the Americans were perceived more as a serious rival than as a possible partner. The Exclusive system gave French merchants a monopoly on trade with overseas French colonies, and they were determined to exploit it. Yet American traders were interloping more and more frequently in the French West Indies and threatening this monopoly. On 29 January 1785, the Parliament of Bordeaux protested to the French King against the 1784 decision to open some colonial ports to American vessels: "We observe with pain that the Nation ...with which we had hoped to establish advantageous relations for our agriculture and industry flows with its vessels [to] our Islands and invade them with its products."[13] Indeed, in 1789-1790 American exports to the French West Indies were greater than to France.

The fragility of Franco-American relations between 1783 and the French Revolution is reflected by the data concerning this trade. French exports towards the United States dropped at the end of the war from $2.3 million (average 1781-1783) to less than $400,000 (average 1784-1789). American exports to France, on the contrary, rose from less than one million dollars to two million dollars.[14] If France had enjoyed a positive balance of trade during the war, this was no more the case after 1783. It is true that French statistics of this time are an inadequate instrument to measure American trade, as probably a great number of French ships going to the United States officially registered the French Caribbean as their destination.[15] Unfortunately, there are no national statistics for the United States before 1789 to correct this possible distortion of French values. However, we can reasonably assume that Franco-American trade in the 1780s was not particularly important, neither for France nor for the United States. According to American sources, exports to France

---

[13]*Lettre du Parlement de Bordeaux au Roi au sujet de l'Arrêt du Conseil d'Etat du 30 août 1784 concernant le commerce étranger dans les Iles françaises de l'Amérique* (Paris, 1785).

[14]Buron, "Statistics." One dollar is approximately five French *livres tournois* or *francs*.

[15]This has been shown for Nantes by Jean Meyer, "Les difficultés du commerce franco-américain vues de Nantes, 1776-1790," *French Historical Studies*, XI, No. 2 (1979), 159-183.

represented only eight percent of the export of United States exports to Europe in 1791.[16]

This picture changed profoundly once war broke out between France and Great Britain in 1793. That war radically disrupted the traditional trade patterns of Bordeaux, and American shipping began to play an important role for France. This was quite consistent with the pattern throughout the eighteenth century, when each new war provoked drastic changes in European maritime trade. The commercial policies of the belligerents and the risk of privateering induced French merchants to use neutral ships. It was in fact generally admitted that a neutral flag protected the cargo from seizure. Trade between enemy countries went on, but cargoes were first brought into a neutral port and trans-shipped, so as to efface any trace of their origin. Moreover, a ship could show a neutral clearance in case she met a belligerent cruiser on her way to Europe. This was known as the so-called "broken-voyage technique."

Thanks to the experience of previous wars, both French merchants and neutral carriers were thus prepared to cope with trade difficulties. American merchants, in particular, were able to reorganize oversea flows of merchandise to their profit and to assume a large role in the West Indian re-export trade to Europe. No less than forty-two American ships arrived in Bordeaux in the first semester of 1793.[17]

We lack detailed information on American shipping to Bordeaux from 1793 to May 1797.[18] However, both French and American national statistics show that 1795 was an excellent year and that trade was also very intensive in 1796 and 1797. In this period, Bordeaux trade recovered considerably from previous difficulties.[19] From 22 May to the end of

---

[16]*Statistical Tables Exhibiting the Commerce of the United States with European Countries from 1790 to 1890* (Washington, 1893), VIII-XIII.

[17]NA, T 164, reel 1, Dispatches from the United States Consul in Bordeaux, J. Fenwick to the American Secretary of State, semi-annual list of American ships, 1 January to 30 June 1793.

[18]The consular register of vessels, 1790 to 1797, NA, RG84, C20, vol. 214, is missing.

[19]Paul Butel, "Les difficultés du commerce maritime bordelais sous le Directoire. Exemple de l'adaptation à la conjoncture de guerre maritime," *Congrès national de Sociétés Savantes*, XCIV (2 vols., Paris, 1969), II, 331-344.

December 1797, eighty-eight American ships entered Bordeaux. In the late summer of 1798, however, the Americans almost ceased to sail to France, as diplomatic relations between the two countries worsened. Since no one could predict whether this would finally lead to war, American merchants deserted the French coasts and concentrated instead on other European countries. If only seven American ships entered Bordeaux in 1799 and two in 1800, other neutral ships, such as Danish and Hanseatic, continued their activities, filling the vacuum left by the absent Americans in trade with French ports.

After Napoleon and the United States settled their differences at the end of the year 1800, American trade with Bordeaux revived. The consul in Bordeaux recorded 173 entries of American vessels for 1801, an average of a ship every two days. By March 1802, however, peace was restored in Europe. France could trade again with her colonies, without having to apply to neutral carriers, and this probably explains the decrease in the number of American vessels entering Bordeaux in this period: on the average, this meant about two ships a week as long as the peace lasted.

In May 1803, Europe was again at war. The conflict between France and Great Britain became more and more intense, and there was an escalation in the commercial policies of the belligerents. As a result, American shipping became essential to French merchants. In fact, as Napoleon expanded his dominion on continental Europe, the number of other neutral flags continuously diminished. Between 1803 and 1807, France either occupied or indirectly controlled all major European ports. Hamburg, which during the 1790s had become the major entrepôt of northern Europe, fell under French control in November 1806, just two days before Napoleon published the decree ordering a continental blockade against British trade.

As a result, by 1807, the United States had become the major commercial partner of France as far as imports were concerned. In that year, 197 American ships entered Bordeaux. The market was apparently profitable, as some merchants did not hesitate to ship their vessels again to France as soon as they came back. The brig *Belleisle* of Salem, John Felt master, was cleared by customs, for instance, to sail from Salem to Bordeaux on 19 September 1806 with a cargo of sugar, cacao and oil, returned from Bordeaux on 5 February 1807 with a cargo of brandy, wine and manufactured goods valued at $20,000, cleared customs again for Bordeaux on 7 March with sugar, pepper and oil, and returned safely from Bordeaux on 13 July 1807 with brandy, wine and dry-goods, valued again at around $20,000.[20] The brig had made two direct voyages in less than nine months.

The prosperous trade between the United States and France after the rupture of the Peace of Amiens came to an abrupt end in 1808. In response to British Orders-in-Council of November 1807, which put the whole European continent under blockade and obliged all ships to stop in England and pay duties, Napoleon declared that any vessel coming from England should be seized. As there was no room left for neutral trade, President Jefferson laid an embargo upon American shipping and closed American ports to European vessels. Only twenty-one American ships entered Bordeaux from 1808 to 1810. It was not until December 1810 that President Madison again authorized trade between the United States and the French Empire. Around forty American ships per year entered Bordeaux in 1811 and in 1812. Still, this trade was essential for the French town. In 1811, for instance, three-quarters of Bordeaux wine exports were bound to the United States, though it should also be noted that wine production was particularly poor that year.[21]

The decline in trade was even greater after 1812, when the outbreak of war between the United States and Great Britain made it dangerous for American ships to venture across the Atlantic. As well, Napoleon had authorized trade between France and Great Britain. American merchants, who now had to pay a high premium to insure their ships and cargo, could no longer compete in the sale of colonial produce. As a consequence of this change in the international context, twenty-five American ships arrived in Bordeaux in 1813, and only eleven in 1814. This was a far cry from the hundreds of American vessels which came yearly to Bordeaux before 1807.

From 1793 to 1815, France played a moderate role in United States foreign trade, in terms both of American imports and American exports. Only in 1795 did American exports to France represent more than fifteen percent of the total exports of the United States; in the whole period of twenty-three years, American exports to France exceeded ten

---

[20]Peabody Essex Museum (PEM), Phillips Library (PL), Salem Customs House Records (SCHR), Foreign Entrances and Clearances, microfilm No. 139, reel 7.

[21]François Crouzet, "La ruine du grand commerce," in F-G. Pariset (ed.), *Bordeaux au XVIIIe siècle* (Bordeaux, 1968), 485-510.

percent of American foreign exports only in nine years.[22] American shipping and trade were however essential to France, especially after 1803. During the 1790s, the United States was far from being the only neutral maritime power: Danish, Prussian or Hamburg shipowners were particularly active in those years. Even in 1796 and 1797, when American trade to Bordeaux was consistent, the number of North European ships entering Bordeaux was two to four times greater than the number of American ships.[23] However, as the different European neutral states were progressively annexed by France or put under its control, this situation changed. Protected by its geographical position, the young American republic was able to escape more effectively the restrictive policies of the belligerents. By the first month of 1812, American ships were the only foreign vessels entering Bordeaux. More than ever, American shipping represented a vital element for the economy of Bordeaux.

The Role of American Shipping in the Bordeaux Trade

American vessels provided different important functions. They engaged both in inter-European as well as in colonial trade. The only shipping service they could not supply was the carrying trade between French ports, as this was forbidden by the British government. If they did arrive at Bordeaux from another French port, American ships were in ballast. This was the case with about one ship in four coming to Bordeaux between 1806 to 1814 in search of a return cargo. But regardless of their origin and their destination, American ships leaving Bordeaux rarely left without wine, brandy and dry-goods on board.

As we have noticed, these vessels did not confine themselves to direct trade between the United States and France. Three American ships out of four entering Bordeaux in the first semester of 1793 had either cleared from or entered a European port before their arrival, and many came in fact from a British seaport. However, this changed very quickly as the belligerent nations restricted the trade opportunities for neutral vessels. By 1797, two American ships out of three entering Bordeaux

---

[22]*Statistical Tables*, VIII-XIII.

[23]Paul Butel, "Charles Fieffé, commissionaire et armateur: contribution à l'étude du négoce bordelais sous la Révolution et l'Empire" (Unpublished PhD thesis, Université de Bordeaux, 1967), 42-43 and 305.

arrived directly from an American port, and this was approximately the case in 1807 as well. In the following years, as British and French legislation became even more restrictive, more than eight American ships out of ten entering Bordeaux came directly from the United States.

This, however, did not prevent them from carrying foreign products. War led to changes in ordinary trade routes, and this was particularly true for colonial trade. Because of the possibilities offered by the "broken voyage," American merchants specialized in the re-export trade. On a national level, over half of American exports from 1796 to 1807 were foreign goods which had previously been imported to the United States.[24] The records of the drawbacks paid to American merchants give an insight into the circuitous re-export trade of those years. The *Brutus* of Newburyport, for instance, entered Bordeaux on 13 November 1803, after a forty-day passage, with sugar and coffee which had previously been imported to Newburyport on fourteen different vessels from Guadeloupe, Martinique and Cap Français.[25] In this case, the *Brutus* was merely carrying produce which would normally have been shipped directly from the French colonies to Bordeaux — a trade which was blocked by British measures during the war. The sugar arriving in Bordeaux in those years came also largely from Cuba. One of the paradoxes of war trade is that the colonial trade escaped more than ever from the restrictive policies of the mother countries.

Maintaining trade in French colonial products was certainly one of the main functions of American ships in Bordeaux during the Napoleonic wars. In fact, in 1807 over half of them transported sugar or coffee. But these ships also enabled Bordeaux to sell regional products to its traditional markets and provided an essential link to the French colonies. On 3 October 1803, Israël Thorndike from Beverly, Massachusetts wrote to John Lewis Brown, a Bordeaux merchant, asking him to charge some "good merchantable wine suitable for the Ile de France market and at a reasonable rate" on the schooner *Two Brothers*, which was expected to

---

[24]Adam Seybert, *Statistical Annals* (1818; reprint, Philadelphia, 1967), 93; and Timothy Pitkin, *A Statistical View of the Commerce of the United States* (1816; reprint, New York, 1967), 36.

[25]PEM, PL, Ms. 282, Newburyport Custom House Records (NCHR), vol. 486.

arrive at Bordeaux from Bilbao.[26] Americans had discovered the Ile de France (Mauritius) trade in the 1780s. In the 1790s, it was still possible for them to sail directly from France to the French colony in the Indian Ocean — fourteen ships made this voyage in 1797.[27] By 1803, however, it had become safer to sail first from Bordeaux to the United States, discharge the cargo there and pay the import duties, load the same ship or another again, and sail to the French colonies with a new clearance and American property on board.

The brandy that the *Brutus* bought back from Bordeaux to Newburyport on 13 March 1804 was shipped in August on the brick *Union* to Guadeloupe. The brandy imported by the schooner *Alert* arrived in Newburyport on 12 February 1805 and was subsequently re-exported to Copenhagen and to Havana. In some cases, French spirits were sold to the British West Indies.[28] All these cases demonstrate the carrying function provided by American ships. It is interesting to note that war made some exchanges possible which, under normal circumstances, would only have been possible through smuggling (such as the sale of French produce into British Caribbean colonies).

The Organization of a Trade Network

The significant number of American ships arriving at Bordeaux raises some questions regarding the modalities of these exchanges. How could merchants organize this important flow of merchandise within a few years? It is generally admitted that international trade in modern times required the acquaintance of merchants with the region where they traded, as well as a regular correspondence with reliable merchant houses. The establishment of contracts was facilitated by merchants' emigration and/or by the commercial training of young merchants' sons in these areas. All this, however, required time. Under normal circumstances, habit probably would have prevailed. To understand the force of tradition, one has but

---

[26]Harvard University, Baker Library, Israel Thorndike Papers, XII.

[27]Auguste Toussaint, *La route des Iles. Contribution à l'histoire maritime des Mascareignes* (Paris, 1967), 295-298. A total of thirty-one American ships arrived at the Ile de France from Bordeaux between 1795 and 1806.

[28]PEM, PL, NCHR, vol. 487.

to recall the drastic decline in Franco-American trade after 1783, when American merchants turned again towards their British colleagues. Only a drastic change in international trade patterns could give the decisive impulse to change. In 1793, this was due to the outbreak of the war. But who took the initiative?

Some additional questions arise. Until now, we have analyzed American shipping and trade globally, but were all American port cities and merchants equally involved in the French trade? Moreover, American vessels were constantly suspected of being the property of some merchants of belligerent powers, as was the case with other neutral flags. Did American ships arriving at Bordeaux also belong to French merchants?

In fact, the central point is to establish whether Americans seized the commercial opportunities that the war offered to them, or, on the contrary, whether these trade networks were mainly due to French initiative. Was the role of French merchants as passive as historians tend to believe, or did they behave as skilful entrepreneurs? The answers to such questions lie basically in merchants' papers. These, unfortunately, are rare in Bordeaux, though the notarial acts can partially make up for this loss. In the United States, in contrast, such papers are superabundant.

American Shipowners and the Bordeaux Trade

The records of the American consul in Bordeaux identify the residence of the shipowners. It is therefore possible to analyze the relative importance of the merchants of different American port cities in the trade with Bordeaux and to establish if there was any evolution in this period.

New England shipowners appear to dominate the American trade at Bordeaux from the very beginning. Boston, Marblehead and Salem played a central role throughout the entire period, though a number of other New England ports sent some ships to Bordeaux with a certain regularity. Forty-two percent of the American ships entering Bordeaux in the first semester of 1793 were owned in New England. This is the case of fifty-seven percent of the ships arriving at Bordeaux from May to December 1797, and of thirty-six percent in 1801. The percentage drops to twenty-four in 1802, when peace was restored, but by 1807 four American ships out of ten arriving at Bordeaux again belonged to New Englanders. From 1808 to 1814, the participation of New England shipowners dropped to 16.8 percent. This relative decline is possibly due to a change in the composition of cargoes, cotton being more often exported to Bordeaux after 1808 (57.7 percent of the vessels) than in 1807 (41.6 percent). Changes in French duties and international policies might also have favoured the export of American domestic products, and thus encouraged merchant-shipowners of the American South to ship to France.

Yet Charleston shipowners were only occasionally present with more than ten percent of the American ships entering Bordeaux, as in 1793 or again in 1802; between 1808 and 1814 their rate was only 2.2 percent. Baltimore, on the contrary, played no important role prior to 1811 — the peak was reached in 1801 with 8.1 percent — but from 1812 to 1814 almost four ships out of ten entering Bordeaux belonged to Baltimore shipowners. Even if Baltimore foreign trade was catching up to Philadelphia in those years, the peculiar strong and late presence of the Maryland shipowners in Bordeaux still needs further investigation, as does the possible shift in the composition of the cargoes.[29] Philadelphia merchants, who owned one American ship out of five of those entering Bordeaux in the first semester of 1793, still scored sixteen percent from 1808 to 1814. The worst year for them was 1807, when they accounted for only nine percent. However, while Philadelphia shipowners maintained a regular trade with Bordeaux, the importance of New York shipowners increased remarkably from 1793 to 1807. In the first half of 1793, only two American ships entering Bordeaux belonged to a New Yorker (4.7 percent). Their ships, however, represented 14.7 percent of the total in 1797, 19.1 percent in 1801, 29.8 percent in 1802 and thirty-six percent in 1807. From 1808 to 1814, New Yorkers owned about one ship out of four of those entering Bordeaux.

This picture differs slightly from that presented by the literature on the rank of American ports at that period.[30] Certainly, the importance of New England shipping and the rise of New York are confirmed, whereas Philadelphia maintains some measure of prominence throughout the period. Yet the growth of Baltimore's share of activity in the last years of war is striking. Evidently, trade to France followed its own patterns of growth and decline, and American merchants probably reoriented their

---

[29]James Weston Livingood, *The Philadelphia-Baltimore Trade Rivalry 1780-1860* (Harrisburg, 1947).

[30]David T. Gilchrist (ed.), *The Growth of the Seaport Cities, 1790-1825* (Charlottesville, 1967).

trade according to the results of previous experiences. Some of them might have abandoned Bordeaux after having grown disillusioned by trade setbacks, whereas others might have been trying their luck in a port they had not yet explored. "It appears to be the decided opinion of all of us that the French markets are so bad and the risk of failure so great we ought to send no more consignments that way...so fare well to shipments to Bordeaux," James Crowninshield of Salem announced on 10 July 1804 to his brother John, who was at that time in Bordeaux.[31] And indeed the Crowninshields did not own any property on the ships arriving from Bordeaux to Salem in the following years.[32]

　　Another element which might explain the relative success of a specific American port in the French trade is the presence of French merchants. New York and Philadelphia were the favourite places for Bordeaux merchants settling in the United States. In fact, trade networks are to a large extent connected to human networks.

The Human Network

The quickest way to establish a new trade in an unknown area was to send a relative there, someone on whom one could rely for shipments and regular payments. It therefore becomes necessary to investigate the transfers of merchants across the Atlantic.

　　There are in fact evidences of many French merchants establishing themselves in the United States before and after the Revolution. The best-known French merchant living in the United States in that period is probably Stephen Girard, who was born near Bordeaux and who settled in Philadelphia in 1776. His success was unique, but Girard was not particularly interested in American trade with France. Many other Frenchmen, however, went to the United States during the French wars and helped to reinforce the commercial network between the main American ports and France. The brother of Daniel Guestier, for instance, one of the most influential merchants of Bordeaux, lived in Philadelphia, and it should therefore come as no surprise that, from 1810 onwards, he sent a ship every year to Bordeaux.

---

[31]PEM, PL, Ms. 4, Crowninshield Family Papers (CFP), box 4, folder 3.

[32]PEM, PL, SCHR, Impost book, microfilm no. 29, reel 5; and NA, New England Region, Salem Custom House Records, Impost House Records, VI.

Some of these French citizens settling in the United States came from Saint Domingue, escaping the slave revolts in the early 1790s. Others, however, came directly from Bordeaux, within a precise commercial strategy of their merchant house. Paul Butel has given some examples, and others could certainly be found through an exhaustive analysis of notarial sources at Bordeaux.[33]

A glance at the passports delivered in Bordeaux from 1806 to 1814 reveals that 475 travelers left this French port bound for the United States, one-fifth of them being merchants.[34] The United States was the most common destination of Bordeaux merchants in this period. We can assume that they found the commercial opportunities in America particularly interesting. Many of them sent their children there to complete their commercial education. Fifteen-year-old François-Auguste Bonnaffé and his younger brother Edouard, for instance, were in New York in 1806. Their grandfather was François Bonnaffé, one of the most successful merchants in eighteenth-century Bordeaux, who had made his fortune in the colonial trade. After the reversal of their fortunes during the French Revolution, his son Bonnaffé de Lance, the father of the two boys, tried to revive their trade in colonial goods, using the United States as neutral intermediary. From 1811 to 1814, Bonnaffé de Lance was the consignee of one American ship per year shipped from the United States to Bordeaux. In 1813, the schooner *Orion* entered Bordeaux in ballast, from Bayonne. Auguste Bonnaffé was one of the owners of the ship, which was consigned to his father. It is reasonable to assume that, in the case of the Bonnaffés, it was the Bordeaux firm which directed this trade under American cover. Other young Bordeaux merchants were sent in those years to the United States. For instance, eleven of them, aged nine to seventeen, left from January to March 1812. Among them were the brothers Brown and Daniel Guestier, both belonging to the merchant

---

[33]Butel, "Guerre et commerce."

[34]Silvia Marzagalli, "Les voyages des négociants bordelais à l'époque du Blocus continental," *Bulletin du Centre d'histoire des Espaces Atlantiques*, VI (1993), 137-150.

houses of Bordeaux to whom a significant number of American ships were consigned at that time.[35]

In the opposite direction, but for similar reasons, some American merchants went to France in order to organize their trade better. The American consul in Bordeaux was always a merchant at that time, and quite often, especially in the early years of the war, he acted as commissioner for American shipowners sending their cargo to Bordeaux. Besides the consul, other American merchants were active in Bordeaux. Some, like Jonathan Jones, had arrived before the French Revolution. Others, however, settled during the war. William Bass of Boston, for instance, declared that he had been living in Bordeaux for a year when he got married in 1807. His bride, Katty Duballet, was born in Boston, and had been living in Bordeaux in the merchant residence quarter of *Chartons* for some years.[36] Robert Andrews of Philadelphia settled in Bordeaux in 1799 and lived there until 1817, when he moved to Le Havre.[37]

If we are unable to measure statistically the merchant immigration to and from Bordeaux in these years, it is a fact that a certain movement took place in both directions. On this basis, it is difficult to attribute an exclusive dynamic impulse to the growth of Franco-American relations either to French or to American merchants. However, this human transfer undoubtedly made relations easier.

Who Owned the Ships and Cargoes?

Most of the American ships entering Bordeaux were built in the United States and belonged to American merchants. Nevertheless, the British government was not completely wrong in its assumption that the American flag covered enemy trade. The abuse of neutralizing French-owned vessels went so far that the American consul estimated that forty-two of the fifty-one ships fitted out in Bordeaux under the American flag and to

---

[35]Archives départementales de la Gironde (ADG), Foreign Passport, 4 M 683 à 692 (1806-1814); and Archives Nationales, F7 3542 (1812-1813). Nineteen-year-old Robert David Brown and his eighteen-year-old brother David left in 1811; Daniel Guestier (sixteen years-old) left in 1812.

[36]ADG, Notarial Archives, 3E 21626, marriage contract, 29 April 1807.

[37]J. Campbell, "San Domingo Refugees in Philadelphia," *Records of the American Catholic Historical Society*, XXVIII (1917), 225.

which he had granted consular certificates between May 1803 and April 1805 were in fact on French account.[38] Even if this were the case, however, these ships bought in Bordeaux and put under the American flag represented only a minor part on the total number of American vessels entering Bordeaux. Although we lack the data for 1805, there were in fact approximately 300 American ships entering Bordeaux from May 1803 to December 1804.

However, even if the ships belonged to an American shipowner, Bordeaux merchants could freight them and let the cargo appear as neutral. In this case, the American shipowner would in fact be a commissioner, acting on the account of the French merchants. An indirect proof that American merchants covered French property comes from the papers concerning the brig *Vigilant* of Boston, George Dodd master.[39] *Vigilant* left Boston in 1805 with a $50,000 cargo of sugar, coffee, pepper and other colonial goods. On her passage to Bordeaux, she was taken to Portsmouth by a British vessel, but as her papers were in order, she was authorized to leave. As the ship arrived in Bordeaux, the Trade Court of the city named some experts to check the expenses sustained by the captain in England, and they divided the loss among the French and American merchants in Bordeaux to whom the cargo was consigned. This shows in fact that the cargo already belonged to the merchants in Bordeaux when it was loaded in Boston: had they just been commissioners, they would not have had to pay these expenses.

In his correspondence with Captain Nicholas Tucker, who was detained on the ship *Spring Bird* at Bayonne, the Bordeaux firm Pelletreau, Bellamy and Co. admitted that Joseph Barker, a Marblehead shipowner, "has several sums to receive for us in America," which meant that the Bordeaux firm did some American trade on its own account.[40] In many other cases, however, the American merchants were the real owners of the ship and the cargo, and they did pay just 2.5 to four percent commission to the Bordeaux merchant who sold the cargo on their account. Both these patterns of trade, on French or on American account, appear to have

---

[38]NA, T 164, reel 1, Dispatches from the United States Consul in Bordeaux, W. Lee to Amstrong, 26 April 1805.

[39]PEM, PL, Ms 0.151, George Dodd Papers.

[40]PEM, PL, Ms. 0.134, Nicholas Tucker Papers, 26 February 1810.

been used in those years. The ship papers, however, carefully dissimulated any trace of French property, as this would have led to the seizure of the ship and of the cargo.

The normal pattern of trade involved the sale of the outward cargo in Bordeaux and the purchase of a return cargo with the amount of the sale. The difference, generally to the profit of the American merchant, was remitted through bills on London, Amsterdam or Hamburg and, occasionally, on New York. The proceeds of the sale of the *Pacific*'s cargo, for instance, which left Newport for Bordeaux on 4 March 1807, were remitted to Dickason and Co. in London (£16,653) and to other firms in New York ($35,000).[41] American merchants trading regularly to Bordeaux would also have an account with a Bordeaux merchant. When the house of Strobel and Martini of Bordeaux failed in January 1804, they owed $20,868 to the Crowninshields of Salem.[42] Bordeaux commissioners were regularly employed from the 1790s onwards. This did not discourage shipowners from giving precise instructions to the captain or supercargo for the sale of the cargo. However, because this process could be very time-consuming, shipowners preferred to entrust it to a local merchant, who could eventually store the merchandise in his warehouse and wait for prices to rise.

A particular difficulty in payments arose during the French Revolutionary period because of the inflation of paper money. The ship *Charlotte*, belonging to the Brown family of Providence, Rhode Island, is a good example of some of the problems of Franco-American relations in those years. In 1795, the *Charlotte* had sailed from Providence to Bordeaux with a valuable cargo of rice and tobacco. In their instructions to the supercargo, the Browns wrote that "The cargo must be sold for specie by no means have any thing to do with the depreciated paper."[43]

In all instances, American shipowners relied upon merchants in Bordeaux to conduct their business. The records of the American consul in Bordeaux give the names of the commercial houses to which cargoes were consigned. From November 1806 to December 1814, eighteen

---

[41]JCBL, BFP, V_P 15, folder 8, Ship *Pacific*.

[42]PEM, PL, Ms. MH-15, CFP, box 1.

[43]JCBL, BFP, Ship *Charlotte*, V__C52, box 49, folder 9, instructions to George Tyler, supercargo, 13 June 1795.

percent of the American vessels entering Bordeaux were consigned to John Lewis Brown, twelve percent to John Archer Morton, while Jonathan Jones and Justin Foussat each received five percent of the incoming ships. John Lewis Brown was a Scottish merchant, but his father had married a Fenwick, a family of American merchants of Bordeaux. Joseph Fenwick of Maryland was the American Consul in Bordeaux from 1790 to the Quasi-War. John Archer Morton, who was an associate of Russel's, was an American merchant, just like Jonathan Jones, who came to Bordeaux from native Philadelphia before 1785, when he married Jeanne Textier, the daughter of a well-known merchant of Bordeaux.[44] Justin Foussat was the only French merchant in this group, but his brother lived in Philadelphia, where he had acquired American citizenship.[45] Other merchants in Bordeaux who received ten or more American vessels during this period included Bizat, Pelletreau, and Ducourneau. Their family links to the United States still need investigation.

Conclusion

There is no doubt that American shipping played a very important role in the Bordelais economy during the French Wars. The steady participation of neutral American vessels prevented the total asphyxia of the economy of this maritime French town by ensuring that a minimal flow of colonial trade was maintained, while the export of French products, in particular wine and brandy, also benefited from these shipping activities. Merchants, vineyard-owners, consumers and the French Customs, everybody took advantage of this trade.

Because the British had blockaded northern French ports, American vessels could sail more safely to such west coast French ports as Bordeaux, Bayonne and Nantes. Bayonne shipping activities depended however largely on Bordeaux merchants and capital. Moreover, from March 1811 to March 1812, the number of American ships entering Bordeaux was four times higher than the number entering Bayonne and

---

[44]P. Meller, *Etat civil des familles bordelaises avant la Révolution; mariages* (Bordeaux, 1909).

[45]Butel, "Guerre et commerce," 438; and NA, T 164, reel 2, Dispatches from the United States Consul in Bordeaux, W. Lee to Armstrong, 26 April 1805.

Nantes.[46] The study of American shipping and trade to Bordeaux offers therefore a deep and representative insight into the mechanism of this trade.

Both American and French merchants were involved in these complex commercial patterns, and it is difficult to ascertain who played the most determinant role. The high profit of neutral shipping and trade, especially in the early years, permitted American shipowners to increase their capital, thus making up for the scarcity of resources in the 1780s. In numerous cases, however, American merchants acted as commissioners for French merchants, who then assumed the risks involved in the hazardous trade. As these transactions were prohibited by the British, they could have led to the seizure of the cargo. Evidence of them is therefore scarce and often hidden in ambiguous statements in mercantile correspondence. Further research will explore the profitability of this trade and try to explain the changes in the relative importance of goods and in the rank of American ports for Bordeaux trade. The significance of the movement of merchants themselves across the Atlantic also must be evaluated.

---

[46]Butel, "Guerre et commerce," 444.

The Challenge of War on Maritime Trade in the North Atlantic: The Case of the British Trade to Iceland During the Napoleonic Wars

Anna Agnarsdóttir

This paper discusses an instance when war compelled merchants to venture into trades that were new to them. Specifically, it examines the introduction during the Napoleonic Wars of British trade to Iceland, a dependency of Denmark, one of England's enemies. War between Denmark and Great Britain broke out officially in November 1807 and continued until a peace treaty was finally concluded in Kiel in January 1814. Why did British merchants become interested in trading with Iceland and how was the trade conducted?[1] This paper will attempt to answer these questions.

Iceland in 1800

At the beginning of the nineteenth century Iceland had a population of only about 47,000. Its society was made up of a small landowning class and a large tenant peasantry. Most Icelanders lived on isolated farms and were engaged primarily in animal husbandry (mainly sheep farming) with fishing as a subsidiary occupation. There were no villages, only trading stations dotted along the coast. Reykjavík, the principal mercantile station and centre of administration, had only three hundred inhabitants. The island lacked both fortifications and a defence force.

In 1788 the "Free Trade Charter" brought two centuries of mercantilist monopoly trade to an end. Henceforth only independent merchants, subjects of the Dano-Norwegian kingdom — with the exception of the Faroes and Greenland but including native Icelanders — would be permitted to participate in the Iceland trade. The basic principle of the new trade system was to exclude foreign merchants from trading to

---

[1]For a fuller treatment of this subject, see Anna Agnarsdóttir, "Great Britain and Iceland 1800-1820" (Unpublished PhD thesis, London School of Economics and Political Science, 1989).

Iceland and strictly to forbid Icelanders from having any direct commercial dealings with "foreigners."[2] Almost all of the merchants active in Iceland during this period were Danes resident in Denmark for the better part of the year. In the spring they and their ships would arrive in Iceland; they would trade during the summer season (the *handel*) and return to their homeland in late summer or autumn. Only a handful of native Icelanders were engaged in trade.

The Iceland trade was a barter trade; little money was in circulation. The principal exports were: fish, including both stockfish (dried cod) and *klipfish* (dried salted cod); fish liver oil (train-oil); wool and woollen products of various kinds, such as stockings and mittens; tallow; salted mutton; eiderdown; feathers; the skins of sheep, fox, and swans; and sulphur. British merchants also sought such items as reindeer antlers, minerals and horses suitable as pit ponies.[3] The main imports were grain (chiefly rye), timber, iron, fishing tackle, salt, linen and cotton goods, alcohol and tobacco. From about 1770, coffee and sugar became valued imports as well.

From the beginning of "free trade" in 1788 until the outbreak of war in 1807, fifty-six merchants ships sailed on average each year to Iceland with an aggregate tonnage of 2300 commercial tons.[4] By the beginning of the nineteenth century, however, the number had declined, with just over forty ships making the voyage in 1807.[5]

War and the Introduction of British Trade

In 1807, following the British bombardment of Copenhagen, Denmark abandoned its neutrality and entered into a formal alliance instead with Napoleon. Denmark was now at war with Great Britain, the foremost sea

---

[2]See Gísli Gunnarsson, *Monopoly Trade and Economic Stagnation. Studies in the Foreign Trade of Iceland 1602-1787* (Lund, 1983), 148-9.

[3]The *Liverpool Mercury* is a good source for lists of Icelandic produce favoured by British merchants; see, for instance, 27 August 1813.

[4]Marcus Rubin, *Frederik VI's Tid fra Kielerfreden til Kongens Död* (Copenhagen, 1895; reprint, Copenhagen, 1970), 118.

[5]See Rigsarkivet, Copenhagen (RA), Rentekammer (Chamber of Rents; hereafter Rtk), 737.121, , *söpas* (sea licences) lists.

power in the North Atlantic. The Royal Navy subsequently captured almost half of the merchantmen bound for Copenhagen from Iceland, bringing them to British ports.[6] The seizure of the vessels was serious enough in itself. But even more disastrous was the fact that their capture would discourage Danish merchants from risking the voyage to Iceland.

Among the passengers on the captured ships was Magnús Stephensen, Chief Justice of Iceland and the leading Icelander of his day. Stephensen understood at once that the Iceland trade was not viable unless it had British sanction and cooperation. Because of his high rank he was permitted to proceed to Copenhagen, where he tried to convince the Danish government to initiate negotiations with the British regarding the future navigation to Iceland. In this, however, he was not successful.[7] Stephensen therefore decided on a bold approach. He would contact the enemy himself by seeking the assistance of a great friend of Iceland — Sir Joseph Banks, the great British naturalist. Following his celebrated voyage to the South Seas in the *Endeavour* with Captain James Cook in 1768-1771, Banks had led the first scientific expedition to Iceland by foreign naturalists to Iceland in 1772. By 1807 he had become President of the Royal Society, a Privy Councillor, and a close friend of both statesmen and the British King, George III.[8] By virtue of his familiarity with Iceland and because of his prominent position in society, Banks was recognised by the British government and individuals alike as *the* authority on Icelandic affairs.

In his letter to Banks, Stephensen stressed that it was of vital importance that the captured ships be released and allowed to continue their trade, if necessary with British licences. Without supplies Iceland would become "an uninhabited desert."[9] Banks proved more than willing to use his influential position to come to the rescue of the Icelanders. As he himself wrote, "the hospitable reception I met with in Iceland made too

---

[6]Agnarsdóttir, "Great Britain and Iceland 1800-1820," 47-49.

[7]Royal Ordinance, 12 February 1808, in Oddgeir Stephensen and Jón Sigurdsson (eds.), *Lovsamling for Island* (21 vols., Copenhagen, 1853-1874), VII, esp. 154-155.

[8]The definitive biography of Banks is H.B. Carter, *Sir Joseph Banks 1743-1820* (London, 1988).

[9]Natural History Museum (NHM), Dawson Turner Collection (DTC), XVII, Magnús Stephensen to Banks, 17 October 1807.

much impression on me to allow me to be indifferent about any thing in which Icelanders are concerned."[10] Throughout the winter of 1807-1808 Banks was besieged by petitions and visits from the Iceland merchants detained in England and he frequently corresponded with both his friend Lord Hawkesbury, Secretary of State for Home Affairs and Viscount Castlereagh, the Secretary of State for War and the Colonies, advocating the release of the Iceland ships.[11] These efforts were successful, for in June 1808 the government released the Iceland vessels and their cargoes "to preserve the inhabitants...from distress and possible famine."[12] The ships were thus released by the government ostensibly on humanitarian grounds, and this was undoubtedly a factor (certainly Banks' motive). The politicians, on the other hand, may have had more pragmatic aims. At Banks' prompting, Earl Bathurst, the President of the Board of Trade, saw an advantage in releasing the Iceland ships and issuing them with licences, as he explained to the War Office.[13] Napoleon's blockade had attempted to close the Continent, one of England's major markets, to British trade. In an effort to evade the "Continental System" the British had instituted a system of licences regulating neutral trade. Neutral vessels to which such licences had been issued were permitted to carry on a trade between Britain and any European ports in blockade.[14] The Iceland vessels, deemed neutral vessels, were now incorporated into this system.

Yet Britain was neither an ideal market for Icelandic produce nor could it easily supply Icelanders with necessities during wartime. A direct and self-contained trade between England and Iceland was therefore not a feasible option. Instead, the Iceland merchants asked for permission to sail their vessels to a Danish port where a traditional market could be

---

[10]Sutro Library, San Francisco (SL), Banks Papers, Iceland, Banks to William Wright, 21 November 1807.

[11]Agnarsdóttir, "Great Britain and Iceland 1800-1820," 35-56.

[12]Public Record Office, London (PRO), Admiralty (Adm) 1/4979, Undersecretary of State Edward Cooke to the master of the *Rennthier*, 30 June 1808.

[13]PRO, War Office (WO) 1/883, Bathurst to [Cooke (?)], 30 May 1808.

[14]See Eli F. Hecksher, *The Continental System. An Economic Interpretation* (Oxford, 1922), especially chapters 2 and 3 and 205-210 on the British licensing system.

found and where suitable provisions for Iceland could be acquired.[15] British commercial policy found little difficulty in agreeing to this request, since it obliged a belligerent, Denmark, to provide the necessities. The compulsory inspection stops in a British port, the cornerstone of the British licensing system, both on the way to Iceland and Denmark, would ensure British control of the trade. Provided the Icelanders obeyed the tenets of the licences, they had little to fear from the Royal Navy.[16]

Thus it was that the Iceland ships were licensed to carry on their trade with Denmark in relative safety. As a Frenchman, living in England during this period, remarked, "no country in the four quarters of the earth has been able to trade for the last ten years (1804-1813) without England's goodwill."[17] Iceland was no exception. During the years 1807-1814 the traditional Dano-Icelandic trade came almost entirely under the control of Great Britain. Even so, and in spite of British protection, the stringencies of war curtailed navigation to Iceland, with the result that Iceland suffered a great deal of hardship, even famine, towards the end of the war period.

British Trade with Iceland Begins: The Voyage of the *Clarence*

The detention of the Iceland merchantmen in England during the winter and spring of 1807-1808 had one important and perhaps not unexpected result. It aroused the interest of British merchants, who were cut off from the Continent and seeking new markets, in an Iceland trade.

In London the Royal Exchange was the centre of commercial activity and a meeting place for merchants from all over the world, including Danes and Icelanders stranded in London.[18] Among those frequenting the Exchange was Jörgen Jörgensen, captain of a Danish privateer captured by the British and by coincidence an acquaintance of Sir Joseph Banks (they shared an interest in the South Seas). A prisoner-

---

[15]SL, Sivertsen to Banks, 18 April 1808.

[16]See for instance the first licences in PRO, Privy Council (PC) 2/177.

[17]Quoted in Fernand Braudel, *The Perspective of the World* (London, 1985), 578.

[18]Ada Polak, *Wolffs and Dorville. Et norsk-engelsk handelshus i London under Napoleonskrigene* (Oslo, 1968), 52-54; Andreas A. Feldborg, *A Dane's Excursions in Britain* (London, 1809), I, 8; and British Library (BL), London, Department of Manuscripts, Eg[erton] 2068, ff. 2-3.

of-war, he was on parole in London.[19] Among those whose ships had been detained was Bjarni Sivertsen, a major native Icelandic merchant. The two met and Sivertsen told Jörgensen about the immense quantities of produce, including tallow, piling up in Icelandic warehouses waiting for a market.[20] Soon after, Jörgensen, by chance "at dinner at a public table," as he described it, met James Savignac, an employee of Phelps, Troward and Bracebridge, leading soap manufacturers and merchants of Cuper's Bridge, Lambeth. Soap-boiling was at a standstill for lack of fats. Savignac would therefore have been very interested to learn from Jörgensen that Sivertsen had 150 tons of tallow waiting in Iceland for a market. Savignac quickly introduced Jörgensen to Phelps, principal partner of the firm, who was immediately interested.[21] Imports of tallow by 1808 had sunk by sixty percent.[22] This had driven up the price, so that a cargo of that article would doubtless be very profitable. Jörgensen explained that Iceland was probably in a state of famine because the ships had been released so late in the season that no trading vessels had reached the island that year. There would therefore be a good market for whatever necessities the English merchants could offer in exchange for the valuable tallow. Phelps was convinced; he wasted no time hiring a ship and obtaining permission from the government to carry a cargo to Iceland.[23]

Applications were made to the Board of Trade, which "much encouraged" Phelps to undertake the voyage.[24] This conformed not only with the British government's clear policy of expanding trade everywhere, but more specifically with government efforts to develop new markets for

---

[19]Agnarsdóttir, "Great Britain and Iceland 1800-1820," 87-89.

[20]Jörgensen does not mention him by name but it was definitely Sivertsen; see Historical Manuscripts Commission, *Report on the Manuscripts of Earl Bathurst* (Bathurst MS) (London, 1923), 85, Savignac to Phelps and Co., 19 March 1809.

[21]BL, Eg 2068, ff. 3-6.

[22]Heckscher, *The Continental System*, 172-173. Tallow was normally imported from Russia.

[23]BL, Eg. 2068, f. 2; and Samuel Phelps, *Observations on the Importance of Extending the British Fisheries, etc.* (London, 1817), 52.

[24]Phelps, *Observations*, 53.

British manufactures to compensate for those closed in Europe by Napoleon's Continental System.[25] Though it was up to the merchants to take the initiative in finding the markets, the government lent all its support to British merchants who did.[26]

The Privy Council granted Phelps's "humble petition" for a licence to trade in late November, permitting him to export a cargo of barley, rum, hats, sugar, tobacco, and coffee and to return with a cargo of tallow, hides, feathers, salted mutton, eiderdown, moss and other Icelandic produce.[27] The cargo, with freight and charges, was estimated by Phelps to be worth £8500. Savignac was to head the expedition as supercargo and Jörgensen would serve as interpreter. Banks told Phelps that they could not have undertaken a more humane project.[28]

The *Clarence*, a 310-ton brig, was chartered. Armed with fourteen guns, it was issued with a letter of marque from the High Court of Admiralty, as well as a set of false American papers and passports, the United States then being the major neutral nation.[29] As Denmark and England were at war this might be necessary to facilitate the trade.[30] So great was their enthusiasm that the *Clarence* — probably the first English ship sent to trade with Iceland since the sixteenth century — did not wait for spring but set sail from Liverpool at the end of December 1808 for the hazardous winter voyage to Iceland.[31]

---

[25]Judith Blow Williams, *British Commercial Policy and Trade Expansion 1750-1850* (Oxford, 1972), 445.

[26]See, for instance, the case of Greenland: PRO, Board of Trade (BT) 3/10, Cottrell to Harrison, 15 May 1809.

[27]PRO, PC 2/178, 29 November 1808.

[28]Phelps, *Observations*, 51-52.

[29]The *Clarence*'s letter of marque is no. 167, PRO, High Court Admiralty (HCA) 25/192.

[30]BL, Eg. 2068, f. 8; and Bathurst MS, 85, Savignac to Phelps and Co., 19 March 1809.

[31]The English had both traded with Iceland and fished Icelandic waters at least from the beginning of the fifteenth century; see, for instance, Wendy Childs, "England's Icelandic Trade in the Fifteenth Century: The Role of the Port of Hull," in Poul Holm,

The *Clarence* reached Iceland safely on 12 January 1809 and found a Norwegian brig at anchor in the harbour.[32] This was the *Justitia* from Trondheim, which had arrived in October 1808 with supplies sent at the expense of the Danish Crown.[33] The Danish administration was worried about the plight of the dependencies in the North Atlantic and, in addition to sending this ship, had tried to encourage merchants to risk the voyage by offering loans, bounties and insurance.[34] Though it was the only merchant ship to arrive in 1808, the *Clarence* met with a discouraging welcome from the Icelandic deputy governor (the governor Count Trampe was away in Denmark). Despite hoisting the American flag, the American papers which were produced proved useless. To Savignac's "great astonishment they produced an old Danish ordinance interdicting the trade with Iceland by foreigners."[35] Neutrals were also foreigners. The British licence was then produced but to no avail.[36] The officials of the King of Denmark were determined to uphold the ban on foreign trade.

Savignac, "exceedingly mortified" at this refusal, felt he had no choice but to resort to force and ordered the captain of the *Clarence* to seize the *Justitia*.[37] This had the desired effect; on 19 January the English were granted permission to trade.[38] Savignac quickly rented a warehouse

---

Olaf Janzen and Jón Thór (eds.), *Northern Seas Yearbook 1995* (Esbjerg, 1995), 11-31. They were subsequently joined by German merchants and throughout the monopoly period it is certain that an illicit trade took place with British, French, Dutch and Spanish fishermen.

[32]Bathurst MS, 85, Savignac to Phelps and Co., 19 March 1809.

[33]Jón Espólín, *Árbœkur Íslands í söguformi* (Copenhagen, 1855), Section XII, 24.

[34]See for example *Lovsamling*, VII, 154-8, 12 February 1808 (on insurance and bounties); and *ibid.*, 220, 19 August 1808 (on insurance).

[35]Bathurst MS, 85, Savignac to Phelps and Co., 19 March 1809.

[36]*Ibid.*

[37]PRO, Adm. 1/692, Savignac to the Resident Governor of Iceland, 14 January 1809; and Savignac to Jackson, 17 January 1809.

[38]National Archives of Iceland (NAI), Bf. Rvk. I, 2, Bréfadagbók 1806-1813 (only extant in Danish and Icelandic), Agreement of 19 January 1809, no. 2305.

in Reykjavík, expecting to carry on a brisk trade with the Icelanders. Yet, despite prices that were far lower than usual and the general lack of supplies in the country, the trade was extremely disappointing.[39] The cargo proved not wholly suitable to Icelandic needs, prompting Savignac to make a list of necessities "in current consumption here" for the benefit of his employers.[40] Of greater significance was the fact that this was simply not the proper time of year. The *handel* or trading season in the Icelandic barter economy was in the summer, when farmers brought in their produce. And though the Danish factors, who supervised the trade during the merchants' absence, had plenty of Icelandic produce in their warehouses, they refused to do business with their English rivals.[41] No doubt they hoped that the English would leave in frustration and not return.

Savignac and Jörgensen used their time to gather information on the Iceland trade. According to Jörgensen, one of Phelps' aims for the voyage was to "procure a thorough knowledge" of the Icelandic commerce.[42] After assessing the situation Savignac and Jörgensen were convinced a profitable trade could be carried out in the summer when the *handel* would be in full swing.[43] Savignac decided to remain in Iceland and try to dispose of the cargo while Jörgensen went back on the *Clarence* to England, returning the following summer with more suitable goods. Accordingly, the *Clarence* set sail on 22 March, not with a cargo of valuable tallow but with a ballast of lava rocks, sold to them by the Danish merchants for 235 *rixdollars*![44]

Notwithstanding this inauspicious end to the first voyage, Savignac's report was enthusiastic in stating that there were about a

---

[39]William Jackson Hooker, *Journal of a Tour in Iceland in the Summer of 1809* (2 vols.; London, 1813), II, 14-15.

[40]Bathurst MS, 85, Savignac to Phelps and Co., 19 March 1809 (this list is not extant); and Hooker, *Journal*, II, 21.

[41]Bathurst MS, 85, Savignac to Phelps and Co., 19 March 1809.

[42]BL, Eg. 2068, f. 5.

[43]Bathurst MS, 85, Savignac to Phelps and Co., 19 March 1809.

[44]BL, Eg. 2068, f. 17. In 1809 there were about five *rixdollars* to the English pound (Hooker, *Journal*, I, xxxv).

thousand tons of the sought-after tallow in Iceland, and suggesting as well that "an immense sum of money may be made" by exporting fish "of the first quality" direct to some Mediterranean port or to England, provided the British government would allow the importation duty free. Two or three ships could be loaded immediately with superb fish.[45]

On his return to London in April Jörgensen, accompanied by Phelps, visited Sir Joseph Banks, delivering "a correct account of the brig *Clarence*'s proceedings in Iceland."[46] Banks was extremely interested in what they had to say. He had communicated frequently with members of the government during 1807-1809, presenting detailed plans for the conquest of Iceland. In Banks' opinion a British annexation was the only solution to the wartime plight of the Icelanders and a very appropriate one at that. In his view, "No one who looks upon the map of Europe can doubt that Iceland is by nature a part of the group of islands called by the Ancients 'Britannia,' & consequently that it ought to be part of the British Empire...."[47] After all, Britain had already seized Heligoland, a Danish island of strategic importance in the North Sea, at the beginning of September 1807, and British forces had moved quickly to occupy the Danish colonies in the West Indies and India. The annexation of Iceland could have served as a further retaliatory measure against Denmark. In a letter to Earl Bathurst, President of the Board of Trade, Banks urged "his Majesty's ministers" to take possession of Iceland, saying that Phelps was prepared "to make the conquest with a privateer."[48] But all the available evidence indicates that by May 1809 at the latest, the government had resolved against taking possession of the island.[49]

Despite this setback — an annexation would certainly have facilitated British trade — Phelps set about preparing the second expedition to Iceland. He lay before the Board of Trade documents concerning the voyage of the *Clarence*, and a licence "for a British ship or ships" to trade

---

[45]Bathurst MS, 85, Savignac to Phelps and Co., 19 March 1809.

[46]NHM, London, Banks' Correspondence (BC), Jörgensen to Banks, 14 April 1809.

[47]NHM, DTC, XII, Banks to Mr. Stephensen of Reikiavick, December 1807.

[48]NHM, BC, Banks to Bathurst, 16 April 1809.

[49]*Ibid.*, Banks to Mackenzie [May 1809].

was immediately granted, stipulating, however, that permission would not be granted to export grain or grain products.[50] Phelps and Co. decided to send two ships the following summer, the *Margaret & Ann* and the *Flora*, the latter chiefly carrying rye and oats worth over £15,000 which had been especially imported for this purpose.[51] This would circumvent the government restriction. There is, however, no record that Phelps received any bounties even though another merchant trading to the Faroes apparently did.[52] Phelps decided to conduct the enterprise himself.

Mindful of the hostility displayed by Danish officials and of the fact that the British licence and letter of marque had not proved sufficient to safeguard their right to trade in January, Phelps turned to the Admiralty for naval support. Protection against enemy action at sea was the province of the Royal Navy and it was always one of the chief aims of British naval policy to keep the seas open to British merchant shipping. The merchants were usually consulted on what kind of protection they preferred.[53]

In a petition submitted to the Treasury, Phelps explained that a convoy would give the best protection, but, failing that, he recommended that "some sufficiently powerful vessel of war...be dispatched...from the Leith station."[54] He hoped to be permitted "in case of need to land a few guns, arms & ammunition" in Iceland.[55] These efforts were eventually rewarded, possibly because Banks had written to the Admiralty in support

---

[50]Phelps, *Observations*, 53; PRO, BT 6/195, no. 4257, 22-24 April 1809. The *Margaret and Ann* received a licence on 2 May 1809 (PRO, PC 2/181) and the *Flora* on 18 May 1809 (PRO, PC 2/181).

[51]The *Flora's* licence had only been granted on the grounds that the grain exported to Iceland was foreign grown. For this the firm had paid £200 in duty; PRO, Treasury (T) 1/1216, Phelps and Co. to Lords of the Treasury, 11 August 1809 and 31 July 1811.

[52]Phelps, *Observations*, 53.

[53]A.N. Ryan, "The Defence of British Trade with the Baltic 1808-1813," *English Historical Review*, LXXIV (1959), 444, 450; and Patrick Crowhurst, *The Defence of British Trade 1689-1815* (Folkestone, 1977), 43 and 80.

[54]NHM, BC, Phelps to Banks, 21 and 22 April 1809; BL, Eg. 2070, Jörgensen to Hooker, 13 December 1810.

[55]*Ibid.*, Phelps to Banks, 21 and 22 April 1809.

of Phelps' petition.[56] However, Phelps did not receive quite the degree of naval protection he desired. At the beginning of May the Admiralty provided the vessels licensed by the British government with some protection by authorizing that a sloop-of-war be stationed off Iceland until the end of the season.[57] On 22 May 1809 Captain Francis John Nott of the *Rover* sloop-of-war received his instructions and set sail from Leith Roads for Iceland to pave the way for the British merchants.[58]

In addition to his licence Phelps also obtained a letter of marque for the *Margaret and Ann* "for the apprehending, seizing and taking the ships, vessels and goods, belonging to the King of Denmark."[59] The merchantman eventually sailed from Gravesend on 2 June 1809.[60]

HMS *Rover* in Iceland

When *Rover* arrived in Iceland on 11 June 1809, several Iceland ships, released and licensed in Britain, had already reached the island, loaded with provisions, and more ships were expected. The supply situation had thus greatly improved. A few days earlier, Count Trampe, the Danish governor, had also arrived back in Iceland on his new ship, *Orion*, recently purchased with a cargo.[61] It is worth noting that Trampe had a personal stake in all matters concerning trade, which he himself termed

---

[56]*Ibid.*, Barrow to Banks, 25 June 1809.

[57]PRO, Adm.3/2589, Special Minutes, 1 May 1809; Adm. 2/1368 (file on secret orders), correspondence between Wellesley-Pole and Nagle, 1 and 9 May 1809; and Adm. 1/692, 5 May 1809.

[58]PRO, Adm. 53/1103, *A Journal of the Procedure of H.M.'s Sloop Rover.*

[59]PRO, HCA 25/194, no. 387, 31 May 1809.

[60]Hooker, *Journal*, I, 1.

[61]PRO, HCA 32/1614, Trampe's Claim in the Admiralty Prize Court, 1 November 1809.

"my very important private affairs."[62] One of Trampe's first actions was to increase the price of a barrel of rye.[63]

The war had forced decentralisation on the Danish realm and thereby greatly increased Trampe's authority in Iceland.[64] Danish ordinances, issued after the outbreak of war, reflected Frederik VI's stringent anti-British policy: British ships were strictly banned from entering any harbour in the Danish kingdom and Danish subjects attempting to trade with the British would risk severe punishments. Accordingly, upon arriving in Reykjavík, Trampe promptly ordered Savignac to stop selling the *Clarence*'s cargo.[65] As well, the governor issued a proclamation warning Icelanders not to have any contact with the Englishmen on pain of death.[66] In this way, Trampe effectively and publicly voided Savignac's trade agreement of 19 January 1809 with the King's officials.

Trampe continued in his unwavering attitude after Nott's arrival, forbidding the British captain to step ashore except under a flag of truce.[67] In view of British naval supremacy, these were hardly sensible actions. Trampe, however, was not only acting according to his sovereign's wishes but doubtless was also influenced by the fact that his own cargo would face competition from the cheaper British goods.

The *Rover*'s arrival was a godsend for Savignac who, as a British subject, could now claim Nott's assistance and protection "at a time when he almost despaired of relief."[68] Phelps' insistence on the need for naval protection was thus vindicated. To gain Nott's sympathy Savignac con-

---

[62]University of Wisconsin Memorial Library, Madison, Rare Book Department, "Iceland, the Danish Colonies and the Polar Regions, 1772-1818" (hereafter Wisconsin), Trampe to Bathurst, 6 November 1809.

[63]Espólín, *Árbækur*, XII, 26.

[64]*Lovsamling*, VII, 217-218, Royal ordinance, 10 August 1808; and PRO, FO 40/1, Banks to Liverpool, 11 December 1809.

[65]PRO, Adm. 1/692, Savignac to Nott, 13 June 1809.

[66]*Lovsamling*, VII, 248-250, Trampe's ordinance prohibiting trade with English subjects in Iceland, 13 June 1809.

[67]PRO, Adm. 1/692, Trampe to Nott, 12 June 1809.

[68]*Ibid.*, Savignac to Nott, 13 June 1809.

cocted an improbable story of an assassination plot directed at him. More
to the point, he stressed the many commodities with which Iceland could
provide Britain, such as cod, salmon, seal, wool, tallow, oil, eiderdown,
and sulphur. Five hundred ships "might trade to this island with advantage" and the Crown could expect revenues of £100,000 a year, no less![69]
This was of course a gross exaggeration, and Nott was not fooled, as his
report to the Admiralty shows.[70] Nevertheless, he came to Savignac's
support, fulfilling his duty to protect British trade. In so doing Nott
assumed a role not uncommon for Royal Navy officers. In remote regions
where England had no diplomatic representatives (such as Latin America
or the African coast) naval commanders often settled disputes between
British merchants and the local authorities.[71] Of course, Nott did not have
the authority to establish the British trade "upon a permanent basis" as
demanded by Savignac.[72] He did, however, insist that in "consequence of
British protection being granted to the trade of the inhabitants of Iceland"
Trampe must unequivocally assist ships licensed by the British government and grant British subjects full liberty to trade.[73] According to Phelps,
Nott forced Trampe to negotiate by threatening to fire upon the town.[74] A
trade convention was signed by Nott and Trampe on 16 June. All vessels
licensed by Great Britain would be permitted to trade. British merchants
would be allowed to establish trading concerns in Iceland and to continue
to trade there until a year after "certain intelligence of peace between

[69]*Ibid.* The alleged assassination plot is documented nowhere else.

[70]PRO, Adm. 1/692, Nott to Nagle, 3 August 1809.

[71]Williams, *British Commercial Policy and Trade Expansion*, 142, 427.

[72]PRO, Adm. 1/692, Savignac to Nott, 13 June 1809.

[73]*Ibid.*, Nott to Trampe, 16 June 1809.

[74]Phelps, *Observations*, 55.

Denmark and Great Britain" had reached Iceland.[75] Considering his duty to be done, Nott left the following day.[76]

Phelps' Trading Expedition on the *Margaret and Ann*

Five days later, on 21 June 1809, Samuel Phelps arrived in Iceland on his vessel, the *Margaret and Ann*, a 271-ton barque armed with ten guns.[77] Savignac immediately went on board, recounting what had happened since the *Clarence* had left.[78] To their surprise there was no sign of the Nott-Trampe convention of 16 June, while Trampe's notice prohibiting trade on pain of death, was still posted.[79] The Icelanders showed no signs of wishing to risk their lives, though the trading season was in full swing and Icelandic farmers were already in town with their goods. After waiting a few days for Trampe to honour his agreement Phelps concluded that the governor had gone back on his word, now that the British man-of-war had left.[80] If Trampe's intentions had been honourable, he could at least have removed the placard prohibiting trade. Phelps believed he had little choice but to arrest the governor or return to England at a great financial loss to himself. As he later explained:

> finding that the same conduct [obstruction of trade] prevailed on my arrival here with another cargo...and that my vessels must again return in ballast, unless I pursued strong measures, I ventured to make Count Trampe prisoner...[81]

---

[75]PRO, Adm. 1/692 and Adm. 1/1995, Copies of the convention of 16 June 1809.

[76]PRO, Adm. 51/1954, *Rover*'s log.

[77]PRO, HCA 25/194, Letter of marque, no. 387.

[78]Hooker, *Journal*, II, 22-23.

[79]*Ibid.*, II, 21 and 23; Phelps, *Observations*, 57; and BL, Eg. 2068, f. 35.

[80]Phelps, *Observations*, 56.

[81]PRO, Adm. 1/1995, Phelps to Jones, 23 August 1809.

Phelps acted "from necessity only, to protect our lives and property" and to force the execution of the Nott-Trampe convention permitting a free trade.[82] In view of his conversation with Banks a couple of months previously on the merits of a British annexation, Phelps probably had no real qualms about the course he felt he had been forced to take. His trading venture had received encouragement from the government and he had reason to hope that the British authorities would later sanction, perhaps even applaud, his actions.

Trampe was duly arrested and confined on board the *Margaret and Ann* throughout the nine-week "Icelandic Revolution," as this episode is called in Icelandic history.[83] With no "tame" Icelander available, and with Phelps aware that he was not empowered to establish a government in another country "without the consent of his own," the political vacuum was obligingly filled by Phelps' interpreter, Jörgen Jörgensen, who was not a British citizen.[84] Styling himself "protector" of Iceland, Jörgensen played the part with great gusto, issuing radical proclamations in the French revolutionary spirit and dramatically proclaiming Iceland an independent country under the protection of Great Britain with its own flag — three white codfish on a blue background! All British subjects could engage in free trade and had the right of residence in Iceland. A battery, Fort Phelps, was erected for "the security of the very considerable property" the soap merchant now had in Iceland.[85]

From the point of view of the British merchants, this so-called "Icelandic Revolution" was a success. The *Orion*, Count Trampe's ship, was declared lawful prize, the warehouses of Danish merchants were closed and their property confiscated. Icelanders now flocked to trade, so that Phelps could write with satisfaction that "in a short space of time, we obtained a most valuable cargo...."[86]

---

[82]Phelps, *Observations*, 58; and Hooker, *Journal*, II, 24.

[83]Much has been written about this event. Primary sources are abundant as all the protagonists wrote their accounts. A fairly impartial contemporary account in English is Hooker, *Journal*, II, Appendix A, 3-63.

[84]*Ibid.*, II, 26; and BL, Eg. 2068, f. 52.

[85]Hooker, *Journal*, II, 40-41.

[86]Phelps, *Observations*, 60.

In August an American ship, the *Neptune & Providence*, arrived.[87] Magnús Stephensen had arranged for it to sail to Iceland during his stay in Norway the previous winter.[88] Americans were of course foreigners but Stephensen had prudently asked Trampe whether he had any objections to permitting neutral Americans to trade. Trampe's response in February 1809 was that he would not obstruct the trade of an American ship, should it come to Reykjavík or Hafnarfjörður. Indeed, he professed himself to be willing to buy the cargo.[89] George Athearn, the supercargo, wanted "as much tallow and wool as possible," saying he would be staying for six weeks.[90] Here, then, was stiff competition for the English merchants — a ship loaded with attractive produce and a demand for the very tallow Phelps wanted. To end the threat Phelps therefore decided to exchange the American cargo for Icelandic goods already acquired by the English.[91] When Magnús Stephensen protested (for the American's prices were considered good), Athearn said he had had no choice if he was to obtain a return cargo.[92] This suggests that Phelps had managed to collect all the tallow in the Reykjavík area, a conclusion borne out by the fact that Stephensen gave the Americans permission to trade in Iceland the following year, saying they would find large stocks of wool and tallow in the north, an area relatively untouched by the English.[93] The Americans also

---

[87]The cargo of rye, oats, barley, indigo, rum, spirits, rice, coffee, sugar, tobacco, flour, bread, beans and salt belonged to Samuel Butler and Son of Providence, Rhode Island; NAI, Bf. Rvk. IV, 3a, Bréfabók 1807-1811, 22 November 1809; and NAI, Stiftamtsjournal, III, box 268, Athearn to Stephensen, 7 September 1809.

[88]RA, Rtk. 373.133, Magnús Stephensen to the Rentekammer, 27 September 1809; and Hooker, *Journal*, I, 323.

[89]RA, Rtk. 373.133, Extract of Trampe to Magnús Stephensen, 24 February 1809.

[90]NAI, Stiftamtsjournal, III, box 268, Athearn to Stephensen, 7 September 1809.

[91]NAI, Bf. Rvk., IV, 3a, Bréfabók 1807-1811, Phelps to Petræus, 26 August 1809.

[92]NAI, Stiftamtsjournal, III, box 270, Athearn to Stephensen, 13 September 1809.

[93]RA, Rtk. 373.133, (draft) Stephensen to Staples, 29 November 1809.

had difficulty obtaining a cargo because they arrived late in the season, when the *handel* was over, so that they experienced the same problems as the *Clarence* earlier in the year.[94]

The *Talbot* Arrives on the Scene

In August the *Talbot* sloop-of-war, sent from the Leith Station to relieve *Rover*, arrived in Iceland. The captain, the Hon. Alexander Jones, was astonished to find that the island had been declared "free, neutral, independent and at peace with all nations" and demanded an explanation.[95] Phelps' response was to warn Jones that it was a matter of the utmost importance that he not "interfere with the arrangements" Phelps had made in Iceland; otherwise he would have to detain the ships ready to sail to Britain and "remain, myself, on the island to protect my right and property until the will of the British government can be known."[96] Convinced that Phelps had far exceeded the authority of his licence and letter-of-marque and had by his actions "not only...transgressed the laws of Great Britain, but of all nations," Jones was understandably hostile. He was reasonably certain that the British government would not approve of the goings-on in Iceland, so he insisted that Phelps depose Jörgensen and restore the former government under a respected Icelander "until his Majesty's pleasure is known."[97] An agreement was eventually reached by Jones, Phelps and the Stephensen brothers, who were the leading Icelanders. In effect, all of Jörgensen's actions in Iceland were declared null and void and the Nott-Trampe convention of 16 June was declared to be in full force, safeguarding the rights of British subjects in Iceland and a free

---

[94]In April 1810, the *Vigilant* from Boston, on its way to Drontheim in Norway, was driven into Reykjavík in distress and discharged its cargo there; see NAI, Stiftamtsjournal, III, box 271, Tyler to the Governor of Iceland, 4 May 1810.

[95]PRO, Adm. 1/1995, Jones to Phelps, August 19 1809.

[96]*Ibid.*, Phelps to Jones, 17 August 1809.

[97]*Ibid.*, Jones to Phelps, 19 August 1809.

British trade. Fort Phelps was subsequently dismantled and Danish rule restored.[98]

The arrival of *Talbot* was therefore a major disaster for the British merchant party. Phelps felt that Adam Smith had been correct in saying that governments, or at least their "agents," should interfere as little as possible in trade matters.[99] A few years later, Phelps would write:

> But for the interference of Captain Jones, I should have made a very large fortune, in a most humane and honour-able way, and by this time have produced some millions of benefit to this country, and have placed the inhabitants of Iceland in the most prosperous and happy situation...[100]

Undaunted, Phelps prepared his departure, determined to continue his trade with Iceland. Savignac would remain in Reykjavík as the agent of Phelps & Co. in Iceland.

Meanwhile Nott had arrived in Leith at the beginning of August. His report of the situation in Iceland went from the Admiralty to Lord Liverpool at the Home Office, who referred it to the Board of Trade, which finally felt competent to deal with the matter.[101] That august body, with Lord Bathurst present, expressed its approval that Captain Nott had preferred to negotiate with the Danish governor rather than "manifesting his resentment at the unjustifiable treatment which British subjects appear to have experienced from the Government of Iceland."[102] The Nott-Trampe convention of 16 June was judged:

---

[98]PRO, Adm. 1/1995, Agreement of 22 August 1809; printed copy in Hooker, *Journal*, II, 99-102.

[99]Phelps, *Observations*, 68n.

[100]*Ibid.*, 67n.

[101]PRO, Adm. 1/692, Nagle to Wellesley-Pole, 4 August 1809; PRO, Home Office (HO) 28/36, Barrow to Beckett, 7 August 1809; and PRO, BT 1/46, Beckett to Cottrell, 11 August 1809.

[102]PRO, BT 5/19, Minutes, 28 August 1809.

> as being well calculated to establish an amicable inter-
> course with Iceland not unfavourable to the interests of
> this kingdom and essentially necessary to the existence of
> that island...

Furthermore:

> their Lordships deem it to be highly expedient that the
> Danish administration of the Government of Iceland
> should be given distinctly to understand, that considering
> that the intercourse, which His Majesty allows to exist
> between this country and Iceland, proceeds from His
> Majesty's generous disposition not to extend the calami-
> ties of war to the defenceless inhabitants of Iceland, to
> whom the Danish Government has been, from the
> commencement of the war unable to give any succour, or
> to secure them from an absolute state of famine, and
> considering that the authority which the Danish adminis-
> trators exercise, is to be exercised only by sufferance,
> His Majesty will give directions, that they shall be
> forthwith dispossessed of their authority and that their
> persons shall be removed from the island, if they endea-
> vour again to interrupt this intercourse. His Majesty
> being resolved, not to allow this His generous purpose to
> be frustrated, or molested by their inconsiderate
> conduct.[103]

Thus the situation was clear: as long as the Danish officials and Icelanders
conducted themselves according to the wishes of Great Britain all would
be well. Should they have proved intransigent, however, England might
well have been obliged to take possession of Iceland. In the final analysis,
the crux of the matter was that Britain was able to take full advantage of
Iceland without the need to seize it. Situated in the Atlantic Ocean, where
the Royal Navy reigned supreme, Iceland was within the British sphere of
influence. And since the Danes were quite powerless to prevent the British

---

[103]PRO, BT 3/10, Cottrell to Beckett, 29 August 1809.

from trading freely with Iceland, there was no compelling reason to incur the extra cost of formally annexing the island.

Jones, however, had taken some risk. Instead of falling in with the wishes of the British merchants who were firmly ensconced in the island and conducting an apparently valuable trade, the intervention of the Royal Navy had restored Danish rule. Jones probably shared the anti-republican sentiments of his fellow aristocrat Trampe and the leading Icelanders, the Stephensen brothers, all of whom he met soon after his arrival. They were profoundly unhappy with this shocking "jacobin" revolution! Jones simply sided with them. William Battine, the Advocate of the Admiralty, later ruled that Jones had "acted upon no authority, but of his own discretion and interfered at his own risk...."[104] While both Jones and Phelps had acted at their own initiative — and risk — Jones' conduct met with approval while Phelps was threatened with criminal lawsuits.[105] The "Icelandic Revolution" was condemned both by the British government and especially Banks. Though an ardent advocate of a British annexation of the island, he was deeply shocked, condemning this attempt at involving his innocent Icelanders in what he called "the horrors of a revolution."[106]

The Revolution, however, had an important consequence for Anglo-Icelandic relations. Trampe had insisted on being taken to England to bring charges against the "revolutionaries" and ask the British government for "a convention...by which the neutrality of the country may be established, and the mutual relations placed on a firm footing."[107] The governor had to bow to the inevitability of British naval supremacy. The Iceland trade could not exist without British support. And the British government was now obliged to state its official policy towards the Danish dependencies in the North Atlantic.

---

[104]PRO, Adm. 1/3899, Opinion of William Battine, Advocate of the Admiralty, 27 March 1810.

[105]See, for example, PRO, FO 83/2293, Sir Christopher Robinson, the King's Advocate, to Wellesley, 10 February 1810.

[106]Banks wrote many memoranda on this subject. See, for instance, PRO, FO 40/1, Banks to Liverpool, 11 December 1809, and "A brief recital of some of the enormities committed in Iceland by the crew of the...Margaret & Ann," 12 January 1810.

[107]Wisconsin, Trampe to Bathurst, 6 November 1809.

Banks was the principal author of the Order-in-Council of 7 February 1810. Iceland, Greenland and the Faroes were firmly placed in a state of neutrality and amity with England.[108] Humanitarian motives were apparently paramount, stating that George III, "being moved by compassion for the sufferings of these defenceless People," exempted them from "the attack and hostility of H.M.'s forces...." Yet again free trade was established between these colonies and Great Britain.[109] Thus Iceland's official position in relation to Great Britain had in effect been changed. Though the Order acknowledged that the sovereignty of Iceland was still vested in the Crown of Denmark, Iceland was now *de facto* under the protection of Britain, an unusual situation for an enemy island. Yet again it was Banks who was behind the scenes.

British Trade in 1809 and the Appointment of a Resident Consul

The volume of British trade in 1809 was considerable. To the chagrin of the Americans — not to mention the Danish merchants — the "Revolution" had enabled Phelps to corner the market. Phelps shipped goods back to England, not only on his own ships but also in Icelandic vessels.[110] He left behind a considerable amount of goods from his three ships and the American ship, valued at about £30,000.[111] His agents were ordered to dispose of them "to safe merchants" in exchange for Iceland goods "on the

---

[108]Drafts in his unmistakable handwriting can be found in the Wisconsin Manuscripts.

[109]The original document is to be found in PRO, PC 1/3901; it was published in the *London Gazette* of the same date.

[110]See, for example, PRO, PC 2/183, petitions for entry, 6 October and 13 November 1809.

[111]On 25 September 1809 the assets of Phelps and Co. in Reykjavík were listed by Petræus. They included 300 barrels of rye, 850 of oats, one hundred of barley, eighty of bread, 200 of various cereals and beans, some iron, coal and tar, 1600 barrels of salt, fishing lines and tackle; NAI, Jörundarskjöl. The value of these goods is mentioned in PRO, Adm. 1/1995, Phelps to Jones, 16 August 1809.

most reasonable terms," Phelps preferring "tallow, salted mutton, woollen goods, down and feathers, oil and saltfish to other articles..."[112]

The centre of British trade was in Reykjavík, where warehouses and houses had been rented and several Icelanders were employed by Phelps and Co. as clerks. Phelps appears mostly to have sold his goods wholesale to factors and merchants in the south and a few in the north and east, sending his agents to arrange contracts.[113] The goods were either transported by small ships or packhorses. *Flora*, the second of Phelps' ships to arrive that summer, was immediately sent to the east and north of Iceland.[114]

Thus a sizable trading concern had been set up and a large stock of British goods had also been left in the island. Phelps and Co. was eager to continue its trade. But as we have seen, it repeatedly encountered serious local opposition to their commercial venture. Nott's convention of 16 June 1809, the agreement of 22 August 1809 and the Order in Council of 7 February 1810 had formally declared that British ships could trade with Iceland. In the opinion of the English merchants, however, these paper agreements had not and would not prove adequate. Only a consul resident in the island could afford the necessary protection. To put pressure on the authorities for such an appointment, Phelps pointed out to the Treasury in early March 1810, while preparing his third commercial venture, that the Danish merchants or even the Icelanders, under orders from the hostile Danes, might refuse to trade or pay their debts, an amount which, according to him, was already "enormous." Phelps and Co. would not take any further risks unless a consul were appointed by the British government with the powers "to interfere officially in the protection of the British trade." Should this request be granted, the British

---

[112]NAI, Bf. Rvk. IV, 3a, Bréfabók 1807-1811, Extract of a letter from Phelps and Co. to Petræus, 26 August 1809.

[113]See, for example, RA, Rtk. 373.133, M. Stephensen to the Rentekammer, 27 September 1809. This practice was continued. In June 1810 Savignac left for a three week journey to Skagestrand and Eyjafjörður; NAI, Jörundarskjöl, Savignac to Icelandic Government, 13 June 1810.

[114]PRO, Adm. 1/1995, Phelps to Jones, 16 August 1809.

trade would become "very considerable." If, however, it were not granted, then they would be forced to abandon the trade.[115]

In March 1810 Phelps and Co. again wrote to the Lords of the Treasury, stressing "the insecurity of the British trade" if no consul were appointed. It hoped for an early decision so it could send off some vessels, which were now ready to sail to Iceland.[116] A consul would both protect the interests of the British merchants *vis-à-vis* the Icelandic officials and discharge necessary bureaucratic duties, such as issuing certificates proving the due landing of certain goods exported from England to Iceland. This was necessary, for without these certificates the Customs in British ports could not cancel the shippers' debenture bonds. The merchants' anxiety was understandable. In the wake of the Revolution Phelps and the Icelandic authorities were hardly on the best of terms. Count Trampe was at the very moment making demands that he pay damages and restitution for his crimes in Iceland.[117]

In April 1810, Lord Bathurst recommended the appointment of a consul for Iceland, and the Marquess Wellesley, Secretary of State for Foreign Affairs agreed.[118] Phelps' arguments had probably been persuasive and the government's policy of supporting new markets would have coincided with his wishes. The decision for this appointment would, moreover, have followed logically in the wake of the Order in Council of February 1810. A consul, serving British interests and resident in the island, would in time probably attract more trade. Besides, Iceland remained a Danish dependency, and therefore difficulties could be expected. The problem of dealing with the consequences of the Icelandic Revolution was also a factor. The prospective consul could take on much-needed policing duties, granting a general amnesty to the people "to

---

[115]PRO, T 1/1121, Phelps and Co. to the Treasury, 3 March 1810.

[116]PRO, T 1/1124, Phelps and Co. to Lords of the Treasury, 23 March 1810.

[117]Wisconsin, Trampe to Bathurst, 6. November 1809.

[118]PRO, FO 40/1, Bathurst to Foreign Office, 14 April 1810. Wellesley informed George III that it was "necessary to appoint a consul to reside in the Island of Iceland." Wellesley to George III, 26 July 1810; and George III to Wellesley, 27 July 1810, in A. Aspinall (ed.), *The Later Correspondence of George III* (5 vols.; London, 1962), V, 625-6.

secure to the whole of the Icelanders the benefits of British protection."[119] Finally, as there is no record of the Admiralty despatching more sloops-of-war to patrol Icelandic waters, a resident consul was a much cheaper solution to the protection of the British trade and probably more effective as he was on the spot.

The new consul was John Parke, a well-connected Liverpool merchant.[120] Consuls were invariably merchants during this period and there were not many of them. According to the *British Imperial Calendar* there were no consuls stationed abroad in 1810, though they would soon increase in number.[121] Parke was thoroughly briefed by Banks before his departure.[122] His instructions have not survived, but his primary duty was of course the protection of the British trade.[123]

As the war progressed British shipowners began attacking the neutral trade. British merchants and shipowners engaged in the Greenland fisheries were quick to oppose the newly licensed Iceland trade, not surprisingly as their chief products were the same: fish and oil. They feared the competition, insisting that if the importation of oil in foreign ships were allowed it would lead to "the entire destruction of the fisheries."[124] Their colleagues in Hull agreed, fearing "utter ruin" if Danish ships were licensed to bring oil into England.[125] Accordingly the Board of Trade had issued "Additional Instructions" to the consul which restricted exports of *klipfish* and fish liver oil from Iceland to 300 tons each, as both

---

[119]PRO, FO 40/1, Smith to Banks, 23 April 1810.

[120]PRO, FO 40/1, James Parke the lawyer (later Baron Wensleydale) to Wellesley, 6 July 1810.

[121]Parke is listed in the 1811 edition; he did not reach Iceland until that year. By then there was also a consul in Algiers.

[122]SL, Parke to Banks, 9 and 13 July 1811.

[123]PRO, FO 40/1, James Parke to Wellesley, 6 July 1810; FO 95/353, Instructions (Entry Book), 12 July 1810; and FO 95/390, Smith to Parke, 13 July 1810. His reports in FO 40/2 demonstrate this.

[124]PRO, BT 1/46, William Mellish and others to the Treasury, 11 August 1809; and BT 3/10, Cottrell to Arbuthnot, 17 August 1809.

[125]PRO, BT 1/46, G.J. Egginton and others to the Treasury, 3 August 1809.

interfered with the interests of the British fisheries. It was up to Parke to decide "fairly and without favour or preference" how much each merchant should be allowed to export.[126] It was not a popular task. He also had to report on the quantities and qualities of linen imported to Iceland from Denmark.[127] This was doubtless to see what kind of a market Iceland would be for British textiles, as these had been hardest hit by the Continental System.[128]

In Iceland Parke quite simply controlled the export trade. Not surprisingly, contemporary Icelandic sources are unanimous in their hostility toward him. He was accused of interfering with the trade and favouring the British merchants.[129] Yet the Icelanders dared not object to his actions for fear of the British authorities.[130]

Parke took his duties seriously, regulating the Iceland trade according to British interests. He regularly sent reports to the Foreign Office, which were then usually sent on to the Board of Trade for consideration.[131] He also became keen on the possibilities that the exploitation of Iceland's resources might offer the British Crown and he favoured an increase in British trade at the expense of the traditional Danish one.[132]

The Extent of British Trade with Iceland

In spite of the creation of the consulship, official British support for the Iceland trade failed to attract many British merchants. Apart from Phelps

---

[126]PRO, FO 40/2, "Draught of Additional Instructions for H.M's Consul in Iceland," 9 July 1811.

[127]PRO, FO 40/2, Parke to Wellesley, 20 August 1811. Parke was able to inform Wellesley that the linens favoured in Iceland were those of Scotland and Ireland.

[128]Ian Christie, *Wars and Revolutions. Britain 1760-1815* (London, 1982), 168.

[129]Espólín, *Árbækur*, XII, 52. Parke freely admitted to "giving a preference to the British" when he began issuing the certificates; see SL, Parke to Banks, 9 July 1811.

[130]Espólín, *Árbækur*, XII, 52.

[131]See his despatches in PRO, FO 40/2.

[132]PRO, FO 40/2, Parke to Castlereagh, 8 September 1813.

and Co. (who traded there from 1809 to 1811) and Consul Parke himself, who engaged in trade from 1811 to 1813, a search through the documents only turns up three other merchant houses: Everth and Hilton, London fish curers and merchants (1811-1812); and the Liverpudlian merchant houses of Horne and Stackhouse (1812-1817) and Titherington and Allanson (1813-1816). Parke and Horne and Stackhouse also conducted trade with the other Danish dependencies, the Faroes and Greenland.[133]

The first year of the British trade, 1809, is well documented because of the Icelandic Revolution; the same cannot be said for the war years from 1810 to 1814.[134] In spite of the dearth of information about tonnage and the value of imports and exports, it appears that British trade with Iceland during the Napoleonic Wars was not extensive, either in comparison to British world commerce or as a supplement to the traditional Dano-Icelandic trade, which was obviously of far greater importance. For instance, during the war years 1808-1813, only about twenty British ships sailed to Iceland, compared to about seventy Danish ones. Roughly speaking, then, the British trade accounted for about twenty-five percent of the total navigation to Iceland during this period.

---

[133]For the Faroes see, for instance, contracts in NAI, Stiftamtsjournal, V, boxes 279 and 280; for Greenland see, for example, PRO, T 1/1456, Horne and Stackhouse to the Treasury, 18 February 1815. On the British trade in Iceland, see Agnarsdóttir, "Great Britain and Iceland 1800-1820," chapter 8.

[134]The paucity of documentary evidence makes research into the extent of British trade with Iceland during the Napoleonic Wars difficult. The vessels sailed mostly from Liverpool or London. There appear to be no official records of ships sailing from London because of the Customs House fire of 1814. The *Liverpool Mercury* often published incomplete lists of the sailings of ships to and from Liverpool. Efforts to trace the records of the major firms trading with Iceland proved unfruitful. The Public Record Office has some relevant records in the Board of Trade, Treasury, Foreign Office and Board of Customs and Excise collections. A shortage of paper during the war years meant that Icelandic records are almost non-existent. There are no official trade statistics from this period and Heckscher remarked about those still extant: "It should be remarked once for all that the British commercial statistics are not only highly uncertain in themselves, but also show inexplicable variations in different sources." Hecksher, *The Continental System*, 172n.. There are some statistical data available in the records of the Board of Customs and Excise in the PRO. The most useful are: Customs 4 recording "values imported into Great Britain and number of ships from from Iceland and the Faroes" (together); Customs 8 records of "exports of British merchandise" to Iceland and the Faroes for certain years; and Customs 10, the ledgers of exports of foreign and colonial merchandise under countries. These records do not always tally with other sources.

It is interesting to note that the English trade did not reach its peak until *after* the war. In 1814 Horne and Stackhouse and Titherington and Allanson together sent eleven ships from Liverpool, far more than during any war year. Altogether from when the trade began in 1809 until 1817 when the last British ship left Iceland, at least thirty-seven British ships and possibly as many as ten or so more sailed to Iceland to trade.

Phelps and Co. and Horne and Stackhouse were the leading merchants trading to Iceland. Phelps' pioneering efforts have already been recounted. That mercantile house sent at least six ships to Iceland in the years 1809-1811, though their accounts were not wound up until 1813.[135] (William) Horne and (Jonathan) Stackhouse of Liverpool carried on the most extensive trade with Iceland, sending at least three ships in 1813 (and informing Banks that they had already "considerable property" in Iceland — perhaps in the beginning in partnership with Parke?[136]) They sent six 1814, four in 1815, two in 1816 and one in 1817. Precisely what induced Horne & Stackhouse to begin trading is unknown, but it may have been connected with the fact that Parke was also a Liverpudlian. Like Phelps and Co., they formed a regular trading establishment in Reykjavík with clerks and assistants, warehouses and other buildings.[137]

British Involvement in the Iceland Fisheries

Given that the major Icelandic exports were fish products, it comes as little surprise that the British merchants were interested in exploiting the fisheries themselves. After all, Englishmen and Scots had been fishing in Icelandic waters since the beginning of the fifteenth century. Phelps had ambitious plans for the Iceland trade and planned to carry the under-developed fisheries "to an extent of perfection never before known to any country..."[138] He had bought a massive amount of salmon fished in the

---

[135]NAI, Stiftamtsjournal, V, box 279, Phelps and Co. to G. Haldorsen, 2 April 1813; Geir Vídalín, *Geir biskup góði í vinarbréfum 1790-1823*, ed. Finnur Sigmundsson (Reykjavík, 1966), Vídalín to Thorsteinsson, 22 August 1813.

[136]Wisconsin, Horne and Stackhouse to Banks, 28 April 1813.

[137]PRO, FO 40/2, Memorial of Henry Nodin on behalf of Horne and Stackhouse to Castlereagh, 16 April 1814.

[138]Phelps, *Observations*, 67n.

neighbourhood of Reykjavík in 1809, 2200 fish, and had cured two-thirds of them for export.[139] The following year Phelps' agent would again be ordered to exploit this resource.[140] As well, the crew of Phelps' ship, the *Elbe*, had cured 112 barrels of cod on shore that year.[141] Everth and Hilton also appear to have had ambitious plans for participating in the Iceland fisheries, asking to export thirty-six bushels of grain and peas "for the support of the fishermen and coopers going out to that place" to fish cod and salmon.[142] And Horne and Stackhouse had ambitious plans for a herring fishery, as will be recounted below.

Phelps and Co. Abandon the Iceland Trade

The reason for Phelps and Co.'s disappearance from the Iceland trade is uncertain. Its last ship was sent in 1811, while Parke wound up the concern in 1813, as has been mentioned, finding Phelps' property "in a state of decay."[143] In Iceland it was believed that Phelps had gone bankrupt.[144] There is some evidence to support this conclusion, though a search through bankruptcy lists has not provided any official

---

[139]Hooker, *Journal*, I, 229-230.

[140]The agent, Edwin Fell, travelled to Borgarfjörður in western Iceland, a region famous for its salmon rivers, to explore the possibilities; Sir George Steuart Mackenzie, *Travels in the Island of Iceland during the Summer of 1810* (Edinburgh, 1811), 194; and Henry Holland, *The Iceland Journal of Henry Holland 1810*, ed. Andrew Wawn (London, 1987), 215 and 225-226.

[141]NAI, Bf. Rvk. IV, 3a. Bréfabók 1807-11, 16 June 1810.

[142]PRO, PC 2/191, Petition of William Andrews and Co. on behalf of Parke, 31 May 1811; Petition of Everth and Hilton, 1 June 1811; and Fawkener to Richmond, 3 June 1811.

[143]NAI, Stiftamtsjournal V, box 279, no. 488, Parke to Castenschiold, 4 May 1813.

[144]Espólín, *Árbækur*, XII, 44. Viscount Dillon, who visited Iceland in 1834, also stated this to be the case. See Arthur Dillon, *A Winter in Iceland and Lapland* (2 vols.; London, 1840), I, 77.

confirmation.[145] In 1810 Abraham Bracebridge, one of the principal partners, spoke of their "unfortunate speculation with Iceland."[146] Phelps and Trampe had finally come to an agreement: Trampe would desist from prosecution if Phelps promised to return all the cargoes confiscated and the monies taken during the Revolution, paying compensation to the wronged Iceland merchants. Henry Holland, who visited the island with the Mackenzie scientific expedition in 1810, stated with truth that Phelps' participation in "the singular revolution...had interfered much with the success of their mercantile speculation in the island."[147] Nor did its luck improve much the following year. In 1811, the merchant firm "suffered very grievous losses in commerce."[148] Its interest in Iceland had been aroused, it will be remembered, first and foremost by the prospect of obtaining tallow for their soap-manufacturing business. Valuable cargoes had been loaded on their ships in 1809 (though the *Margaret and Ann* had gone down with its freight). In fact they appear to have almost exhausted the supplies, as has been seen in connection with the American ship. In 1810 *Flora* was sent to the east and north of Iceland in an unsuccessful search for a cargo.[149] Little tallow was brought to Reykjavík, as a shortage of butter had led to increased domestic consumption of that article.[150] Scarcity meant a price increase. In 1812 alone tallow rose by over thirty percent.[151] To make matters worse, the salmon fishery in the neighbourhood of Reykjavík, exploited so successfully in 1809, only yielded about a thousand fish in 1810, being "more unproductive than it has ever

---

[145]A search through PRO, B 7/23 Court of Bankruptcy for the years 1812-1815 did not reveal any mention of Phelps.

[146]PRO, FO 40/1, Bracebridge to Smith, 27 July 1810.

[147]Holland, *Iceland Journal*, 305.

[148]PRO, T 1/1216, Phelps and Co. to the Treasury, 31 July 1811.

[149]Mackenzie, *Travels*, 259.

[150]Holland, *Iceland Journal*, 225.

[151]PRO, FO 40/2, Castenschiold, Einarsson and Frydensberg to Parke, 11 May 1812.

before been recollected."[152] To obtain a cargo in 1811, Phelps' agents resorted to buying timber, imported into Iceland from Norway, to take to England, much against the wishes of the Iceland authorities.[153] All this, coupled with the restrictions placed by the Board of Trade on Icelandic exports, together with the fact that Phelps encountered difficulties with importing Icelandic produce into England, more or less appears to have forced it to abandon its Iceland trade.[154] It seems likely that, through a series of misfortunes, Phelps and Co profited little from its Iceland venture. This was a sorry end considering Phelps' enthusiasm and pioneering efforts in 1809.

Assessment of the British Trade in Iceland

The question then is why Iceland did not attract more British trade during the Napoleonic Wars. There were many contributing factors. While the problem of finding markets for Icelandic produce does not seem to have been a source of worry to the British merchants, Britain itself was not an ideal market. Some articles, such as wool (after the Spanish market closed), sulphur, eiderdown, swan quills and skins, were permitted for home consumption. The quantities, however, were small and the major Icelandic exports, klipfish and fish liver oil, while selling well on the traditional Danish market (mostly shipped on to the Mediterranean), did not find a ready market in England. This was primarily due to the opposition of the British merchants engaged in the Atlantic fisheries. Nonetheless, the fish fetched a high price during the war. Though documents have not revealed where the English merchants found their major markets, they were successful at one time or another in exporting

---

[152]Holland, *Iceland Journal*, 225; and Mackenzie, *Travels*, 205. "The salmon fishery of Iceland appears to be an admirable object for speculation, while the rents of our British rivers are so high."

[153]NAI, Stiftamtsjournal, V, box 277, Fell to Castenschiold and Frydensberg, 26 June 1811.

[154]For instance, Phelps and Co. had no luck in regaining the duty on rye and oats imported into England for the sole purpose of exporting the grain to Iceland; see many letters on the subject from 1809-1810 in PRO, T 1/1216 and T 11/49, Phelps and Co. petition, 18 August 1809.

Icelandic fish to Sicily, the Baltic and even the East Indies.[155] Phelps also had had ambitions of opening up a trade via Iceland with the United States.[156]

Secondly, the trade was faced with many difficulties. Duties on Icelandic products were high. There were various problems over regaining drawbacks on imports. Furthermore, the general restrictions placed on the export of klipfish and fish liver oil by the Board of Trade during these years must have had a discouraging effect on the English trade. The continuous hostility of the Danish merchants and the Icelandic authorities would not have helped matters. For example, Horne claimed in 1814 that the Icelandic state physician, Tómas Klog, had been induced to denounce the British imported coffee as "injurious to health."[157] Furthermore, the fact that the traditional Dano-Icelandic trade continued, though at a reduced rate, under British protection would have acted as a deterrent to some degree. Parke suggested to Castlereagh in 1813 that the number of licences issued to the Iceland merchants be limited or even suspended, "thereby...[giving] encouragement to British merchants, who might and I have no doubt would employ their shipping successfully and afford the country the required relief."[158]

Most important, however, Iceland could not always offer the ideal produce. It seems clear that in some years there were severe shortages, as in 1810-1811 when tallow was in short supply. In 1812 the fisheries were disastrous, compelling the governor to ban the export of fish. Both Phelps and Co. (1811) and Everth and Hilton (1812), who returned in ballast, abandoned their trade. The competition for the limited Icelandic produce had also increased, as in 1811-1812 Danish navigation to the island grew to half its former size (about twenty ships). However, when the fisheries improved in the following years, there was a good basis for an Anglo-Icelandic trade; Horne and Stackhouse and Titherington and Allanson sent

---

[155]PRO, BT 6/211, no. 56,665, August 1814; BT 6/204, no. 35,950, September 1811; PC 2/218, 19 September 1811.

[156]Phelps, *Observations*, 67n.

[157]Wisconsin, Extract of Mr. Horne's letter in Stanley to Banks, 13 January 1814.

[158]PRO, FO 40/2, Parke to Castlereagh, 8 September 1813.

eleven ships in 1814 and wanted an exclusive trade with Iceland. As will be seen below, they were to campaign diligently for this privilege.

As already mentioned, contemporary Icelandic accounts of the British trade are mostly negative, finding Parke's control of the trade insufferable. The Danish merchants, insisting that the English mainly imported luxuries, were of course totally opposed to the trade, although it is clear that they were not capable of importing enough for the needs of the Icelanders. However, in 1809 Magnús Stephensen conceded that rye, salt and coal had been very cheap, and that the coming of the *Clarence* had given employment to many people that winter and spring curing fish for the English.[159] The bishop of Iceland, Geir Vídalín, was certainly sorry to see the English trade brought to an end.[160] As well, the English trade with Iceland, though hardly extensive, was an important supplement to the declining Danish navigation. Besides, its positive features — the import of necessities, good prices and the competition it offered the Danes — were important factors in preventing widespread starvation in Iceland, which had been threatened by the reduced Danish navigation.

The leading merchants were Phelps and Co., seeking tallow for its soap-boiling industry, and Horne and Stackhouse, interested in establishing a herring fishery and an exclusive trade with Iceland and the Faroes. Both were of the opinion that, given the right conditions — those of peace — there was a sound basis for a lucrative Anglo-Icelandic trade, though a British annexation of Iceland would certainly be the best solution.

In 1817 Phelps published *Observations on the Importance of Extending the British Fisheries etc.* in which he proposed the establishment of an Iceland Fishing Society on the grounds of the "immense value" of the Iceland fisheries as "the finest nursery in the world for seamen."[161] To this Phelps added:

> The possession...of Iceland, would not have cost Government a farthing, and the acquisition would have been

---

[159]RA, Rtk. 373.133, Stephensen to the Rentekammer, 27 September 1809.

[160]Vídalín to Thorsteinsson, 6 October 1817, in Vídalín, *Geir biskup góði í vinarbréfum*, 154.

[161]Phelps, *Observations*, viii, 2-4.

invaluable to the British trade, and for establishing the
finest fishery in the World![162]

The following year Phelps turned philosopher, publishing *The Analysis of
Human Nature* in London in two volumes in 1818, after which he
disappeared from the historical scene.

　　　In February 1815 Horne and Stackhouse had "the chief part of the
proceeds of their trade" from Iceland and the Faroes. It was immense.
They successfully asked for permission to import into England from the
Danish Atlantic islands and warehouse for exportation no less than 500
tons of fish, 500 tons of oil, 200,000 pairs of woollen mittens and
stockings, 50,000 pairs of woollen frocks and fifty tons of woollen and
worsted yarn.[163] This was a huge amount when compared to the aggregate
quantity of fish and oil allowed to be exported from Iceland during the
war, namely 300 tons of each. Indeed, they were so eager to continue
their trade with Iceland after peace was declared in 1814, that, as will be
discussed below they appealed to the British government to annex Iceland.

The End of British Trade with Iceland

On 14 January 1814 a peace treaty was finally concluded between
Denmark and Great Britain. The Danish colonies seized during the war
were returned and Iceland reverted to its former status — a dependency
under the undisputed sovereignty of the King of Denmark, its trade
reverting to its pre-war pattern. At the peace negotiations at Kiel in
January 1814 Great Britain obtained Heligoland, occupied during the war,
but made no demand for Iceland, though the British negotiators ensured
that the three Danish North Atlantic dependencies remained in Denmark's
hands, which the British Crown preferred to a Swedish takeover of these
islands.[164] The question might also be asked why, after the Peace of Kiel,

---

[162]*Ibid.*, 69.

[163]PRO, T 1/1456, Horne and Stackhouse to the Treasury, 18 February 1815. See
also T 1/1419, Horne and Stackhouse to the Treasury, 26 August 1814, and T 1/1456,
Decision of Lords of the Privy Council, 16 July 1814.

[164]Finn Gad, "La Grönlande, les isles de Ferröe et l'Islande non comprises. A
new look at the origins of the addition to Article IV of the Treaty of Kiel of 1814,"
Scandinavian Journal of History, IV, No. 3 (1979).

the British government did not insist on maintaining freedom of trade in Iceland, and thereby indirect political domination.

Though Phelps and Co., Everth and Hilton, and Parke had abandoned their Iceland trade before the peace, it continued to be of great commercial importance to the Liverpool merchant houses Horne and Stackhouse and Titherington and Allanson to continue their Iceland/Faroe trade.[165] Early in February 1814 the merchants petitioned the Privy Council for protection for their unsold property in Iceland and a continuation of the freedom to trade. The matter was referred to Lord Castlereagh at the Foreign Office.[166] Then, and again in April, Castlereagh was treated to a glowing description of the advantages inherent in an Icelandic trade.[167] Horne and Stackhouse in particular had ambitious plans. They wanted to develop an extensive herring fishery for the valuable oil. They were interested in the long wool of the Icelandic sheep, described as "an article of great moment to an important branch of British manufacture," mentioning that Yorkshire manufacturers had dismissed many workers simply because of an insufficient supply of wool.[168] They were convinced that a mutually advantageous trade could be conducted between England and the North Atlantic Islands, with the Icelanders providing a market for colonial goods and British manufactures.[169] They were also prepared to take on single-handedly the provision of grain for both the Faroes and Iceland.[170]

---

[165]Agnarsdóttir, "Great Britain and Iceland 1800-1820," chapter 11.

[166]PRO, BT 1/84, William Horne's and Jonathan Stackhouse's petition to the Privy Council, 4 February 1814; BT 5/23, Minutes, 8 February 1814; and FO 40/2, Lack to Hamilton, 9 February 1814.

[167]PRO, FO 40/2, Memorial of Henry Nodin on behalf of Horne and Stackhouse to Castlereagh, 16 April 1814.

[168]When Napoleon invaded Spain, the Spanish market for merino wool became closed to the British.

[169]PRO, FO 40/2, Henry Nodin's memorial on behalf of Horne and Stackhouse to Castlereagh, 16 April 1814.

[170]Wisconsin, extract from Mr. Horne's letter in 13 January 1814, Stanley to Banks, [late 1813].

Castlereagh decided that as soon as an envoy could be sent to Copenhagen he would be instructed respecting the interests of Horne and Stackhouse; as usual the opinion of the Lords of the Council for Trade was sought.[171] Their attitude was understandable, if not exactly encouraging. They found it difficult to see how the Danish government could be asked to grant an unrestricted trade between her dependencies and Great Britain "while the British colonial system is maintained in full rigour..:"

> [If] however, Lord Castlereagh shall be of opinion that Denmark may be induced to grant any facilities for trade between Great Britain and Iceland, without requiring any inconvenient reciprocity, the Lords of this Committee would not be sorry to see that object effected.[172]

Probably the sheer insignificance of the Iceland trade was the major factor in the government's decision not to press the matter greatly.[173] In Heligoland, retained by the British, £500,000 pounds had been spent during the war on erecting fortifications and a port in which two hundred merchants settled.[174] In Latin America the same number of merchants was already established in Rio de Janeiro alone as early as August 1808 and in 1810 the British concluded a Treaty of Navigation and Commerce with the Prince Regent of Portugal.[175] These were important markets to which Iceland does not compare. Besides, Britain and Denmark were now friends.

The Liverpool merchants, however, disappointed, behaved as Magnús Stephensen had behaved in 1807 in the face of governmental indifference. They decided on a bold approach, successfully making a

---

[171]PRO, BT 1/84, Hamilton to the Clerk of the Council, 10 February 1814; and FO 95/391, Cooke to the Clerk of the Council, 20 April 1814.

[172]PRO, BT 3/12, Lack to Cooke, 14 June 1814.

[173]See though the appointment of the second British consul in Iceland; Agnarsdóttir, "Great Britain and Iceland 1800-1820," chapter 12.

[174]Heckscher, *The Continental System*, 178-179.

[175]Leslie Bethell (ed.), *The Cambridge History of Latin America* (11 vols.; Cambridge, 1985), III, 172-173.

direct application to the Danes themselves. On 19 August 1814 Frederik VI officially permitted the Liverpool merchants to import necessities in Iceland during 1814 and 1815 to enable them to close their accounts. This was in recognition of the contribution of the English trade in provisioning the island during the war.[176]

In 1815 Horne and Stackhouse offered to pay the Danish government an annual sum for the exclusive right to the Iceland trade.[177] This the Danes refused.[178] It had always been of paramount importance to the King to protect his own subjects' trade.[179] The Iceland trade continued to be of great importance to Denmark. As the Russian *chargé d'affaires* in Copenhagen explained to Nesselrode, the Russian foreign minister, in 1816, Iceland was one of Denmark's "meilleures ressources ...et ...très conséquent pour la balance de son commerce."[180]

In the autumn of 1816 the British trade was in practice brought to an end by the Danish trade ordinance of 11 September. Its first article auspiciously enough permitted the granting of licences to a certain number of foreign vessels to trade with Iceland. However, the duties and costs of the licences were so high that they would successfully cancel any profit made by the foreign merchants.[181] A British trade could not henceforth be profitably carried out with Iceland.

As has been seen, the introduction of a British trade with Iceland began as a chance encounter at the Royal Exchange in 1808 between an

---

[176]RA, Island and Færöer, Rosenkrantz to the King with the King's assenting signature,19 August 1814; *Lovsamling*, VII, 512-513, the Rentekammer to Governor Castenschjold, 30 August 1814.

[177]RA, Departement for udenlandske anliggender (D.f.u.a), Rapports au Département des Affaires Étrangéres 1814-1817, Island og Færöer, Bourke to Rosenkrantz, no. 27, 11 July 1815; Island og Færöer, Bourke to D.f.u.a., 8 August 1815.

[178]*Lovsamling*, VII, 563-564, the Rentekammer to the Governor and Deputy Governors of Iceland, 30 September.

[179]See note, *Lovsamling*, VII, 590.

[180]RA, USSRs Udenrigsministeriums arkiv, Moskva, Danica 485, Von Brienen to Nesselrode, despatch no. 18, 25 March/6 April 1816.

[181]*Lovsamling*, VII, 614-620; copy in PRO, FO 22/74 with translation (shortened version).

adventurous Danish prisoner-of-war and an Icelandic merchant owning supplies of tallow in his beleaguered island which were waiting for a market. The Dane then met by chance one Savignac who happened to work for Phelps and Co., a firm of soap manufacturers in need of fats for their soap-boiling. Phelps decided to chance a voyage to Iceland. Supported by government licences and letters of marque and later by naval protection and a resident consul they initially carried on a profitable trade and were joined by a few other merchant firms. However, the rigours of wartime with all its rules and regulations regarding trade and navigation, proved too much. A small population of only 50,000 people, producing mostly goods for their own consumption due to unfavourable natural conditions and a reduced navigation, were not an ideal market. In peacetime, however, conditions were such that an Anglo-Icelandic trade could be carried on profitably — as was indeed the case later in the century after the Iceland trade had been opened up to all nations.

[The following material was trimmed:

From the end of the first part. This summary paragraph seemed redundant:

"The Royal Navy could have severed all communication between Denmark and her North Atlantic dependency. Instead Iceland was placed under the *de facto* protection of Britain.[182] This was mainly due to Sir Joseph Banks who took on an active role, as self-appointed benefactor and patron to the Icelanders, smoothing the way for their trade during the Napoleonic Wars and ensuring the British government gained both sympathy and understanding for the wartime plight of the Icelanders. Partly, this was also due to the government policy of using neutral ships to evade Napoleon's Continental System."]

---

[182]Agnarsdóttir, "Great Britain and Iceland 1800-1820," chapter 7.

Merchant Organization and Maritime Trade in the North Atlantic, 1660-1815: Some Reflections

Henry G. Roseveare

In a well-known opening passage of his *Essay upon Projects* (1697) Daniel Defoe rhapsodised upon the ingenuity of merchants, forced by the pressures of recent maritime conflict to devise novel strategies of survival. Living by their wits, every venture they undertake is a project:

> ...ships are sent from Port to Port, as Markets and Merchandizes differ, by the help of strange and universal Intelligence; wherein some are so exquisite, so swift, and so exact, that a Merchant sitting at home in his Counting-house, at once converses with all Parts of the known world. This, and Travel, makes a True-bred Merchant the most Intelligent Man in the World, and consequently the most capable, when urg'd by necessity, to contrive New ways to live.

It is a romantic, almost Faustian, image this — the merchant as *magus*, contriving remote levitations and transmutations from the cloistered privacy of his wharfside offices — and it may seem rather far removed from the prosaic realities conveyed to us by a score of contemporaneous manuals on mercantile practice and brought to life most recently by Jacob Price and David Hancock.[1] In their vivid accounts of eighteenth-century Atlantic-merchant partnerships we are placed in a severely practical world, of disciplined procedures, meticulous record-keeping and cautious calculation. Surrounded by the ordered hierarchies of waste-books, bill-books, letter-books, journals and ledgers we are in an environment of

---

[1] Jacob M. Price, "Directions for the conduct of a merchant's counting house, 1766," *Business History* XXVIII (1986), 134-150, reprinted in J.M. Price, *Overseas Trade and Traders: Essays Upon Some Commercial, Financial and Political Challenges Facing British Atlantic Merchants, 1660-1775* (Aldershot, 1996); David Hancock, *Citizens of the World: London merchants and the integration of the British Atlantic community, 1735-1785* (Cambridge, 1995), Chapter 3, "Managing from a 'Merchant's Public Counting-House'."

constraints — constraints imposed by time, distance, law and the overriding necessity to reduce risk. It does not seem an environment attuned to strenuous adventure or novel enterprise.

Yet, Defoe was right. Implicit in his characterization is the timeless truism that knowledge is power. The well-ordered merchant-house, sustaining a large correspondence and capable of efficient information-retrieval, was the organization most advantageously placed to conduct its affairs with least risk of disappointment or surprise, and if it could convey a reputation for the reliability of these attributes to its clients and competitors then it stood to gain one of the highest prizes in the game of commerce — sound credit. From this all else could flow — business, profit, confidence, the momentum of self-sustained growth.

I

Unsurprisingly, the force of these simple truths re-emerges, again and again, from these collected papers. Despite the competing, autarchic state-system — English, Spanish, Dutch or French — which sought to monopolize the transatlantic trades, the eighteenth-century North Atlantic was a trading environment distinctively exploited by individual initiatives. Unlike the Far East or the Levant, and to a greater extent than northern or southern Europe, its commercial traffic was mainly independent of large-scale, corporate organization. No centralized structures comparable to those of the great East India Companies, and remarkably few formal associations of the kind which regulated trades to many European destinations, supported the initiatives of the Atlantic merchant.[2]

In such a context it can be argued that a higher than usual premium attached to the merits of a sound individual reputation for competence and reliability. In "Credit, Risk and Reputation in Late Seventeenth-Century Colonial Trade," Dr. Nuala Zahedieh supplies ample support for such an assertion, depicting as she does the exceptional

---

[2]For the English Atlantic context, see K.G. Davies, *The North Atlantic World in the Seventeenth Century* (Minneapolis, 315 or Jacob M. Price and Paul G.E. Clemens, "A Revolution of Scale in Overseas Trade: British Firms in the Chesapeake Trade, 1675-1775," *Journal of Economic History* XLVII, 1 (March 1987), 1-43. For a wider context, see E.L.J. Coornaert, "European Economic Institutions and the New World; the Chartered companies," in *The Cambridge Economic History of Europe*, Vol. IV, *The Economy of Expanding Europe in the Sixteenth and Seventeenth Centuries* (Cambridge, 1967), 223-274.

incentives which English Atlantic merchants were habitually obliged to offer to their captains and factors in order to ensure loyalty and punctual performance. Coupled with freight and commission rates some four to five times greater than those which were customary in west European sectors, the Atlantic merchant was also obliged to concede a greater discretionary latitude to his agents or suppliers, and to repose considerably greater trust in their honesty. It was this compulsion which, at any time and in any sector, did much to drive mercantile correspondence, for amid the routine exchange of information about markets, prices, qualities and seasons, there is always the anxious inquiry about reputation and reliability — the "informal character references" to which Dr. Zahedieh refers. But in the Atlantic sector, exaggerated by time and space, this compulsion to acquire accurate information and establish reliable personal contacts may, she suggests, have played into the hands of the larger, sounder, more experienced firms which tended to dominate late seventeenth-century London's export trades to the West Indies and North America.[3]

This may be a debatable conjecture worth further examination, but another inference finds strong support among these papers — support which is all the more welcome for being broadly founded. This is the role played by confessional allegiances. Dr. Zahedieh finds no difficulty in endorsing traditional views of those very special cohesions and collaborations always discernible among both Quaker and Jewish business communities. Highly efficient networks of communication and the regular exchange of confidential information were as much parts of their commercial, as of their spiritual, communion, and endowed them with strong competitive advantages which were as important in the Atlantic world as in their traditional fields of operation. The same was of course true for the French Huguenot diaspora which, passing through England and the Netherlands to Canada and the North Atlantic colonies, formed its own complex networks.

It is therefore salutary to be reminded by Professor Bosher that powerful countervailing forces were successfully brought to bear against the pervasive, cosmopolitan commercial culture of early seventeenth-century Huguenots. In his study of "The Gaigneur Clan" he has shown how the Church and State of seventeenth-century France combined to

---

[3]*V. infra*, N. Zahedieh, Table 2, confirming similar findings for the Chesapeake tobacco trade by Price & Clemens, *op. cit.*.

eliminate the Huguenot dominance of trade between La Rochelle and New France during the middle and later years of the century. Business alliances between French and foreign Protestants, at home and abroad, were vigorously displaced by Catholic merchants, such as the Gaigneurs, whose clerical and office-holding affiliations gave them overwhelming advantages in securing government contracts and commercial privilege. Carried through with genuine missionary zeal, this planned and sustained strategy of Catholicization forms a distinctive phase in the history of French imperial policies — although whether this facet of policy belongs within or outside the conceptual framework of "mercantilism" is another intriguing question which deserves debate.

Certainly there was no rigidly exclusive boundary which could be sustained indefinitely between the requirements of faith and the temptations of profit, and Professor Bosher goes on to record some of the late seventeenth-century evidence for collaboration and exchange between Catholic and Protestant merchants. Under the necessity to hire shipping, the Gaigneurs could not for long ignore the preponderantly Protestant ownership of commercial tonnage; nor could they evade the obligation to borrow from Protestant sources. A pattern of dependence was established which evidently endured well into the next century, for — as John G. Clark has shown — La Rochelle's greatly reduced group of Protestants in the 1730s still provided "most of the city's entrepreneurial leadership and dominated the maritime sector."[4] There is indeed a reassuring congruence between Bosher's elaborately traced findings for the Gaigneur clan and Clark's more broadly sketched portrait of eighteenth-century La Rochelle. In both accounts, intricate family networks and strategic alliances form an essential basis for long-term commercial success in the Atlantic world, and in both cases confessional ties were a strong and very enduring constraint. As Clark found, "kinship ties never, and socializing but rarely, crossed religious lines" despite the informal arrangements which allowed Catholics and Protestants to collaborate in mercantile and political initiatives.[5]

---

[4]John G. Clark, *La Rochelle and the Atlantic Economy during the Eighteenth Century* (Baltimore, 1981), 5.

[5]Clark, *La Rochelle*, 43. For a similar observation, see J.F. Bosher, "Success and Failure in Trade to New France, 1660-1760," *French Historical Studies* XV (1988), 456-457.

This makes it all the more interesting to follow Professor Nash's exploration of the Huguenot diaspora in South Carolina for, drawn initially from western France and from La Rochelle in particular, there must have been some intimate links between Bosher's seventeenth-century cohorts and those examined by Nash. However, what was at issue here was not so much the temporary submergence of opposing religious allegiances as the permanent social and cultural absorption of one ethnic group in another — a process of much profounder significance and greater complexity. One can therefore readily accept that Huguenot assimilation was not only slow but qualified by several contingencies — by the predominately urban and largely mercantile background of the first wave of Huguenots from Atlantic France; by their superior vitality and fecundity in comparison with their English contemporaries; and even by the fortuitous loss of their long-serving pastor.

But working alongside these random factors were the kind of ineluctable commercial compulsions with which so many of these papers are concerned. The most important and characteristic in the Atlantic context was the need for reliable European correspondents — either as agents or principals — and it is no great surprise to learn that with only one exception the Huguenot merchants of Charleston dealt with one or the other of the élite London firms of English extraction which specialized in commerce between London and South Carolina. Although the potential importance of credit founded upon kinship and shared religious affiliation cannot be ignored, and although there is evidently substantial strength in Bosher's depiction of a Huguenot international trading culture in the seventeenth century, it must be questionable how far such affiliations of blood and faith could override the material attractions of experience, superior financial resources, and connections.[6] For the young Henry Laurens, in Professor Nash's telling example, there was no contest.

II

In contrast to these intensely human and often unpredictable relationships, it is good to be reminded by Uriarte of the importance of reliable institutional structures and legal disciplines to the operations of commerce.

---

[6]J.F. Bosher, "Huguenot Merchants and the Protestant International in the Seventeenth Century," *William & Mary Quarterly*, LII (1995), 77-102.

The Bilbao case-study reflects on a marginal but not insignificant sector of late seventeenth-century Atlantic trades, the importance of which is indicated by French and English anxiety to establish consulates at Bilbao. Indeed, I believe there is much more to be learned of this issue by closer attention to English diplomatic correspondence, with particular reference to Westcombe's role in superintending English interests both in Spain and France during the embargo on French trade. The bill of exchange — by far the most vital yet neglected commodity in international trade history — was probably not of paramount importance in Bilbao's overseas settlements. My own experience of Bilbao's late seventeenth-century dealings suggested that bills of exchange accounted for less than ten percent of English returns from Bilbao, as against more than eighty percent in gold and silver, but this is a narrowly-based finding.[7] However, the difficulties which Bilbao experienced in establishing the conventional "usance" allowable on settlements, and the nature of the few "protests" Uriarte describes, is suggestive of an immature but ambitious commercial environment struggling hard to establish its international credit. That it had succeeded by the 1730s, when its commercial Ordinances were again revised, is convincingly argued by Uriarte and well-supported by eighteenth-century commercial manuals, and although Bilbao remained outside the front-rank of European exchange centres, its proximity to French and south of England ports made it an important channel of communications for North Atlantic trades.

This role is incidentally illustrated in one of Ralph Davis' selections of commercial correspondence where, in 1693, a London-based merchant gives precise and pressing instructions for the purchase and disposal of a prospective Newfoundland fish cargo.[8] The relevance of this example to Professor Janzen's case-study will be at once apparent for here, in the 1720s, is an unusually vivid and instructive illustration of the same staple trade, though in this instance directed from post-Union Scotland. Janzen is surely right to stress the exploratory nature of this Newfoundland venture for a partnership of Edinburgh merchants, familiar

---

[7]Henry Roseveare (ed.), *Markets and Merchants of the Late Seventeenth Century: The Marescoe-David Letters 1668-1680* (Records of Social and Economic History New Series XII, The British Academy/Oxford University Press, 1987), 199.

[8]Ralph Davis, *The Rise of the English Shipping Industry in the Seventeenth and Eighteenth Centuries* (Newton Abbott, 1962), 169.

with Spanish markets but novices on the cod-fishing grounds. That their initiative was ill-rewarded was certainly not due to a lack of sensible preparation, and their prudent alignment of victuals, credit facilities, end market and return cargo deserved a better fate. Edward Burd's *Journal of a Voyage*, on which Janzen has based his illuminating story, is a poignant lesson in the universal hazards of all long-distance trades and particularly those of the Atlantic which were dependent on accurate timing with such perishable commodities as fish. However, although incompetence, ill-luck, war and rumours of war all played their part, it would seem that Burd's travails as supercargo were largely the fault of a slow, leaky and inadequate vessel in which to traverse Atlantic waters. There could be no more basic failure than this, and it is indeed little wonder that this Newfoundland venture of the partners was their last!

III

A much longer record of commercial venture is the subject of Johannes Postma's important study, and the context is a narrower but more strictly controlled traffic than that of Bilbao. The Surinam Corporation, with its links to the Dutch West India Company, is a distinctive, if not unique, trans-Atlantic example of corporate organization, firmly backed by state power and sustained by an elaborate administrative system which has left its invaluable legacy of correspondence and records. Out of this evidently rich material Postma reconstructs more than a century-long analysis of ship traffic in which the slave trade — largely absent from these papers — figures as a crucial component of Surinam's plantation system. But it is another, hitherto more shadowy, dimension of trade in the Americas which is the focal point. Illicit and licit North American trade with Dutch and Spanish emporiums in the Caribbean and Central America has for long been an acknowledged but largely unquantified feature of the British colonial economy. Postma is not only enabled to give some valuable precision to this traffic but to indicate its real significance for the participants. For it is not merely the scale of this traffic in horses or molasses which matters but the favourable colonial balance of trade with Surinam which is the striking centrepiece of Postma's findings. The contribution this made to the American economy and its demand for English manufactures has to be conjectural at this stage, but Dr. Postma is surely right to hold out the very exciting promise of further illumination from this work. It will be eagerly awaited.

An exceptionally long and privileged interlude of neutrality between 1715 and 1780 protected this dimension of Dutch colonial trade, and although Postma argues that the outbreak of the Revolutionary War did not seriously impair American shipping-arrivals in Surinam, it is less surprising to learn of the devastating consequences of the Anglo-Dutch War of 1780-1784. It is war, and its ambivalent implications for participants and neutrals alike, which provides the common theme of three further papers by Rabuzzi, Marzagalli and Agnarsdóttir. With these it is again demonstrated just how much illumination can be gained from closely focused micro-analyses, founded upon the papers of individual merchants or consuls, and in each case, we are brought back to the issues with which these reflections began: the importance of information, contacts, timing, and credit to the operations of successful commerce. In Rabuzzi's wide-ranging study there is a particularly valuable bonus in his demonstration of how far the need for such operative advantages could transcend the short-term barriers of national hostilities. Admittedly, his merchant examples belong to the same Anglo-Saxon community, only recently divorced by revolution, but to a student of seventeenth-century international trade there is something familiar in the dependence of his novice Americans on their more experienced British counterparts as middlemen in the specialized milieux of northern Europe, for it closely mirrors the dependence of English intruders on their Dutch mentors a century before. Then, as later, certain institutional factors counted heavily in the mentors' favour: established entrepôts, secure merchant-banks and large-scale exchange networks, but — as at all times — the pathways were open to the energetic and bold, regardless of national allegiance. Rabuzzi's story is thus a pleasingly up-beat celebration of early American enterprise, establishing its self-confident presence in international trade upon a growing foundation of personal contacts, local knowledge and commercial credit.

Neatly complementary to this is Marzagalli's account of American shipping and trade in Bordeaux, where after 1793 the profit incentives were rather more obvious and the obstacles less complex than in Hamburg or the Baltic. Nevertheless, the vicissitudes of American traffic with France during the changing circumstances of the decades up to 1815 make an interesting study, founded upon consular records and a large secondary literature. Dr. Marzagalli asks some penetrating questions of this evidence. Not content with mere quantitative findings, useful though they are, she has sought to know answers which are fundamental to this symposium on merchant organization: *how* did her merchants, French or American, organize their trade networks; what strategies did they use; and who took the incentive? By challenging the data in this way, she brings to light something less than complete answers but at least certain important possibilities which will need serious discussion. For she offers some tentative, but intriguing evidence, reminiscent of the papers by Bosher and Nash, of the human networks which supported French interests in America and American interests in France. It justifies her observation — central to the whole conception of this conference — that "trade networks are to a large extent connected to human networks."

The last but not least exploration of these perceptions is Dr. Agnarsdóttir's account of that curious episode in British trade history when a chance encounter on the Royal Exchange inaugurated an abortive experiment in Anglo-Icelandic trade. Thanks to a prevailing state of war, the respective merchant networks of Britain, Denmark and Iceland were not easily reconciled, and although British interests flourished briefly under the revolutionary Icelandic flag, its three white codfish on a blue background failed to appease the dissentient islanders or impress the imperial government in London. Thus, despite the enterprising commercial efforts of Phelps & Co. and their Liverpudlian colleagues under the protection of a British consul, trade with Iceland failed politically as well as economically.

Given the context, of overwhelming British naval power and undisputed control of the North Atlantic, this is ironic, for in virtually all the instances cited in these papers we have seen mercantile enterprise succeed in the face of the serious adversities posed by distance, by religious allegiance, by national antagonisms and exclusive systems of economic autarchy. The generous boundaries of the Atlantic and the richness of its desirable resources seem, more often than not, to have produced, in the Atlantic merchant, manifestations of economic man at his most ingenious. But clearly there must be exceptions, and it is not easy to subsume under one explanatory model the diversity of instances which this conference has produced. Nevertheless, there are intriguing opportunities offered by these thoughtful and original studies to extend our understanding of mercantile enterprise in general and to refine our appreciation of Defoe's "True-Bred Merchant" in particular.

Printed and bound by CPI Group (UK) Ltd, Croydon, CR0 4YY

16/04/2025

14658576-0002